**DELICIOUS RECIPES
FROM THE HIT TV SHOW**

itv 1

Published by PP Publishing Ltd, 2011
2 Marylebone Road, London NW1 4DF

Distributed by Littlehampton Book Services Ltd,
Faraday Close, Durrington, Worthing, West Sussex BN13 3RB

British Library Cataloguing in Publication Data
A catalogue record for this book is available from the British Library

The publishers would like to thank everyone at The Good Food Guide and
ITV Studios for their help in producing this book.

Project manager: Emma Callery
Designer: Blânche Williams, Harper Williams Ltd
Recipe testers: Margaret Clancy, Ann Reynolds, Sian Stark
Proofreaders: Kate Parker, Kathy Steer
Indexer: Christine Bernstein
Photography: Tim Feak, Philippa Gedge, Jo Hanley, Justin Harris, Neil Hurley,
Gary Moyes, Helen Turton

Printed and bound by Charterhouse, Hatfield
Paper: Tauro Offset is a totally chlorine free paper produced using timber from
sustainably managed forests. The mill is ISO14001 certified.

PEFC
PEFC/16-33-160

www.itv.com/food
www.thegoodfoodguide.co.uk

Foreword

Britain's Best Dish has built a formidable reputation for unearthing the very best amateur cooks from all corners of the nation. Along the way we've tucked into a staggering 848 different dishes – not to mention thousands more during auditions.

Now we've upped the ante and thrown down the gauntlet to the nation's professionals for the first time. The result is the most exciting competition yet – **Britain's Best Dish: The Chefs**.

The cream of the country's professional talent has stepped up to the plate, hailing from the humblest bistros to the glitziest fine-dining restaurants.

In total, 112 gifted chefs laid their hard-won reputations on the line in the famous Best Dish kitchens. And what a standard they set. Sensational serving followed sensational serving, as they plated up mouth-watering mains and desserts to die for. And all of them created especially for this competition.

Now, with the team behind the culinary bible that is **The Good Food Guide**, we've recreated every single dish featured in the series in this unique recipe book.

True to the flavour of the show our professionals have kept their dishes accessible, retaining those no-nonsense principles that underpin all great British cooking. They may sizzle with the flair that a professional chef brings to the table, but every recipe in this book can be recreated in a domestic kitchen.

We want the chefs to inspire the cooks, to bridge the gap between seasoned professional and talented amateur, so that the next time the nation's best home cooks line up in the nation's greatest cookery contest, the standard will be higher than ever.

We heartily believe that the recipes in this book will do that, so get reading, get inspired and get cooking.

ED SAYER
Executive Producer
Britain's Best Dish

Recipe notes

● The recipes in this book have been specially adapted to make it easy for you to replicate the chefs' dishes in your own kitchen. To this end, in some recipes, ingredients such as pastas and stocks are listed as shop-bought ingredients, rather than home-made.

● Additional elements, trimmings and serving ideas that are shown in the photographs but not included in the recipes are listed at the end of each recipe. More adventurous home chefs can visit www.itv.com/food to find the chefs' own recipes for each of these components.

● Eggs are large unless specified otherwise.

● All herbs are fresh unless specified otherwise.

● Specific equipment that may be required, including cake tins, can be found on page 236.

● The symbol ⏱ at the top of some of the ingredients lists means that elements of this dish need preparing at least one day before serving.

Contents

Introduction

Our island nation has one of the most abundant natural larders in the world, from the humble potato to the highly prized truffle, from the heartiest game to the finest fish. And what better way to celebrate Britain's culinary wealth than this collection of brand new British classics from some of the country's top professional chefs.

You'll find in these pages a feast of main courses that celebrate the diversity of the British dining table. Global influences breathe new life into classic British produce, while exotic ingredients give a twist to cherished heritage dishes. Go nostalgic with 'lobster fish and chips', update a classic pork roast with ham hough bonbons, or fire up your British lamb with a kick of wasabi. (And if you've ever wanted to cook a kangaroo, go straight to page 118.) To help you on your way you'll find tips galore, from getting the crunch into crispy crackling to baking the perfect pastry case.

And when it comes to the nation's best desserts, our chefs have had fun with confections and crumbles of every variety, be it a popcorn panna cotta or sloe gin crème brûlée. Vegetables make a sweet appearance by way of a pumpkin and blueberry tartlet, while British fruits appear in silky soufflés, refreshing granitas, and delicious purées and jellies.

From Scotland to Australia, Catalonia to the Punjab, our chefs have taken inspiration from far and wide – but what unites them all is a distinctly British sensibility: a pride in local sourcing; a resolve to support artisan producers; and a determination to fly the flag for great British food.

Mains...

VEGETABLE DUM BIRYANI
Minal Patel

Prashad means 'blessed food' in Gujarati, and Bradford diners at this restaurant have long been blessed with some of the finest vegetarian Indian cuisine Britain has to offer. Head chef Minal Patel works alongside her mother- and father-in-law in their family business, specialising in Gujarati and Punjabi dishes whose complex, intense flavours have led diners to label them 'masterpieces'. Minal comes from a family of rice farmers, and this vegetable dum biryani pays homage to the fact. Although it 'exudes simplicity', the tastes therein are intricate.

1 **To make the vegetable dum biryani,** put the clarified butter or ghee into a heavy-based pan and gently heat through until it is clear and runny. Add the bay leaves, cloves, cinnamon, cumin seeds, mustard seeds, asafoetida and curry leaves and leave for a few seconds. Add the onion and cook for a few more seconds. Then add the vegetables, one at a time, starting with the hardest first, potato, and then the pepper, cabbage, peas, courgettes and aubergines, and stir.

2 Put the ginger, chillies and garlic in a mortar, add the salt and crush to a pulp using the pestle. Add to the pan together with the turmeric, garam masala, lemon juice, coriander, rice and 150ml of water. Stir together, bring to the boil, cover with a lid and cook over a low heat, adding more water if necessary, for 15–20 minutes until the rice is cooked through.

3 **For the garlic-infused yogurt drink,** put the cumin seeds into a small pan and roast on a low heat for about 1 minute. Once the seeds start to brown, remove from the heat, transfer to a mortar and crush to a fine powder with the pestle. Put the yogurt in a bowl, add 115ml of water and whisk for about 1 minute to a smooth consistency. Then add the salt and the cumin powder from the mortar together with the garlic, green chilli and coriander and whisk again. Put in the fridge until needed.

4 **To make the tomato sauce,** put the oil in a pan over a medium heat. Add the mustard seeds, 1 tsp of the cumin seeds and the onion and cook for a few minutes. Put the tomatoes in a food processor to blend to a purée and then add to the pan with the ginger, turmeric, salt, coriander, remaining cumin seeds and the chilli powder. Cook for 5 minutes on a medium heat.

5 **To serve,** put the biryani, tomato sauce and yogurt drink into separate dishes for each person, arrange on large warmed plates and garnish with coriander. The chef suggests serving this dish with homemade chapattis and you may also wish to make up your own garam masala (see page 6).

Serves 4

For the vegetable dum biryani
2 tbsp clarified butter or ghee
2 bay leaves
2 cloves
1cm cinnamon stick
1 tsp cumin seeds
1 tsp black mustard seeds
1/4 tsp asafoetida
6 curry leaves
1 onion, peeled and finely diced
20g finely diced potato
20g finely diced red pepper
20g finely chopped cabbage
20g shelled peas
20g finely diced courgettes
20g finely diced aubergines
3cm fresh root ginger, peeled and finely chopped

4 green chillies, deseeded and chopped
5 garlic cloves, peeled
1 tsp salt
1/2 tsp turmeric
1 tsp garam masala
Juice of 1 lemon
Small handful of coriander, chopped
250g basmati rice

For the garlic-infused yogurt drink
1 tsp cumin seeds
240g plain yogurt
1 tsp salt
1 garlic clove, peeled and finely chopped
1 green chilli, deseeded and finely chopped

Small handful of coriander leaves, chopped

For the tomato sauce
1 tbsp sunflower oil
1 tsp black mustard seeds
2 tsp cumin seeds
1 onion, peeled and finely chopped
5 vine tomatoes
1 tsp chopped fresh root ginger
1 tsp turmeric
1 tsp salt
1 tsp dried coriander
1 tsp red chilli powder

To garnish
Small handful of coriander, finely chopped

Redolent with the aromas of Gujarat, a fragrant and tastebud-tantalising curry.

WILD MUSHROOM SUET PUDDING
with port & red wine jus
Lisa Walker

Lisa Walker describes herself as a 'rarity' in the restaurant industry – a female head chef cooking vegetarian food. At Brighton's legendary veggie haunt Food for Friends, Lisa uses her Northern heritage to put a twist on her dishes and extols the culinary possibilities of vegetables. Her wild mushroom suet pudding references her upbringing, while communicating how exciting, interesting and appealing vegetarian food can be, to veggies and meat-eaters alike.

1 **For the port and red wine jus,** place the oil in a large pan and gently heat. Add the carrot, celery, onion, leek, mushroom, garlic and sun-dried and fresh tomatoes. Cook on a low heat for 5 minutes, stirring occasionally. Add the dates, tamarind, wine and port and bring to a rolling boil, then reduce the liquid by half. Add the remaining ingredients, season with salt and pepper and reduce to a gentle simmer. Cover with a lid and reduce over about 40 minutes to 1 litre. Strain the jus through a sieve and set aside.

Serves 4

For the port and red wine jus
50ml olive oil
½ carrot, peeled and chopped
½ celery stick, trimmed and
  chopped
1 onion, peeled and chopped
½ leek, trimmed and chopped
1 portabella, roughly chopped
1 garlic clove, peeled and
  chopped
1 sun-dried tomato, roughly
  chopped
1 tomato, roughly chopped
4 whole dried dates, pitted
20g tamarind paste
150ml red wine
200ml ruby port
50ml tamari soy sauce
Sprig of rosemary

Sprig of thyme
1 vanilla pod, split lengthways
50g tomato purée
1.5 litres vegetable
  stock
Salt and freshly ground black
  pepper

For the filling
2 tbsp olive oil
1 small carrot, peeled and
  finely diced
1 celery stick, trimmed and
  finely diced
1 small onion, peeled and
  finely diced
2 garlic cloves, peeled and
  crushed
100g ceps, chopped
100g chestnut mushrooms,
  chopped

100g chicken of the woods
  mushrooms, chopped
50g porcini, chopped
4 sun-dried tomatoes,
  chopped
2 sprigs of thyme, leaves
  finely chopped
Sprig of rosemary, leaves
  finely chopped

For the pastry
300g self-raising flour
½ tsp baking powder
Pinch of English mustard
  powder
1 tsp grated horseradish or
  horseradish cream
100g vegetarian suet

To serve
4 bunches of redcurrants

2 **For the filling,** heat the oil in a pan over a medium heat, add
   all the vegetables (except the mushrooms) and garlic, and sauté
   for 5–8 minutes until tender. Add all the mushrooms and cook
   for about 5 minutes until they start to soften slightly. Then add
   the port and red wine jus, the tomatoes and herbs. Cook for a
   further 5 minutes and remove from the heat. Allow to steep for
   5 minutes. Drain the mixture, reserving the jus and the
   mushroom filling separately.

A rich and juicy savoury pudding to warm the hearts of veggies and meat-eaters alike.

3 **To make the pastry,** preheat the oven to 190°C (Gas 5) and butter four 225ml metal
   pudding basins and dust with flour. Mix all the ingredients in a bowl, seasoning with some
   salt and pepper, and add enough cold water to make a firm paste. Roll out the pastry on
   a well-floured work surface to about 3mm thick. Cut out four circles of pastry the size of the
   top of the basins and four larger circles to fit inside the basins. Line the basins with the larger
   circles of pastry, gently easing it around the sides to ensure a snug fit.

4 Spoon the mushroom mixture into each basin, leaving a 1cm gap at the top. Pour in the
   reserved jus, just level with the top of the mushrooms (still allowing a 1cm gap at the top).
   Some of the jus will be left over; reserve it for serving. With a sharp knife, trim the pastry
   around the rim of each basin, then place the smaller circles on top and gently push down.
   Press the edges together to make a firm seal. Place the puddings in a deep roasting tin and
   fill halfway up the basins with water. Cover the roasting tin with foil and bake for 35 minutes
   until hot through and golden.

5 **To serve,** unmould each pudding and place in the middle of warmed plates. Top with
   a bunch of redcurrants and drizzle over the remaining port and red wine jus. The chef
   suggests serving this dish with a potato and parsnip gateau, braised red cabbage, chestnut
   purée and a redcurrant jus (see page 6).

CATALAN FISH STEW
with almonds and aïoli
Andres Alemany

It's all about sharing at Spanish-born chef Andres Alemany's idyllic Hampshire country pub, where his popular tapas and Catalan-inspired menu contribute to the convivial atmosphere. After spells at the Oxo Tower and the Fifth Floor Restaurant at Harvey Nichols, Andres became excited by the innovative food being served in London's pubs, eventually bringing that enthusiasm to bear with the purchase of his own pub, the Purefoy Arms in Hampshire. Andres' Catalan fish stew with almonds and aïoli typifies his passion for premium ingredients and Catalan cuisine.

1 **For the stew base,** remove and discard the fish gills and eyes. Remove the bones and rinse in cold running water for 10 minutes then put them into a large pan. Chop the flesh into generous bite-sized pieces and set aside in the fridge.

2 To make the stock, cover the fish bones with cold water. Add the vegetables, bring to the boil, then reduce the heat and simmer for 20 minutes. Remove the pan from the heat and squeeze the lemon juice into the stock, adding the squeezed lemon halves. Then

add the parsley and leave for 5 minutes to infuse. Pass the fish stock through a sieve and return the liquid to the heat to reduce by half over about 15 minutes. Meanwhile, preheat the oven to 180°C (Gas 4).

3   Break the bread into small chunks and place on a baking sheet with the almonds. Drizzle over the olive oil. Roast in the oven for 10–15 minutes until golden brown, making sure they don't burn. Then pound the bread and almonds until fine using a pestle and mortar; they will be used later to thicken the stew.

4   Pour the vermouth into a pan and simmer for about 10 minutes to reduce by half.

5   In a separate large pan, heat the extra-virgin olive oil until smoking. Then add the garlic and salt and cook for about 30 seconds until lightly toasted and golden. Add the tomatoes and cook for a further 5 minutes. Pour in the reduced fish stock and reduced vermouth and bring to the boil. Put the stew base into a food processor (in batches if necessary), add the saffron and blend until smooth. Return to the large pan and keep warm.

6   **To make the aïoli,** smash the garlic and salt using a pestle and mortar until it forms a smooth paste. Transfer to a bowl and add the egg yolk, then slowly add the oil, whisking in a little at a time, until it is a mayonnaise consistency.

7   **For the seafood,** heat the vegetable oil to 180°C in a large pan or a deep fryer. Simmer the cuttlefish in boiling water for about 15 minutes. Drain and, once cool enough to handle, remove the tentacles and set aside the flesh. Deep fry the tentacles for about 2 minutes until crisp, drain on kitchen paper and keep warm.

8   Meanwhile, heat the olive oil in a large heavy-based pan over a medium heat. Take the fish from the fridge and fry in the oil, skin-side down, starting with the thickest fish and ending with the langoustines. When the fish and langoustines are almost cooked, flip them over and transfer to the large pan with the stew base. Add the clams and mussels to the stew pan and cook until the shells open and the sauce thickens slightly.

9   **To serve,** put the fish in warmed bowls, skin-side up and the clams and mussels open shells face up, finishing with the langoustines and cuttlefish. Pour over the remaining sauce and top with a spoonful of aïoli.

Serves 4

For the stew base
1 side of hake weighing about 600g on the bone
330g sea bass on the bone
330g red mullet on the bone
1 Spanish onion, peeled and finely sliced
½ leek, trimmed and finely sliced
½ head of celery, trimmed and finely sliced
1 unwaxed lemon, halved
Small bunch of flat-leaf parsley, chopped
70g unsliced white bread
170g almonds
1 tbsp olive oil
250ml vermouth
170ml extra-virgin olive oil
½ head of garlic, divided into cloves and peeled and sliced
Pinch of salt
600g vine-ripened plum tomatoes, chopped
½ tsp saffron threads

For the aïoli
1 garlic head, divided into cloves and peeled
1 tsp salt
1 egg yolk
200ml extra-virgin olive oil

For the seafood
500ml vegetable oil
250g cuttlefish
1 tbsp olive oil
4 langoustines
200g clams
200g mussels

A joyful Catalan dish with luscious tomatoey juices – you'll make this dish again and again.

SOUND OF MULL FISH PIE

Liz McGougan

Named fish restaurant of the year in *The Good Food Guide 2012*, Tobermory's Cafe Fish leads by stunning example, with head chef Liz McGougan preparing the freshest of seafood in simple style. Liz, who has been in the restaurant trade since she was 13 years old, cites the 'abundance of ingredients on our doorstep' as the inspiration for this luxurious fish pie.

Serves 6

For the béchamel sauce
½ small onion, peeled
3 cloves
1 bay leaf
6 whole black peppercorns
450ml full-fat milk
300ml double cream
50g unsalted butter
50g plain flour

For the mash topping
1.25kg floury potatoes, preferably
   King Edward or Maris Piper, peeled
   and chopped
50g unsalted butter
100ml double cream
180g mature Cheddar cheese
80g Parmesan cheese
Pinch of nutmeg
100g cooked spinach, chopped
Salt and freshly ground white pepper

For the filling
200g fillets of smoked haddock,
   skinned, boned and cut into chunks
200g fillets of haddock, skinned,
   boned and cut into chunks
150g fillets of salmon, skinned, boned
   and cut into chunks
20 queen scallops, shelled
26 squat lobsters or prawns, shelled
160g white crab meat

To serve
1 head of kale, shredded
1 head of broccoli, cut into florets
150g peas, fresh or frozen
Knob of butter

1   **For the béchamel sauce,** stud the onion with the cloves and put in a large pan with the bay leaf, peppercorns, milk and cream and bring to the boil. Melt the butter in a separate large pan, add the flour and cook for 1 minute. Gradually add the warmed milk and cream and bring slowly to the boil, stirring all the time. Simmer for about 10 minutes until the flour is cooked and the sauce thickened.

2   **For the mash topping,** boil the potatoes in a large pan for 15–20 minutes. Drain, mash and add the butter and cream. Add 100g of the Cheddar cheese together with the Parmesan, nutmeg and spinach and mix together well. Season with salt and pepper. Preheat the oven to 180°C (Gas 4).

3   **For the filling,** put the two types of haddock and the salmon into the béchamel sauce and warm for 2 minutes to infuse the flavours. Then add the scallops, squat lobsters or prawns and crab meat and gently cook for a further 2–3 minutes until the prawns are cooked. Place the fish mix in six individual pie dishes and top with the spinach mash and remaining Cheddar cheese. Bake in the oven for 20 minutes until golden brown.

4   **To serve,** blanch the kale, broccoli and peas for 5 minutes and toss with butter. Place the pies on warmed plates and add the vegetables. The chef suggests serving this dish with warm granary bread (see page 6).

RAY & LANGOUSTINES
with fennel purée & clam emulsion
Mark Stubbs

Opened in 1856, Wheelers Oyster Bar in Whitstable is a bona fide British institution and a much-celebrated local gem. Catering for the tiny dining room in the back parlour, head chef Mark Stubbs cooks 'from the heart'. This imaginative chef serves subtle modern fish dishes using produce straight from the boat, earning him a dedicated following among locals and visitors alike.

> Fresh-tasting, punchy fennel makes the perfect partner for seafood.

1   **To make the fennel purée,** sweat the fennel in a little oil over a medium heat for about 5 minutes. Add the fennel seeds and continue to sweat for a few more minutes. Add the pastis and simmer for about 1 minute to cook off the excess alcohol. Cover the fennel with water and reduce until almost all of the liquid has evaporated. Transfer to a food processor and blend to a purée, then pass through a sieve, adjust the seasoning and keep warm.

2   **For the clam emulsion,** sweat the carrot, leek, celery, shallot and garlic in the oil over a medium heat. Then add the dill, wine and clams, cover with a lid and cook for about 3 minutes until the clams have opened.

3   Strain all the liquid through a muslin cloth, remove the clams and pick them out of their shells. Reserve the clams in a little of the liquid and set aside. Reduce the remaining liquid over a medium heat by a third, then add the double cream and whisk in the cold butter. Finish with a little lemon juice, if needed. Keep warm.

4   **To cook the ray and langoustines,** first blanch the langoustines or prawns in boiling salted water. Refresh in cold water, then peel off their shells and reserve the flesh.

5   Fillet the ray (if using) from the cartilage, keeping the flesh intact. If using ray, trim it into portions. Then put the ray or plaice onto individual pieces of cling film. Season lightly with salt and pepper and add a few drops of lemon juice.

6   Roll the shelled langoustines in the tarragon and place evenly along the centre of the fish fillets. Roll each tightly in cling film to make a sausage shape. Tie both ends of the cling film, place in the fridge and leave the rolls for at least 10 minutes to set. To cook the fish, bring a pan of water to the boil and add the fish rolls. Reduce the heat to a gentle simmer and cook the rolls for 10–12 minutes. Remove the rolls from the pan and allow to rest for 1 minute.

Serves 4

For the fennel purée
2 young fennel bulbs, trimmed and
    diced
Splash of olive oil
12g fennel seeds
100ml pastis
Salt and freshly ground black pepper

For the clam emulsion
15g diced carrot
15g diced white part of a leek
1 celery stick, trimmed and diced
1 shallot, peeled and finely diced
2 garlic cloves, peeled and finely
    diced
Splash of olive oil
3 fronds of dill, snipped
120ml dry white wine
20 clams in their shells
20ml double cream
20–30g cold unsalted butter, diced
Few drops of lemon juice (optional)

For the ray and langoustines
12 langoustines or large tiger prawns
    in their shells
1 medium-sized wing of ray, skinned,
    or 4 fillets of plaice
Drizzle of lemon juice
8 sprigs of tarragon, leaves chopped

For the baby leeks
12 baby leeks
Knob of unsalted butter

For the baby carrots
12 baby carrots
60g butter

To serve
Coastal herbs, such as sea purslane,
    stonecrop and samphire (optional)

7   **To cook the baby leeks,** blanch them in boiling salted
    water and then refresh in cold water.

8   **For the baby carrots,** put them in a pan, pour in
    enough water to come halfway up the carrots, add the
    butter and a pinch of salt and bring to the boil. Reduce
    the heat to medium and cook for 5–6 minutes until all the water has evaporated
    and the carrots are tender.

9   **To serve,** reheat the leeks in a pan by melting the butter and adding an equal
    portion of water. Pick the little pearls from the herbs (if using) and add them to the
    clam emulsion. Divide the fennel purée between warmed plates and add the baby
    vegetables. Remove the cling film from the fish rolls, then cut into slices, arrange
    on the plates and finish with the clams and spoonfuls of the clam emulsion. The
    chef suggests serving this with pieces of pork belly and crackling (see page 6).

RED SPICE CRUSTED HAKE
with white tomato velouté
Michael Smith

Australian-born Michael Smith was lured to St Ives by the surf and is now executive chef and partner in the Porthminster Beach Café. Perched on the beach, the Porthminster's relaxed, no-rules vibe and stunning backdrop is the perfect setting for Michael's globally inspired modern seafood. This dish takes its inspiration from the locals of St Ives, who have long been known as 'hakes'.

A milky white fish gets a fiery kick in a sophisticated springtime dish.

1 **The tomato consommé** is an important part of the white tomato velouté. To make it, first preheat the oven to 120°C (Gas ½). Put all the ingredients into a roasting tin, cover with foil and cook in the oven for 1½ hours. Remove from the oven and transfer the contents of the tin into a muslin cloth. Wrap the mixture in the cloth and place in a colander over a large bowl with a heavy weight on the top of the cloth-wrapped mixture and leave in the fridge overnight so the liquid drains into the bowl. Pick out the herbs from the muslin and reserve. Adjust the seasoning of the consommé with salt, sugar and white wine vinegar and then measure out 300ml for the white tomato velouté (store any remaining consommé to add to a soup or stock).

2 **For the white tomato velouté,** melt the butter in a heavy-based pan. Add the shallots, garlic, bay leaf, thyme and a pinch of pepper and sweat over a medium heat for 4–5 minutes until the shallots and garlic are translucent but not coloured. Add the vermouth and reduce by half over 5–10 minutes. Add the tomato consommé and cream and cook for about 20 minutes until it is thick enough to coat the back of a spoon. Remove from the heat and leave to cool.

3 To clarify the velouté, beat the egg whites until stiff and add the egg shells, peppercorns and reserved herbs. Stir this into the cold velouté and gently bring to the boil. Reduce the heat and simmer for 25–30 minutes. Strain the mixture through a sieve and set aside.

4 **For the red spice crust of the hake,** hold the red pepper over a flame and blacken all over. Place in a bowl and cover with cling film and leave to stand for a few minutes. Pull off the skin, cut in half and remove the seeds. Transfer to a food processor and add the spices, garlic, breadcrumbs, the 60g of butter and a pinch of sea salt and blend until smooth.

5 To cook the hake, preheat the grill to hot. Heat the butter and oil in a pan until hot and then pan fry the fish, skin-side down, for 2–3 minutes until golden. Flip the fish over, spread the crust thinly over the crispy skin and then finish under the grill for 3 minutes to caramelise the crust.

6 **To serve,** blanch the samphire in a pan of boiling water, then drain and refresh in a bowl of iced water. Spoon the white tomato velouté into warmed bowls. On the other side of the plate, place a spoonful of samphire and lay a piece of hake on top. The chef suggests serving this dish with crab and prawn cannelloni garnished with shrimps and capers (see page 6).

Serves 4

For the tomato consommé
2kg ripe tomatoes
1 tbsp white peppercorns
15 parsley stalks
3 tsp finely chopped basil
3 tsp finely chopped tarragon
3 tsp finely chopped thyme
3 tsp finely chopped oregano
2 heads of garlic
Sea salt and freshly ground black pepper
Caster sugar, to taste
White wine vinegar, to taste

For the white tomato velouté
½ tbsp unsalted butter
6 very small shallots, peeled and chopped
½ garlic clove, peeled and chopped
1 bay leaf
Sprig of thyme
125ml dry vermouth
250ml double cream
3 egg whites
3 egg shells, crushed
1 tbsp whole black peppercorns

For the red spice crusted hake
½ small red pepper
1 tsp ground sumac
1 tsp sweet non-smoked paprika
Pinch of cayenne pepper
½ garlic clove, peeled
50g Panko white breadcrumbs
60g unsalted butter, softened
Knob of unsalted butter
Splash of olive oil
4 fillets of hake, about 160g each

To serve
100g samphire

POACHED SQUID INK MONKFISH
with basil linguini & saffron mayonnaise
Robert Brittain

The views from 1539 over Chester racecourse may be spectacular, but there's plenty of distraction on the plate, where head chef Robert Brittain's globally influenced dishes deliver heavyweight flavours.

Despite wavering between whether to join the armed forces or become a chef, the young Robert – with the help of grandmother Marjorie – couldn't resist the lure of the professional kitchen. 'There's something about working with food,' he says. 'There's always something going on …'

> A vibrant, colourful dish that's as big on flavour as it is on visual impact.

1 **For the basil linguini,** put the basil, egg yolks, egg and oil into a bowl and, using a hand-held blender, mix to a smooth paste. Put the flour in a food processor and add three-quarters of the basil and egg mix and pulse to bring together. Add the rest of the mix to increase the pliability of the dough, remove from the processor, cover with cling film and allow to rest for 30 minutes.

2 Roll the pasta through a pasta machine to setting number 2, then roll through the linguini cutter. Blanch the pasta in boiling salted water for 20 seconds and refresh in iced water. Remove from the water, roll in a little oil and set aside.

3 **For the chorizo,** put the chorizo in a pan of water, bring to a simmer and cook for 10 minutes. Drain and allow the chorizo to cool before slicing it into lozenges about 1.5cm thick. Set aside.

4 **For the saffron mayonnaise,** combine the saffron with 2 tbsp of water in a small pan and warm gently to make saffron water. Mix the egg yolks with the mustard in a bowl and slowly add the oil. Whisk in the saffron water, add a squeeze of lemon juice and season with salt.

5 **To cook the monkfish,** roll up each piece of monkfish as tightly as possible. Then roll the fish in the squid ink (wear a pair of disposable gloves to avoid staining your hands) and, using pieces of cling film, roll the fish even more tightly so that they will keep their shape well. Tie the ends and put the monkfish rolls in the fridge for at least 30 minutes and preferably up to 24 hours.

6 Bring a pan of water to the boil, then add the monkfish (still in the cling film). Reduce the heat and simmer for 6–10 minutes, depending on the thickness of each roll. Check the fish

is cooked by inserting a cocktail stick into each roll. If it is cooked through, the cocktail stick will not meet any resistance. Remove the monkfish from the water with a slotted spoon and leave on a plate to rest.

7   **For the battered squid,** whisk together the flour, bicarbonate of soda and egg, then add 250ml of iced water to form a batter. Heat the oil to 180°C in a large pan or a deep fryer. Roll the tentacles in a little flour, then dip them in the batter and deep fry for 1–2 minutes until crisp. Drain on kitchen paper.

8   **To finish,** put the chorizo in a warm pan with the oil and brown gently on each side. Reheat the pasta in a pan of boiling salted water and transfer to another pan with the pesto. Gently mix together with a carving fork, then split into 12 small piles, scoop each one on the end of the fork and roll it against the edge of the pan to form a scroll.

9   **To serve,** put the scrolls of pasta on warmed plates. Take the monkfish out of the cling film and trim the ends. Slice each roll into three, lightly season with salt and place on the plate leaning against the scrolls of pasta. Top the pasta with the squid tentacles and add some mayonnaise and chorizo to the plates. The chef suggests serving this dish with saffron-poached tomatoes and red pepper caramel; you may also wish to make your own pesto (see page 6).

Serves 4

For the basil linguini
75g basil leaves
8 egg yolks
1 medium egg
1 tsp olive oil, plus extra for moistening
250g '00' pasta flour
Salt
1 tbsp green pesto

For the chorizo
130g soft chorizo
Splash of vegetable oil

For the saffron mayonnaise
Small pinch of saffron threads
2 medium egg yolks
1 tsp Dijon mustard
300ml light olive oil
Squeeze of lemon juice

For the monkfish
4 monkfish loins or tails, bone removed, about 180g each
4g packet of squid ink

For the battered squid
125g plain flour
½ tsp bicarbonate of soda
1 medium egg
500ml vegetable oil
2 squid, tentacles only

BLACK SESAME MONKFISH
on a quinoa, mushroom & miso risotto
Tina Pemberton

A unique and idiosyncratic dining experience, the Café at Brovey Lair is a restaurant in Tina Pemberton's own Norfolk home. The no-menu approach sees Tina cooking dishes according to each diner's own preference, with a focus on pan-Asian fusion and spectacular seafood. This monkfish dish with quinoa, mushroom and miso risotto takes influences from Japan and the Mediterranean, resulting in a complex symphony of flavour and texture and the thrilling contrasts for which Tina's cooking is renowned.

Notes of ginger and wasabi give this toothsome fish dish some serious bite.

1   **For the black sesame monkfish,** trim the monkfish tail and remove the membrane, then cut it into 8–12 small medallions. Coat the monkfish with sesame oil and then spread the ginger and garlic over the fish. Place the medallions in a shallow dish and generously sprinkle the sesame seeds over the fish until it is covered. Drizzle over the tamari, mirin and sake and add the chopped chilli (if using). Cover and set aside.

2   **To make the quinoa, mushroom and miso risotto,** first remove the mushroom stalks and discard, then slice the remaining mushroom flesh. Heat the oil in a stainless steel pan over a medium heat, add the leek and sauté for 5–8 minutes until soft. Add the mushrooms and sauté for a few minutes, then add the ginger and garlic, followed by the sea vegetables and the quinoa. Stir together and remove from the heat.

3   Put the barley miso in a bowl and add the boiling water. Stir to mix, then pour into the quinoa and mushroom mixture, return to the heat and simmer, uncovered, for about 20 minutes. When it starts to thicken, add a splash of boiling water, then stir. If necessary, repeat to stop the mixture from sticking. Simmer for a further 5 minutes. Cover with a lid and keep warm.

4   **For the roasted beetroot, mooli and hijiki salad,** preheat the oven to 200°C (Gas 6). Coat the beetroot in the oil and sprinkle with sea salt. Place in a roasting tin and cook for 45 minutes. Remove from the oven and coarsely grate. It will be extremely hot, so wear rubber gloves to protect your hands. Leave to cool.

Serves 4

For the black sesame monkfish
1kg monkfish tail, untrimmed
2–3 tbsp blended sesame oil
3cm piece fresh root ginger, peeled
  and grated
2 garlic cloves, peeled and crushed
25g black sesame seeds
2 tsp tamari soy sauce
2 tsp mirin
2 tsp sake
¼ chilli, deseeded and finely chopped
  (optional)

For the quinoa, mushroom and miso
  risotto
60g shiitake mushrooms
60g oyster mushrooms
Splash of blended sesame oil
1 leek, white part only, chopped
Small piece of fresh root ginger,
  peeled and grated
1 garlic clove, peeled and crushed
1 tsp dried sea vegetables
50g quinoa, rinsed
30g barley miso
200ml boiling water

For the roasted beetroot, mooli and
  hijiki salad
200g uncooked beetroot, peeled and
  cut in half
2 tbsp extra-virgin olive oil
Pinch of crushed sea salt
20g hijiki
½ small mooli or 1 radish, peeled and
  grated

For the wasabi and honey dressing
½ tsp wasabi mustard paste
2 tsp rice wine vinegar
20ml toasted sesame oil
20ml extra-virgin olive oil
1 tsp dark honey
Juice of ½ lime

To finish
1–2 tbsp groundnut oil

To serve
4 spring onions, trimmed and
  chopped in half

5   Meanwhile, soak the hijiki in water for 30 minutes. Bring a
    stainless steel pan of water to the boil, drain and rinse the
    soaked hijiki and add to the water in the pan. Reduce the heat
    and simmer for 20 minutes. Add the mooli or radish to the
    grated beetroot, then drain the hijiki and add to the vegetables.
    Set aside while you make the dressing.

6   **To make the wasabi and honey dressing,** put all the
    ingredients in a glass bowl and blend together. Set aside until
    you are ready to serve.

7   **To finish,** heat the groundnut oil in a steel wok until hot and
    stir fry the monkfish in its marinade for 2–3 minutes until sticky
    outside and soft in the middle.

8   **To serve,** toss the roasted beetroot, mouli and hijiki salad in
    the wasabi and honey dressing and make a shallow pile on
    each warmed plate. Oil a small mould or coffee cup, fill with
    the quinoa risotto and carefully place the mould on top of the
    salad. Press down to form a circular bed for the fish and put
    several medallions on top. Between the medallions of monkfish
    place a cross made from two slices of spring onion.

SEA BASS AGNOLOTTI
with a velvet crab sauce
Giorgio Alessio

'I'm a Yorkshire pudding now,' says Giorgio Alessio with pride, having fully embraced the marriage of Yorkshire produce with his fine Italian *cucina*. Chef-proprietor of Scarborough's enduringly popular Lanterna Ristorante, Giorgio is as renowned for his passion and vigour as for his sublime cooking of sparklingly fresh fish. An early champion of local sourcing and foraging, Giorgio has long been found choosing fish at the market every morning, and picking herbs from his allotment, mushrooms from the forest and winkles from the beach.

Serves 4

For the fish stock
4 portions of sea bass, about 125g each, skinned, filleted and bones set aside
1 carrot, peeled and roughly chopped
1 celery stick, trimmed and roughly chopped
1 onion, peeled and roughly chopped
2 bay leaves

For the pasta filling
250g ricotta cheese
5 large basil leaves
Salt and freshly ground black pepper

For the pasta
500g '00' pasta flour
5 medium eggs

For the sauce
Knob of unsalted butter
½ onion, peeled and finely chopped
1 garlic clove, peeled and chopped
250g velvet crab meat, finely chopped
100ml dry white wine
100ml whipping cream
Large pinch of chopped flat-leaf parsley, plus extra to garnish
Salt and freshly ground black pepper

To serve
Dry-cured ham, grilled and broken into pieces

1   **To make the fish stock,** put the fish bones and remaining ingredients in a large pan and cover with boiling water. Bring back up to the boil, then reduce the heat and simmer for 10 minutes. Drain the fish stock into a clean pan, reserving 100ml for the sauce, and set aside.

2   To cook the fish, put the sea bass into a steamer and cook for 5–6 minutes until it is opaque and flakes easily.

3   **For the pasta filling,** put the ricotta cheese and basil into a food processor. Add salt and pepper and blend. Flake the sea bass into the mixture and blend to a purée. Transfer the mixture into a bowl and place in the fridge for 15 minutes to chill. Clean the food processor.

4   **To make the pasta,** put the flour and eggs into the food processor and mix to make a dough. Leave to rest for 5 minutes, then divide the dough into four. Using a pasta machine, roll each quarter into long sheets about 1mm thick.

A pasta dish to die for, dressed in a luxurious crab sauce.

5   Spoon 1 tsp of the filling every 5cm across one of the pasta sheets. Then brush a little water around each heap of the filling to help to seal the agnolotti. Place a second sheet of pasta on top. Seal the pasta around each teaspoon of sea bass filling using your fingers and, using a ravioli wheel, cut to make little parcels. Repeat this with the rest of the pasta and filling. (You will end up with about 40 very small agnolotti.) Bring the fish stock to the boil, then add the pasta parcels, reduce the heat and cook the agnolotti at a simmer for 3–4 minutes until they rise to the surface.

6   **For the sauce,** heat the butter in a pan over a medium heat, then add the onion and fry for 2–3 minutes until translucent. Add the garlic and crab meat and cook for 2 minutes. Add the white wine and allow it to reduce for a couple of minutes and then add the reserved 100ml of fish stock and the cream. Reduce the sauce for about 10 minutes until slightly thickened.

7   **To serve,** drain the agnolotti and stir them into the sauce together with the flat-leaf parsley. Season with salt and pepper and divide between warmed bowls, garnishing them with the remaining parsley and topping with the ham.

PAN-FRIED SEA BASS
with a cockle toastie
Ben Griffiths

From chief runner-bean peeler in his mum's kitchen at the age of five, to head chef at Parkmill's Maes-Yr-Haf in Swansea, Ben Griffiths' passion for cooking is equalled only by his passion for Wales. Located in the heart of the Gower peninsula, Maes-Yr-Haf enjoys the pick of fresh local produce and Ben's cosmopolitan culinary approach sees classic combinations enlivened by modern twists, as seen in the cockle toastie that accompanies this stunning sea bass dish.

1   **For the cockle toasties,** put the sea bass trimmings in a food processor with the egg white and blend until smooth. Pass through a sieve into a small bowl. Fold in the double cream, cockle meat and herbs and season with salt and pepper. Cover and chill in the fridge for 20 minutes.

2   Roll out the bread to a 3mm thickness and cut off the crusts. Brush along the edges with water, then place 1 tsp of the cockle mousse in the centre of each slice and fold over the bread to seal into a parcel, expelling any air. Chill in the fridge until ready to serve.

3   **For the potatoes,** bring a large pan of salted water to the boil. Add the potatoes and cook for 20–25 minutes until tender. Drain, then crush with the butter and chives. Season with salt and pepper and keep warm.

4   **For the samphire,** bring a pan of salted water to the boil, add the samphire and cook for 3 minutes. Drain and keep warm.

5   **For the tomato concassé,** with a paring knife, score the tomatoes with an X at the opposite end to where the stem was once attached. Immerse the tomatoes in boiling water for 10 seconds or until they start to blister, then plunge them into iced water immediately until cold. Peel off the skin and cut in half crossways. Hold the tomato halves cut-side down and squeeze to rid them of their seeds and any water. Finely dice.

6   Put the oil in a bowl with the lemon juice and stir together. Stir in the chopped herbs followed by the diced tomatoes.

7   **For the fillets of sea bass,** remove any bones from the fillets and score the skin with a sharp knife, then season with salt and pepper. Heat the oil in a pan and add the sea bass, skin-side down. Cook for 3 minutes and then turn the fillets over and cook for 1 minute more. Remove from the heat.

8   **To finish the cockle toasties,** heat the rapeseed oil in a pan over a medium heat and cook the toasties for 3 minutes until golden brown. Remove from the pan and drain on kitchen paper, then season with salt and pepper.

9   **To serve,** spoon the crushed potatoes into a ring mould on each warmed plate, carefully removing the mould each time. Lay the samphire next to the potato and place the sea bass on top of the crushed potatoes and the toastie on top of the samphire. Spoon around the tomato concassé.

Serves 4

For the cockle toasties
60g sea bass trimmings
1 egg white
25ml double cream
25g picked cockle meat
20g mixed herbs, chopped
Sea salt and freshly ground white
   pepper
4 slices of white bread
50ml rapeseed oil

For the potatoes
400g new potatoes, peeled
25g unsalted butter, diced
10g chives, chopped

For the samphire
200g samphire

For the tomato concassé
2 tomatoes
120ml olive oil
25ml lemon juice
10g basil, chopped
10g chives, chopped
10g tarragon, chopped

For the sea bass
4 fillets of wild sea bass, about 150g
   each
50ml rapeseed oil

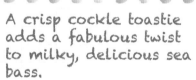

A crisp cockle toastie adds a fabulous twist to milky, delicious sea bass.

SMOKED SEA BASS
with steak & oyster pudding
Grant Nethercott

A refurbished lifeboat house on the harbour front at St Ives is home to Alba, where head chef Grant Nethercott masterminds some of the finest seafood cooking in Cornwall. His classical French training underpins a contemporary menu that uses the best local produce. He defines his sea bass with steak and oyster pudding as a 'seventies retro surf and turf'.

1. **To make the steak and oyster pudding filling,** dust the fillet steak in the flour and heat the oil in a large heavy-based pan. Fry the steak for a couple of minutes on each side until browned, then add the carrot, onions, garlic, red wine and thyme and cook for about 5 minutes until the liquid has reduced to almost nothing. Add the beef stock and cook again for about 5 minutes to achieve a thick sauce consistency. Remove from the heat and set aside. Take the oysters out of their shells, reserving the juices for step 4.

> Don't cook the fish stock for longer than 20 minutes as the flavour won't improve, it will just go bitter.

2. **For the suet pastry,** sift the flour and a pinch of salt into a large bowl, add the suet and season with pepper. Add about 2 tbsp of cold water and bring together to form a dough, kneading until it forms a smooth ball. Allow to rest for 5 minutes, then roll out the pastry on a floured surface until it is 1cm thick.

3. Butter four individual pudding moulds and cut out four large discs from the pastry to line the moulds and four small discs to make the lids. Line the moulds with the large discs and fill to halfway with the steak filling. Place an oyster on top of the steak filling and cover with more steak filling to just below the top of the mould. Wet the rim of the mould with a little water and place the smaller pastry disc on top. Crimp the edges to seal, wrap the moulds in cling film and place in a steamer for 15–20 minutes.

4. **To make the oyster jus,** place the fish bones or stock cube in a large pan and add 1 litre of cold water. Stir in the fennel, onion, bay leaf and peppercorns and bring to the boil. Reduce the heat and simmer for 20 minutes, then skim any scum off the top and pass the stock through a sieve. Return the stock to the pan and, over a high heat, reduce the liquid to 100ml. Add the cream and reduce by half again. Finally, add the oyster juices and the butter.

5. **To cook the smoked sea bass,** preheat the oven to 180°C (Gas 4). Heat the oil in an ovenproof pan, then add the sea bass, skin-side down, and cook for 2 minutes. Transfer to the oven and cook for 7–8 minutes.

6. **To serve,** steam the leeks for about 2 minutes until al dente and sauté the mushrooms for about 5 minutes in the butter. Turn out the beef and oyster puddings onto warmed plates. Place the leeks in a pile, top with the sea bass and scatter the sautéed mushrooms around the plates.

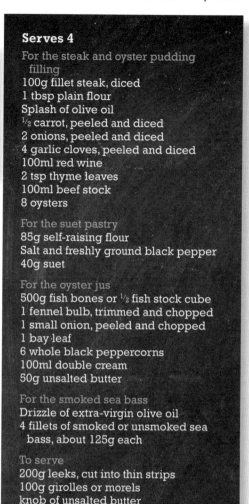

Serves 4

For the steak and oyster pudding filling
100g fillet steak, diced
1 tbsp plain flour
Splash of olive oil
½ carrot, peeled and diced
2 onions, peeled and diced
4 garlic cloves, peeled and diced
100ml red wine
2 tsp thyme leaves
100ml beef stock
8 oysters

For the suet pastry
85g self-raising flour
Salt and freshly ground black pepper
40g suet

For the oyster jus
500g fish bones or ½ fish stock cube
1 fennel bulb, trimmed and chopped
1 small onion, peeled and chopped
1 bay leaf
6 whole black peppercorns
100ml double cream
50g unsalted butter

For the smoked sea bass
Drizzle of extra-virgin olive oil
4 fillets of smoked or unsmoked sea bass, about 125g each

To serve
200g leeks, cut into thin strips
100g girolles or morels
knob of unsalted butter

PAN-FRIED SEA BASS
with textures of cauliflower
Tony Parkin

At just 27, Tony Parkin's youth belies the experience that this chef has already garnered in restaurants such as Gordon Ramsay's Royal Hospital Road and Northcote Manor. Now head chef at Sheffield's Wig & Pen by the Milestone, Tony's robust modern British menus are a platform for the freshest local ingredients, whether it's pork from the restaurant's own rare-breed herd of pigs or produce from local allotment growers.

Serves 4

For the cauliflower samosas
1 tbsp vegetable oil
2 banana shallots, peeled and chopped
2 garlic cloves, peeled and chopped
25g fresh root ginger, peeled and chopped
½ red chilli, deseeded and diced
½ tbsp mild curry powder
½ tsp yellow mustard seeds
½ tbsp cumin powder
½ tsp madras powder
½ tsp ground cumin
½ tsp ground ginger
½ head of cauliflower, chopped
50g coriander leaves, chopped
2 sheets of filo pastry
1 egg, beaten

For the cauliflower tempura
250ml vegetable oil
50g cornflour
250ml sparkling mineral water
½ head of cauliflower, separated into small florets
Sea salt

For the cauliflower carpaccio
½ cauliflower

For the pan-fried sea bass
4 fillets of sea bass, about 150g each
Salt
50g unsalted butter

To garnish
Handful of coriander cress

1 **For the cauliflower samosas,** preheat the oven to 180°C (Gas 4). Heat the oil in a pan over a medium heat, add the shallots and garlic and cook for about 4 minutes to soften. Then add the ginger, chilli and all the spices and cook for 1 minute, stirring continuously, to release the flavour. Add the cauliflower and cook for about 5 minutes until tender. Stir in the coriander leaves and leave for 5–10 minutes to cool.

2 Cut a strip lengthways from a single sheet of filo pastry that is about 2.5cm wide. Lay on a work surface with the narrow ends at the top and bottom. Place 1 tsp of the filling about 3cm from the bottom of the sheet of pastry. Take the bottom left-hand corner of pastry, brush the edges with a little water, then fold it up over the filling and press the pastry together to seal. Fold over again, then continue folding the triangle up the strip of pastry adding water to seal. You will be left with a triangle-shaped samosa. Repeat with more strips, until you have eight samosas. Brush with beaten egg, transfer to a baking sheet and cook for about 5 minutes until golden.

3 **For the cauliflower tempura,** heat the oil to 180°C in a large pan or a deep fryer. Mix the cornflour with the mineral water in a bowl and add the cauliflower florets. Deep fry the florets for about 2 minutes until golden, then drain on kitchen paper and season with salt.

4 **To prepare the cauliflower carpaccio,** slice the cauliflower as thinly as you are able.

5 **For the pan-fried sea bass,** season the fillets with salt. Heat the butter in a pan until hot and then pan fry the sea bass, skin-side down, for 2–3 minutes. Flip the bass over, turn off the heat and let it carry on cooking for about 1 minute.

6 **To serve,** cut each sea bass fillet into two and position two pieces on each warmed plate with two samosas resting next to them. Scatter the tempura cauliflower around the plates, add pieces of the carpaccio and garnish with the coriander cress. The chef suggests serving this dish with cauliflower purée, cumin milk and a lime vinaigrette (see page 6).

When you flip over the fish and turn off the heat, the fish carries on cooking - but it won't overcook.

33

PAN-FRIED WILD SEA BASS
with spinach & potato gateau & moilee sauce
Sudha Shankar Saha

'Cooking is like love,' says Saffron's head chef Sudha Shankar Saha. 'It should be entered into abundantly or not at all.' Sudha pushes the boundaries of multi-cultural cuisine, fusing local produce with global influences to refine his predominantly Indian fare. The results of this East–West love affair are spectacular, and a world away from Birmingham's infamous baltis. This dish of pan-fried wild sea bass with spinach and potato gateau and moilee sauce takes its inspiration from south India. It exemplifies Sudha's preoccupation with balance, nutritional value and the intertwining of ethnic styles.

1   **For the marinade,** mix together the ginger garlic paste, turmeric, coriander, lemon juice, mustard powder and a pinch of salt in a small bowl. Put the fillets of wild sea bass on a plate and coat with the marinade. Cover and leave to marinate for 30 minutes.

2   **To make the moilee sauce,** heat the oil in a pan over a medium heat, add the mustard seeds and, when they start to crackle, add the curry leaves and onion. Cook for 4–5 minutes until the onion is soft and translucent. Add the spices, sauté for few minutes, adding water, if necessary, to prevent them from drying out, and wait for about 5 minutes until the spices emit their oil. Then pour in the coconut milk and bring to the boil. Reduce the heat and leave to simmer for about 10 minutes until the sauce has reduced to 250ml. Add the tamarind extract and check the seasoning, adjusting with sugar to taste. Keep warm.

3   **For the spinach and potato gateau,** bring a pan of salted water to the boil, add the potatoes and cook for about 20 minutes until tender. Drain and mash roughly, then set aside. Heat the oil in a pan over a medium heat, add the mustard seeds and curry leaves and cook for about 2 minutes until the mustard seeds start to crackle. Add the spinach and chickpeas and cook for 2 minutes. Then add the coriander and turmeric and cook for a further 3 minutes, stirring continuously to avoid burning. Pour in a little water, if necessary, to prevent sticking. Add the mashed potato, mix well and check the seasoning, adding salt if necessary. Keep warm.

4   **To serve,** heat the oil in a non-stick pan over a medium heat. Add the fillets of wild sea bass, skin-side down, and cook for 2 minutes. Turn over and cook for a further 2 minutes. Place a square of spinach and potato gateau on each warmed plate. Top with the fish and pour the moilee sauce halfway around the plate. Garnish with micro herbs. The chef suggests serving this dish with spiced samphire and garnishing it with red caviar achar (see page 6).

Serves 4

For the marinade
40g ginger garlic paste
1 tsp turmeric
½ tsp ground coriander
50ml lemon juice
1 tbsp English mustard powder
Salt
4 fillets of wild sea bass, about 180g each

For the moilee sauce
2 tbsp sunflower oil
½ tsp mustard seeds
5 curry leaves
½ onion, peeled and chopped
½ tsp turmeric
1½ tsp ground coriander
500ml coconut milk
60g tamarind extract (see the tip, below)
Pinch of granulated sugar

For the spinach and potato gateau
2 potatoes, peeled and chopped
2 tbsp sunflower oil
Pinch of mustard seeds
6 curry leaves
80g baby leaf spinach
80g canned chickpeas, drained
½ tsp ground coriander

To serve
3 tbsp sunflower oil
Micro herbs

To make 60g of your own tamarind extract, boil 25g dry tamarind in 150ml of water. Leave to cool, then mix the pulp thoroughly in the water and strain.

PAN-FRIED SEA TROUT
with laverbread potato cakes, samphire & cockle sauce
Louise Gudsell

Attached to the Theatr Brycheiniog in the canal basin just outside Brecon, Louise Gudsell's Tipple'n'Tiffin specialises in plates of eclectic, globally influenced food. As chef-proprietor, Louise prides herself on the excellence of her ingredients, sourcing from local organic farms, as well as smoking chicken and salmon on-site. Admonished by her grandmother for peeling too much skin from her potatoes, Louise has learnt her lesson well and accompanies this stunning dish of wild sea trout with flavoursome laverbread potato cakes.

1. **To make the fish stock,** rinse the fish bones, heads and trimmings and put into a large stock pot. Add the remaining ingredients and enough cold water to cover the fish and vegetables, then put the pot on a high heat and bring the liquid to the boil. After 5 minutes, remove the scum that forms on the surface with a slotted spoon and discard. Reduce the heat and simmer, covered, for about 15 minutes, skimming as necessary. Remove the stock from the heat and strain into a jug, discarding the fish trimmings and the vegetables.

2. **To make the laverbread potato cakes,** put the potatoes in a pan of water. Bring to the boil, then reduce the heat and leave to simmer for about 20 minutes until soft. Drain, mash and leave to cool. Preheat the grill to hot, then grill the bacon for about 10 minutes until crispy and chop into small pieces. Combine the potato, bacon, laverbread and pepper and form into eight rounded and slightly flattened cakes. Coat in flour and shallow fry in the hot oil for about 5 minutes on each side until heated through and golden. Set aside and keep warm.

3. **For the cockle sauce,** heat the oil in a pan over a medium heat. Add the shallots and cook for about 4 minutes until softened. Then add the cockles and white wine, cover with a lid and cook for about 5 minutes until the cockles open. Remove the cockles from the pan with a slotted spoon, then remove the cockles from their shells, discarding the shells. Add 400ml of the fish stock and the lemon juice to the pan and simmer for about 20 minutes until the liquid has reduced by half. Remove from the heat, strain the liquid and set aside.

4. **To cook the sea trout,** heat the butter in a pan. Add the fillets, skin-side down, and cook for 1½–2 minutes. Turn the fillets over, add the reserved liquid from the cockles and cook for a further 1½–2 minutes until the fish is opaque and cooked through. If the sauce is not thick enough, remove the sea trout and keep warm while cooking the sauce for a further few minutes. Just before serving, add the cockles and some pepper to the sauce.

5. Add the samphire to a pan of boiling water. Bring back to the boil, then remove the pan from the heat and drain.

6. **To serve,** place two potato cakes in the middle of each warmed plate. Add some of the samphire, top with a fillet of sea trout, drizzle over the cockle sauce and garnish with a little more samphire.

Serves 4

For the fish stock
White bones, heads and trimmings reserved from the sea trout
1 onion, peeled and chopped
2 celery sticks, trimmed and roughly chopped
1 lemon, cut into quarters
2 bay leaves
16 whole black peppercorns

For the laverbread potato cakes
4 large potatoes, preferably Maris Piper, peeled and chopped
4 rashers of streaky smoked bacon
100g laverbread
Freshly ground black pepper
Plain flour, to coat
2 tbsp light olive oil

For the cockle sauce
2 tbsp olive oil
2 shallots, peeled and finely chopped
600g cockles in their shells
200ml dry white wine
2 tbsp lemon juice

For the sea trout
100g unsalted butter, diced
4 fillets of sea trout, about 120g each
200g samphire

Simply lovely – a wonderful, light supper dish that salutes a traditional Welsh delicacy.

SALMON PINWHEEL
with spiced couscous & langoustine tempura
Debbie Robson

'It runs through your blood,' says Debbie Robson of her passion for cooking. It's the 'sheer buzz' of the restaurant kitchen and the ecstatic reaction from customers that inspires Debbie's fine-dining take on Scottish seafood, for which the Seafood Restaurant in St Andrews is renowned. Debbie is now head chef, after beginning her tenure in the kitchen aged 19. Her salmon pinwheel dish epitomises her love of local Scottish seafood and the imaginative cooking that has won her such acclaim.

Don't remove the cling film before cooking the salmon as it keeps the salmon in the shape of a pinwheel.

Serves 4

For the salmon
450g side of salmon
Grated zest of 2 unwaxed lemons
50g parsley, chopped
Salt and freshly ground black pepper
Splash of olive oil

For the couscous
15g butter
75ml chicken stock
30g raisins
1 tbsp harissa paste
1 spring onion, trimmed and snipped
30g pine nuts
130g couscous

For the langoustine tempura
12 langoustines
50g plain flour
50g cornflour
Sea salt
200ml sparkling mineral water
Pinch of chopped parsley
500ml vegetable oil

For the curry vinaigrette
1 tsp Dijon mustard
1 tsp curry powder
1 tbsp lemon juice
½ garlic clove
Pinch of grated fresh root ginger
⅛ tsp harissa paste
2 tbsp white wine vinegar
80ml olive oil

To garnish
Micro herbs, such as mustard frills,
    red amaranth, sorrel

1   **To prepare the salmon,** skin the fish and lie it lengthways in front of you. Cut it horizontally almost to the edge of one side and open it up so it is twice as wide and half as thick as it was. Sprinkle the lemon zest and parsley over the salmon, season with salt and pepper and cut widthways into eight portions. Roll each portion in cling film from one narrow end, like a fish roll, and place in the fridge for 30 minutes to chill.

2   **For the couscous,** warm the butter, stock and 150ml of water in a small pan. Combine the remaining ingredients in a bowl with the couscous and once the liquid in the pan begins to boil, pour it over the mixture. Cover and leave for 5 minutes.

3   **For the langoustine tempura,** remove the head from each langoustine, then carefully remove the inner track. Remove the meat from the shell and set aside. Put the flour, cornflour and a pinch of salt into a bowl and gently whisk in the mineral water. Sprinkle the parsley into the batter. Place the langoustines into the batter and coat well. Heat the oil to 170°C in a large pan or a deep fryer and deep fry the langoustines for about 2 minutes.

4   **To make the curry vinaigrette,** put all the ingredients except the oil into a food processor and blend until smooth. Then slowly drizzle in the oil, mixing continuously. Pass through a sieve and set aside.

5   **To cook the salmon,** preheat the grill to high. Add a small amount of the oil to a pan over a medium heat and, once hot, place the salmon rolls in the pan, still in their cling film wraps, and cook for 2–3 minutes until golden. Turn and repeat. Remove from the pan and place on a baking sheet to finish cooking under the grill for about 1 minute on either side.

6   **To serve,** fold 3 tbsp of the curry vinaigrette into the couscous and divide the couscous between warmed plates. Top with two salmon pinwheels. Arrange the langoustines along the front and finish with a drizzle of the curry vinaigrette and a garnish of micro herbs. The chef suggests serving this dish with pineapple chutney and paprika crisps (see page 6).

FILLET OF WILD SALMON
with a Wensleydale & white chocolate crust
Tony Borthwick

A serious injury in 1987 prompted Tony Borthwick to reconsider his job with the water board and turn his passion for cooking into a career. With stints at top restaurants, including the Savoy, under his belt, he is now the chef/patron of Edinburgh's Plumed Horse where his produce-driven, innovative food has won him much acclaim. Tony's clear flavours and inventive techniques are shown to their best advantage in this delicious wild salmon dish.

Rich and indulgent; an unusual marriage of flavours that really sing.

1   **To prepare the salmon,** cut the salmon fillet into four 150g portions and reserve the remaining 100g portion for the salmon mousse. Place the 150g portions in the fridge until ready to use.

2   **For the salmon mousse,** put the reserved 100g of salmon in a food processor with the egg white and cream and blend to a purée. Pass through a sieve, season with salt and pepper and set aside.

3   **To sear the salmon fillets,** heat the oil in a pan and, when hot, briefly sear the salmon fillets all over and season with salt and pepper. Place in the fridge for 20 minutes to cool. Then spread the raw mousse on top, wrap each portion in cling film and set aside.

4   **For the fish velouté,** bring the fish stock to the boil and reduce over 5–10 minutes by three-quarters, then add the vermouth or wine and reduce again by half. Add the whipping cream, bring back up to the boil, season with salt and pepper and set aside.

5   **For the breadcrumb crust,** put the brioche into a food processor and pulse to make crumbs. Pass through a sieve and leave for about 10 minutes to dry out. Transfer to a bowl and mix in the cheese and chocolate, then season well with salt and pepper, adding the lemon zest and mint.

6   **To prepare the saffron potatoes,** mix the potatoes with a little olive oil and the saffron and set aside.

7   **For the spinach,** blanch the spinach in boiling salted water for 1 minute. Refresh in iced water, squeeze dry and set aside.

8   **To cook the salmon,** preheat the oven to 150°C (Gas 2). Poach the fish, still wrapped in cling film, in simmering water in a pan for 4 minutes. Remove from the water, unwrap the fillets and place them in a roasting tin. Cover the mousse with the breadcrumb crust and cook in the oven for about 10 minutes until the fish is pink in the middle and the cheese and chocolate have formed a crust.

9   **To cook the saffron potatoes,** sauté them in the remaining oil for about 10 minutes until crisp. Season with salt and pepper and keep warm.

10 **To serve,** reheat the spinach in the butter in a pan, divide between warmed plates and place the fish on top. Add the potatoes and serve with the reheated velouté alongside.

Serves 4

For the salmon
700g fillet of wild salmon, skin removed
Splash of olive oil

For the salmon mousse
1 egg white
100ml whipping cream
Sea salt and freshly ground white pepper

For the fish velouté
200ml fish stock
50ml vermouth or dry white wine
100ml whipping cream

For the Wensleydale and white chocolate crust
50g brioche
50g Wensleydale cheese, finely grated
50g white chocolate, finely grated
Grated zest of 1 unwaxed lemon
25g mint leaves, finely chopped

For the saffron potatoes
280g large new potatoes, peeled and cut into 12mm dice
Dash of extra-virgin olive oil
Pinch of saffron threads

For the spinach
400g baby leaf spinach
50g unsalted butter

LOBSTER & CHIPS
with mushy peas
Rob Green

Rob Green converted this old fish and chip shop in the historic fishing port of Whitby into Green's restaurant over ten years ago, and what a decade it has been. Loyal North Yorkshire diners flock to Green's for food that plunders the treasures of the coast. Rob buys his seafood directly from skippers at the quayside, and the fish from these boats is the mainstay of menus that change according to the day's catch, cooked with passion and imagination.

1   **To cook the lobster,** first kill it by inserting a sharp knife into the cross on the back of the head and plunging it into boiling water for 30 seconds to release the meat from the shell. Take the meat from the lobster tail and crack the claws. Rinse and set aside.

2   **For the chips,** heat the oil to 140°C in a large pan or a deep fryer. Peel the potatoes and chop into regular chip shapes then deep fry (in batches, if necessary) for 4–5 minutes until soft, but not coloured. Drain on kitchen paper and set aside. Heat the oil to 180°C.

3   **To make the tempura batter,** mix together the 150g of flour, cornflour and baking powder in a large bowl and then, using an electric hand-held mixer, whisk in the soda water to create a thin smooth batter (it should coat your finger when dipped in). Season with salt.

4   Put the 1 tbsp of flour on a plate and season with salt and pepper. Slice three 5mm pieces of lobster from the tail and choose the smaller of the claws. Dust each piece of lobster in the seasoned flour, then dip in the batter and deep fry for about 2 minutes until crisp and golden. Re-fry the blanched chips (in batches, if necessary) for about 2 minutes until cooked. Drain on kitchen paper.

5   **To make the tartare sauce hollandaise,** put the vinegar, peppercorns and bay leaf into a pan and bring to the boil. Then turn off the heat and allow the mixture to infuse for a few minutes. Strain into a glass bowl and then whisk in the egg yolks. Place the bowl over a pan of simmering water, whisking continuously, and slowly add the melted butter until you have a smooth sauce. Add the lemon juice, capers, gherkins and parsley. Season with salt and pepper and set aside in a warm place.

6   **For the mushy peas,** boil the peas in salted water for 4–5 minutes until they are just cooked and retain their bright green colour. Transfer to a food processor and blend until 'mushy', then season with sea salt, white pepper and a dash of malt vinegar.

7   **To serve,** put the chips and lobster in food-safe newspaper and add mushy pea quenelles and the tartare sauce hollandaise. The chef suggests that you may also wish to make a lobster 'ice cream', a lobster and seaweed 'sandcastle' salad and lobster candyfloss.

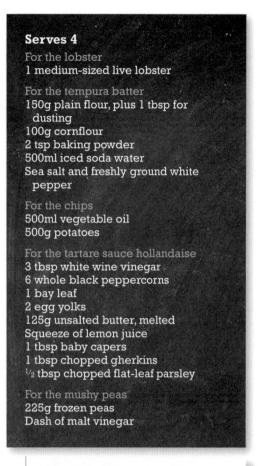

Serves 4

For the lobster
1 medium-sized live lobster

For the tempura batter
150g plain flour, plus 1 tbsp for dusting
100g cornflour
2 tsp baking powder
500ml iced soda water
Sea salt and freshly ground white pepper

For the chips
500ml vegetable oil
500g potatoes

For the tartare sauce hollandaise
3 tbsp white wine vinegar
6 whole black peppercorns
1 bay leaf
2 egg yolks
125g unsalted butter, melted
Squeeze of lemon juice
1 tbsp baby capers
1 tbsp chopped gherkins
½ tbsp chopped flat-leaf parsley

For the mushy peas
225g frozen peas
Dash of malt vinegar

All the flag-waving flavours of the Great British seaside.

BENGALI SPICED LOBSTER
with a mustard sauce
Abdul Yaseen

Abdul Yaseen remembers how cooking an omelette as a child sparked off his passion for cooking – and he's never looked back. His new-wave Indian food marries traditional ingredients with modern techniques to dazzling effect. Head chef of Cinnamon Kitchen in the heart of the City of London, Abdul borrows elements from all over India, using a scientific approach with time-honoured, robust flavours to produce meticulous, creative dishes that satisfy traditionalists and fashionistas alike.

1   **For the lobsters,** first kill them by inserting a sharp knife into the cross on the back of the head, then blanch them for 3 minutes in boiling water. Place the lobsters in ice-cold water to avoid further cooking. Twist off the claws (then cook them for another 1½ minutes in boiling water and return to the water). Use kitchen scissors to carefully cut open the shell of each lobster. Take the tail meat out of the shells and de-vein. Reserve the shells for the stock. Set the claws to one side to use as an extra part of the recipe, if you wish (see step 7).

2   **To make the lobster stock,** heat the oil in a large pan and sauté the lobster shells, then add the remaining ingredients. Cover with water and bring to the boil, then reduce the heat and simmer for 20 minutes. Remove from the heat, sieve half the stock into a bowl and set aside. Leave the rest of the stock in the pan and add a metal steamer over the top for the lobsters.

3   **For the lobster marinade,** mix all the marinade ingredients, except the banana leaves, in a large bowl together with 1 tsp of salt. Add the lobster tails and evenly apply the marinade over them. Wrap each tail in a banana leaf and set aside for 10 minutes. Reserve the remaining marinade to use as a base for the sauce.

> A marinade of ginger, chilli and mustard delivers a shellfish spiced to perfection.

4   **For the mustard sauce,** heat the oil in a heavy-based pan and sauté the onion, ginger garlic paste and chilli over a medium heat for 2–3 minutes. Add the turmeric and curry leaves, sauté for 2 minutes and deglaze the pan by adding 240ml of the reserved stock. Allow it to simmer for 3–4 minutes, then add the remaining lobster marinade. Simmer for a further 2–3 minutes and finish the sauce with the sugar, coconut milk and 1 tsp of salt. Stir in the coriander leaves and remove from the heat.

5   **To make the mushroom and samphire poriyal,** heat the oil in a pan, add the mustard seeds and roasted chana dal or dharia dal (if using) and allow them to splutter. Then add

Serves 4

For the lobsters
4 live lobsters

For the lobster stock
1 tbsp vegetable oil
1 tsp ginger garlic paste
5–6 whole black peppercorns
1 bay leaf
1 tsp coriander seeds
5–6 fresh curry leaves
Small bunch of coriander, leaves
  chopped

For the lobster marinade
1 tbsp vegetable oil
1/2 tbsp ginger garlic paste
2 green chillies, deseeded and
  finely chopped
5 curry leaves, chopped
1 tsp turmeric
2 tbsp Kasundi mustard
  sauce

3 tbsp coconut milk powder,
  mixed with water
Pinch of sugar
Dash of lemon juice
Small bunch of coriander leaves,
  finely chopped
4 banana leaves, each cut into
  a square
Salt

For the mustard sauce
1 tbsp vegetable oil
1 onion, peeled and finely
  chopped
1 tsp ginger garlic paste
1 green chilli, deseeded and
  finely chopped
1/2 tsp turmeric
3 whole curry leaves
Pinch of sugar
4 tbsp coconut milk
Bunch of coriander leaves, finely
  chopped

For the mushroom and samphire
  poriyal
1 tsp vegetable oil
1/4 tsp mustard seeds
1/2 tsp roasted chana dal or
  dharia dal (optional)
3 ceps, sliced
3 girolles, sliced
1/2 red onion, peeled and thickly
  sliced
1/2 tsp chopped fresh stem ginger
1/2 tsp deseeded and chopped
  green chillies
1 tsp chopped coriander leaves
100g shredded coconut
50g samphire
Small pinch of sugar
Dash of lemon juice

To garnish
Coriander cress and baby
  samphire

the vegetables, spices and coconut and cook for about 5 minutes to soften. Finally, add the samphire and stir fry over a medium-high heat. Finish with the sugar, lemon juice and a pinch of salt and set aside.

6   **To cook the lobsters,** unwrap the tails and put them in a steamer above the simmering stock and gently increase the temperature for 5–7 minutes while they cook through.

7   **To serve,** put a portion of stir-fried vegetables on one side of each warmed plate. Split the lobster tails and place them on the vegetables with their reverse sides on top of each other. Drizzle the mustard sauce around the plate and, finally, garnish with the coriander cress and baby samphire. The chef suggests serving this dish with kadhai spiced scallops with a tomato broth and spiced battered claws; for added authenticity, you can also make your own ginger garlic paste (see page 6).

PAVE OF TURBOT & LOBSTER CLAW
with fennel risotto & mussel & vermouth broth
Jean-Philippe Bidart

'The fusion of Anglo-French food with pub food,' is Jean-Philippe Bidart's culinary ethos at the Millbrook Inn, a proudly 'proper' village pub in South Hams, Devon. His rural auberge-style menus make the most of premium Devon produce by way of classical techniques, flair and much-loved family recipes. Jean-Philippe embraces the variety that cooking offers: 'There's always something different to do. I'm still learning, never bored; always searching for new dishes.'

1. **To make the fish stock,** first rinse the fish bones. Briefly cook the leek, onion and celery in the oil in a pan, being careful not to brown any of the ingredients. Add the fish bones (or stock cube), deglaze with wine and add the thyme, bay leaf and cardamom pods. Cover the ingredients with water, bring to the boil and leave to simmer for 20 minutes, skimming off any scum from the surface. Pass the stock through a sieve and set aside.

2. **For the fennel risotto,** heat the oil in a pan. Add the bay leaf and thyme and then the onion and sauté for about 3 minutes until soft and just taking on a golden colour. Add the rice and continue to cook over a medium heat for 2 minutes. Deglaze with the wine and add 250ml of the fish stock and a pinch of salt and pepper. Stir the ingredients and leave to cook on a low heat until the stock is absorbed into the rice, adding more stock if necessary, and the rice is cooked through.

3. Quickly sear the fennel in a pan with a splash of oil and stir into the risotto with 50ml of the fish stock and the butter. Finish off with the dill and some salt and pepper.

4. **For the mussel and vermouth broth,** pour the vermouth into a pan and heat until reduced by half. Add 200ml of the fish stock and reduce again by a third. Then add the cream, bring to the boil and add the mussels. Cover and cook over a high heat for about 5 minutes until the mussels have opened. Add the tomatoes, then season with salt and pepper. Discard any mussels that haven't opened.

5. **To cook the lobsters,** first kill them by inserting a sharp knife into the cross on the back of the head, then blanch them in boiling salted water for 8 minutes. Drain and set aside to cool. Slice the lobsters in half lengthways and remove the meat. Twist off the claws and carefully remove the meat from the tails. Preheat the oven to 180°C (Gas 4). Put the lobster meat and claws in a roasting tin, drizzle with oil to stop them drying out and put in the oven for 15 minutes to warm through.

6. **For the turbot,** trim each fillet of turbot to form a square. Pan fry the fish, skin-side down, in the oil for 3 minutes. Immediately turn the turbot over and cook for a further 2 minutes. Remove from the heat and set aside to rest.

7. **To serve,** place some risotto in the centre of each warmed plate. Remove the lobsters from the oven, position a pavé of turbot on top of the risotto and lean a lobster claw against it. Cut up the lobster meat and arrange it on the fish. Finally, add the mussels and pour a little broth over the top and around the plates. The chef suggests serving this dish with crispy pancetta and a cornet of Parmesan (see page 6).

Serves 4

For the fish stock
Fish bones from the turbot (see below) or 1 fish stock cube
1 leek, trimmed and chopped
1 onion, peeled and chopped
2 celery sticks, trimmed and chopped
25ml olive oil
250ml dry white wine
15g thyme leaves
1 bay leaf
2 cardamom pods

For the fennel risotto
2 tbsp extra-virgin olive oil
1 bay leaf
2 sprigs of thyme
30g diced onion
200g Arborio rice
200ml white dry wine
Sea salt and freshly ground black pepper
100g fennel, diced
Olive oil
20g unsalted butter
40g dill, chopped

For the mussel and vermouth broth
100ml vermouth
100ml double cream
200g mussels in their shells
100g tomatoes, deseeded and diced

For the lobsters
2 live lobsters, about 500g each
Splash of olive oil

For the turbot
4 fillets of turbot, about 160g each, with the skin left on
Splash of olive oil

Leave the lobster to cool by itself after cooking. It will continue to cook once taken out of the boiling water.

PAN-FRIED TURBOT
with chicken boudin & watercress
Simon McKenzie

A hugely talented chef who has worked under the likes of Gordon Ramsay and Marco Pierre White, Simon McKenzie is now head chef at the elegant Isle of Eriska Hotel. Simon favours classical combinations but takes a modernist approach, experimenting with texture and seasoning, and exploring the balance of salt, sweet, sour and acid flavours in each mouthful.

Simple, stylish turbot makes the perfect foil for an indulgent chicken boudin.

1   **For the chicken jus,** preheat the oven to 200°C (Gas 6). Put the lamb jus and chicken stock into a heavy-based pan and reduce over a high heat for 8–10 minutes to 200ml. At the same time, roast the the chicken wings in the oil in an ovenproof pan for about 15 minutes until slightly golden. Remove and set aside.

2   Add the shallot and butter to the pan the chicken wings have been cooked in and fry over a medium heat for about 3 minutes until a good golden colour is achieved, making sure the butter does not burn. Strain off the butter and return the wings to the pan. Deglaze with the tomatoes and vinegar, scraping the bottom of the pan to get all the flavours. Add to the chicken jus and simmer to a sauce consistency. Remove from the heat, add the tarragon and chervil and leave to infuse for 5 minutes. Pass through a sieve and set aside. Remove the meat from the chicken bones and reserve for the mousse.

3   **For the chicken boudin,** first make a chicken mousse. Cut the chicken breast into 2cm pieces. Put in a food processor with a pinch of salt and blend on full power until the chicken is puréed, stopping from time to time to scrape down the sides of the bowl. Add the cream and blend at full power for 30 seconds. Push the mousse through a sieve using a plastic spatula or a ladle.

4   Place a pan on a medium heat. Add the unsalted butter and then the onion. Season with salt and pepper and slowly sweat the onion for about 10 minutes, stirring occasionally, until evenly browned. You may also need to add a little more butter at times. When almost caramelised, drain the onion, spread it thinly on a plate and leave to cool for 15 minutes.

5   Mix the onion in a bowl with 2 tbsp of of the chicken jus, tarragon, vinegar and some salt and add 100g of the chicken mousse and 40g of the chicken wing meat. Lay a piece of cling film on a work surface and transfer the mixture to a piping bag with a 2cm nozzle. Pipe a 30cm-long sausage shape along the cling film and roll it up tightly. Poach for 8–10 minutes in a pan of boiling water, then plunge into iced water to refresh. Remove the cling film, cut the sausage into four 7cm-long boudins and then roll them twice through the flour, eggs and breadcrumbs. Heat the oil to 180°C in a large pan or a deep fryer and deep fry the boudins for 2–3 minutes until golden brown. Drain on kitchen paper.

6   **For the pan-fried turbot,** heat the oil in a pan and then fry the fish for 3–4 minutes on each side before adding the butter to finish off. Sprinkle with sea salt.

7   **To serve,** wilt the watercress in the butter in a pan and season with salt. Lay a line of it on a warmed plate and place a portion of turbot alongside. Add a chicken boudin on top of the watercress and drizzle some of the chicken jus over the boudin, watercress and around each plate. The chef suggests serving this dish with sweetcorn purée, mushrooms and artichoke hearts and a muscatel espuma (see page 6).

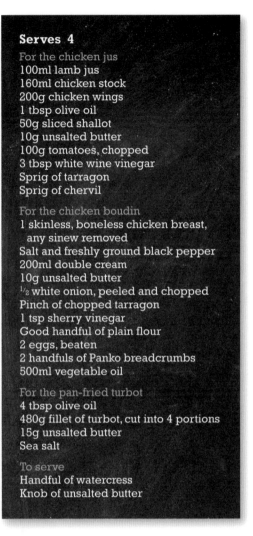

Serves 4

For the chicken jus
100ml lamb jus
160ml chicken stock
200g chicken wings
1 tbsp olive oil
50g sliced shallot
10g unsalted butter
100g tomatoes, chopped
3 tbsp white wine vinegar
Sprig of tarragon
Sprig of chervil

For the chicken boudin
1 skinless, boneless chicken breast,
   any sinew removed
Salt and freshly ground black pepper
200ml double cream
10g unsalted butter
½ white onion, peeled and chopped
Pinch of chopped tarragon
1 tsp sherry vinegar
Good handful of plain flour
2 eggs, beaten
2 handfuls of Panko breadcrumbs
500ml vegetable oil

For the pan-fried turbot
4 tbsp olive oil
480g fillet of turbot, cut into 4 portions
15g unsalted butter
Sea salt

To serve
Handful of watercress
Knob of unsalted butter

49

CHICKEN BREAST & CRISPY WINGS
with parsley dumplings & onion purée
Paul Heathcote

A Lancashire culinary legend, Paul Heathcote was pioneering in resurrecting some of the region's most celebrated dishes, including Lancashire black pudding. His flagship, the Longridge Restaurant, continues to deliver fine dishes of reinvented British regional food with great panache. Paul trained for two years with Raymond Blanc at Le Manoir aux Quat'Saisons, and says that this apprenticeship, along with stints at Sharrow Bay and the Connaught, sculpted him into the chef he is today.

1. **For the chicken breasts,** gently poach the fillets in enough water to cover them with the butter, thyme and some salt for about 15 minutes until just cooked. Test by inserting the tip of a sharp knife into the thickest part of the breast to see if there is any blood.

2. **For the crispy wings,** roughly chop four of the chicken wings. Heat a dash of the oil in a pan and then sauté all the wings, including the chopped ones, until golden. In a separate pan, sauté the celery, shallot, garlic and carrot in some more oil for about 5 minutes until golden. Combine the vegetables with the chicken wings and add the herbs. Deglaze the chicken pan with the wine and top up with water so the wings and vegetables are covered. Cook for 25 minutes and then strain into a clean pan, reserving 100ml of the stock for later. Reduce the remaining stock for the sauce. Cook the girolles in 4 dessertspoons of the sauce in a small pan for about 5 minutes until soft.

3. Remove the meat from the eight whole chicken wings, then fry the flesh and skin in the butter for about 8 minutes until they are a good colour and have crisped up. Add the remaining sauce and reduce until sticky.

4. **For the onion purée,** put the onion and garlic in a pan with a little water, bring to the boil and cook for about 15 minutes to soften. Boil the cream in a separate pan until thick. Drain the onion and garlic and transfer to a food processor. Add the cream and blend to a purée. Season with salt and pepper.

5. **To make the parsley dumplings,** preheat the oven to 180°C (Gas 4). Put the shallot in a pan and add just enough water to cover it. Boil for about 1 minute, then drain. Mix the flour and suet together in a bowl, add the parsley and mustard and bind together with about 80ml of water. Season with salt and pepper and roll the dough out on a lightly floured surface to about 8cm long and 2cm thick. Cut into 2cm-thick rounds and put in an oiled baking tin. Add the reserved 100ml of chicken stock and bake for about 5 minutes until the dumplings are risen and cooked. Transfer to lightly greased greaseproof paper and cook in a steamer for about 5 minutes until light and fluffy.

6. **To cook the vegetables,** boil the peas and carrots in separate pans of boiling water for about 5 minutes until tender. Drain and keep warm.

7. **To serve,** sear the skin on the chicken breasts in the oil in a hot pan until crispy. Slice each breast in two and serve on warmed plates with the onion purée and the dumplings, vegetables and crispy wings. Spoon over the juice and garnish with pea shoots.

Serves 4

For the chicken breasts
4 boneless chicken breasts, skin on, about 130g each
100g butter, diced
4 sprigs of thyme
Sea salt and freshly ground black pepper

For the crispy wings
12 chicken wings
Olive oil
1 celery stick, trimmed and chopped
1 large shallot, peeled and thickly sliced
1 garlic clove, peeled and lightly crushed
1 small carrot, peeled and roughly chopped
Sprig of thyme
$\frac{1}{2}$ bay leaf
Dash of red wine
12–16 girolles, cut in half if large
150g butter, diced

For the onion purée
1 onion, peeled and chopped
1 garlic clove, peeled
125ml whipping cream

For the parsley dumplings
1 shallot, peeled and finely chopped
60g self-raising flour
30g vegetable suet
Small bunch of parsley, finely chopped
1 tsp English mustard powder

For the vegetables
200g peas
12 baby carrots, cut in half

To serve
Splash of olive oil
Pea shoots

If a sauce tastes like it has enough salt and pepper, yet it still feels like it is missing something, add a few drops of lemon juice, which really brings out the flavours of the dish.

POT-ROAST GUINEA FOWL & LOBSTER
with tarragon butter sauce
Hefin Roberts

Hefin Roberts's career began at the age of 14 as a pot-washer. Before long he was helping out in the kitchen and, after training in the hospitality industry, he is now cooking at the Loft Restaurant at Ye Olde Bulls Head Inn, bringing beautifully orchestrated, inventive food to the restaurant scene in Beaumaris. The 15th-century building plays atmospheric host to Hefin's modern British fare, which utilises the best of seasonal, native Welsh ingredients.

1   **For the pot-roast guinea fowl,** first trim the fat off the bacon and fry the fat in a pan. Reserve the bacon. Pan fry the guinea fowl wings and legs in the bacon fat, along with the vegetables, garlic and thyme, for about 10 minutes until golden brown. Cover with the stock and leave to simmer for 30 minutes.

2   Preheat the oven to 160°C (Gas 3). Strain off the stock from the meat, vegetables and herbs, then return the liquid to the pan. Place the guinea fowl crowns in a roasting tin, cover with foil and put in the oven to cook for about 40 minutes until cooked through.

3   **For the potatoes,** sauté the potatoes in oil over a medium heat. Add the garlic, onion and thyme together with a little butter and seal for about 5 minutes until coloured on both sides. Transfer the potatoes to a roasting tin and cook in the oven for about 20 minutes until golden.

4   **To make the tarragon butter sauce,** put the butter in a pan and heat very gently until the butter separates, the oil rising and the butter solids staying on the bottom. Remove from the heat. In a separate pan, heat the vinegar and reduce it by half. Put the egg yolk in a metal bowl, add the vinegar and whisk until pale and frothy. Season with salt and pepper and then slowly pour in the oil from the top of the clarified butter (discarding the solids left in the pan). Finish with the tarragon. Keep warm.

5   **To cook the lobsters,** first kill them by inserting a sharp knife into the cross on the back of the head, then blanch them in a large pan of boiling water for 5 minutes. Drain the lobsters and place in a roasting tin. Cover with cling film and set aside.

6   **For the vegetables,** bring a pan of salted water to the boil and cook the carrots and peas for about 4 minutes until al dente. Refresh in cold water and set aside.

7   Chop the reserved bacon and sauté until crispy.

8   **To finish,** remove the guinea fowl from the oven and seal them in butter in a hot pan to colour well. Let them rest for a minute or two. Transfer some of the stock into a pan, boil to reduce and then add the cream and reduce further. Season with salt and pepper. Take the tail pieces and claws off the lobsters, crack open and discard the shells.

9   **To serve,** sauté the spinach in the butter for about 2 minutes to wilt. Transfer to warmed plates and top with a piece of potato. Slice the guinea fowl in half and place on the potato. Lay half a lobster tail next to it together with a claw, then add the vegetables and bacon and spoon over the tarragon butter. The chef suggests serving this dish with smoked pancetta, and you might also choose to make your own guinea fowl stock in place of the chicken stock (see page 6).

Serves 4

For the pot-roast guinea fowl
200g smoked bacon rashers
2 whole guinea fowl, wings and legs jointed
3 carrots, peeled and chopped
1 onion, peeled and chopped
1 leek, trimmed and chopped
2 celery sticks, trimmed and chopped
1 garlic bulb, peeled and chopped
2 sprigs of thyme, leaves chopped
500ml chicken stock
Knob of butter
50ml double cream

For the potatoes
2 large baking potatoes, peeled and cut into 1cm-thick slices
Splash of olive oil
1 garlic clove, peeled and chopped
1 onion, peeled and chopped
25g thyme leaves, chopped
Knob of butter

For the tarragon butter sauce
170g butter
15ml white wine vinegar
1 egg yolk
Salt and freshly ground black pepper
15g tarragon, finely chopped

For the lobsters
2 whole live lobsters, about 675g each

For the vegetables
10 Chantenay carrots, finely chopped
125g shelled peas

To serve
100g baby leaf spinach
Knob of butter

Slightly undercook your guinea fowl. It's very easy to over cook and become dry.

ASSIETTE OF LAMB
with sweet potato & wasabi purée
Sean Le Roux

'It's not about trial and error,' says the Five Horseshoes' head chef, Sean Le Roux. 'It's about understanding the trial and coming up with something else.' This deeply individualist chef trained at Claridges and works his magic in the kitchens at this hidden gem in the Chilterns. Lamb and deer graze just beyond the pub's 16th-century buildings and the menus change daily according to the offerings from local producers and foraging in the wild.

Serves 4

For the sweet potato and wasabi purée
200g unsalted butter, diced
600ml boiling water
2 garlic cloves, peeled and crushed
1.2kg sweet potato, peeled and chopped
20g wasabi paste
Salt and freshly ground black pepper
Pinch of cayenne pepper

For the smoked cannon of lamb
4 cannon of lamb, about 150g each
2 tsp rapeseed oil
50g unsalted butter, diced

For the hot-smoked rack of lamb
2 racks of lamb, French trimmed, about 350g each
2 tsp rapeseed oil
50g unsalted butter, diced

For the vegetables
8 baby carrots
2 bunches of asparagus, trimmed and peeled
15g unsalted butter, melted

To serve
2 small handfuls of pea shoots

A gorgeous, succulent lamb dish that gets the cooking juices flowing.

1   **For the sweet potato and wasabi purée,** put the butter and boiling water in a pan and heat until the butter has melted. Add the garlic and sweet potato and simmer for 15–20 minutes until soft, then add the wasabi. Transfer to a food processor, blend to a smooth purée and pass through a sieve. Season with salt and cayenne pepper and set aside.

2   **To smoke the cannon of lamb,** first caramelise the meat in a very hot pan with the oil and butter for 8–12 minutes. Place in a hot smoker for 10–15 minutes or until medium rare. Alternatively, to smoke in the oven, preheat the oven to 200°C (Gas 6). Take a large tray and cover the base with oak chippings, lay a perforated tray on top and set the chippings alight to start smoking. Put the meat on top of the perforated tray and cover with foil. Lightly smoke in the oven for 8 minutes or until medium rare. (If you don't wish to smoke the lamb, simply roast in the oven for the same length of time.) Remove from the smoker or oven, rest on a chopping board for 4–5 minutes and then slice each into four pieces.

3   **To cook the hot smoked rack of lamb,** first fry the meat in a very hot pan with the oil and butter for 8–10 minutes all over until caramelised. Season with salt and pepper and then finish in the smoker or oven with the cannon of lamb for about 10 minutes until medium rare. Rest for 4–5 minutes, then slice into cutlets.

4   **To cook the vegetables,** blanch the carrots and asparagus separately in boiling salted water for 1–2 minutes. Drain and then warm through in a pan with the melted butter mixed with 1 tbsp of boiling water. Season with salt and pepper.

5   **To serve,** reheat the sweet potato and wasabi purée in a pan with a splash of water then divide between warmed plates. Add two cutlets with their bones pointing to opposite corners of the plate and lay the sliced smoked cannon of lamb over the centre of the cutlets. Add the vegetables and garnish with the pea shoots. The chef suggests serving this dish with pea and mint velouté and spiced aubergine, pine nut and raisin relish (see page 6).

SHOULDER OF LAMB
with peas, beans & onion rings
Charlie Lockley

Renowned for its stunning lake views and calm, candlelit ambience, the Boath House restaurant in the Highlands delights in classic cuisine with a modern inflection. Head chef Charlie Lockley came to Scotland over 20 years ago and has taken the local larder to heart, regularly foraging and capitalising on native wild produce. This dazzling lamb dish is a 'marriage of all the things he loves'.

Serves 4

For the lamb
1.5–2kg shoulder of lamb, boned
150g sea salt
Large sprig of summer savory, thyme or rosemary
100ml olive oil

For the onion rings
100g '00' pasta flour
50g cornflour
25g baking powder
200–300ml sparkling mineral water
Salt and freshly ground black pepper
1 large onion
500ml peanut oil

For the vegetables
8 baby onions
150g garden peas
150g broad beans (podded weight)
Wild sweet cicely, roughly chopped (optional)

To garnish (optional)
Chickweed
Pea flowers

1   **To prepare the shoulder of lamb,** trim off excess fat. Dissolve the salt in 2 litres of water in a large lidded container to make the brine. Add the lamb, cover with the lid and leave in the fridge for 24 hours.

2   Preheat the oven to 180°C (Gas 4). Remove the meat from the pan, wash away the brine and pat dry. Put the meat in a small roasting tin with the summer savory or other herbs. Cover with the oil and some foil and cook in the oven for 4–5 hours until the meat is tender, basting occasionally.

3   **For the onion rings,** first make the batter. Place all the dry ingredients in a bowl, add 200ml of mineral water and mix with a hand-held blender until smooth, adding more water if needed. You don't want the batter to be too thick. Season with salt and pepper.

4   Peel the onion and slice very thinly into rings. Take eight rings, remove any thin membrane and pat dry. Heat the oil to 190°C in a large pan or a deep fryer. Drop the onion rings into the batter, two at a time, then lower them into the hot oil, making sure they don't touch each other, and deep fry for about 1 minute until they are golden brown. Drain on kitchen paper and then place in the oven with the lamb on a baking sheet to keep warm.

The best of British ingredients in a Sunday lunch to swoon over.

5   **To cook the vegetables,** bring a pan of salted water to the boil. Drop in the baby onions and cook for about 5 minutes. Place on kitchen paper and leave to cool until ready to handle. Cut in half, peel, divide the segments and put into the oven with the onion rings. Using the same water, cook the peas for no longer than 20 seconds, then transfer into iced water to stop the cooking. Again using the same water, cook the broad beans for about 1 minute and transfer into the cold water. Peel off the broad bean skins, then put the beans in a small bowl and pulse with a hand-held blender until roughly chopped.

6   Transfer the lamb from the roasting tin and set aside in a warm place to rest. Put the baby onion segments, chopped broad beans and the peas into a pan. Then skim the lamb's cooking juices and add just enough to the pan to bind the vegetables together. Heat through, season with salt and pepper and stir in the sweet cicely (if using).

7   **To serve,** trim the lamb into four portions and place on the centre of warmed plates. Place the bean mix and lamb juices around the lamb and add onion rings on top. Garnish with the chickweed and pea flowers (if using). The chef suggests serving this dish with lamb's tongues, pickled chanterelles and a drizzle of onion oil (see page 6).

LOIN OF LAMB & DUMPLINGS

with winkle & lamb gravy

Billy Boyter

Growing up in a small fishing village, Billy Boyter fully expected to follow in his family's footsteps and become a fisherman – until he discovered that cooking provided an outlet for his creativity. With coveted roles at some of Scotland's finest restaurants, he is now head chef at the prestigious The Balmoral, Number One, where his refined modern Scottish dishes populate a sophisticated fine-dining menu – complemented by Billy's passion for locally foraged produce.

1 **To make the hogget or lamb stock,** preheat the oven to 200°C (Gas 6). Put the bones in a roasting tin and cook for about 25 minutes until golden.

2 Put the vegetables in a stock pot with the oil. Cook for a few minutes to colour and then add the roasted bones with the herbs, peppercorns and red wine. Bring to the boil, then lower the heat and reduce the liquid until a small amount is left in the pan. Add 1.5 litres of cold water, bring back up to the boil, reduce the heat and simmer for 3–4 hours. Strain the stock and put back in the pan to reduce by half. This will take about 30 minutes.

3 **To make the dumplings,** preheat the oven to 180°C (Gas 4). Rub the suet and flour together until a crumble starts

to form. Add 50ml of water to bring it together, add the lemon zest, rosemary and parsley and combine to a dough. Roll into four small balls and cook in the oven for 15 minutes in just enough of the hogget or lamb stock to cover. Keep warm in some of the stock.

4 **For the gravy,** sweat the vegetables and garlic in the oil and spice. Add 250ml of the hogget or lamb stock and reduce for 2–3 minutes to intensify the flavour. Blitz with a hand-held blender and pass through a sieve. Keep warm.

5 **To cook the winkles,** place them in a pan with the herbs, garlic, wine and vinegar. Bring to the boil, reduce the heat and simmer for about 3 minutes. Transfer the winkles from the pan and keep the liquid. Remove the winkles from their shells, taking off the back section of each winkle just to leave the foot. Slice this and set aside.

6 Pour about 40ml of the winkle stock into the gravy. Taste to check the balance of the flavour, adding salt and pepper as necessary. The lamb stock has an intense flavour balanced by the winkle stock.

7 **For the broccoli purée,** bring the chicken stock to the boil then blanch the broccoli in the stock with the butter and a little salt for about 2 minutes until tender. Using a slotted spoon, transfer from the stock into a food processor and blend until smooth, adding stock as necessary. Check seasoning and pass through a sieve. Keep warm.

8 **To cook the lamb,** preheat the oven to 190°C (Gas 5). Season the meat with a pinch each of salt and pepper. Heat the oil until almost smoking in a heavy-based ovenproof pan. Sear the lamb on each side for 30 seconds, then transfer to the oven for 5 minutes, turning the lamb once. Remove the lamb from the oven and allow it to rest for 5 minutes.

9 **To serve,** add the dumplings to the gravy and warm through, adding the winkles to finish. Slice the lamb and put in the centre of warmed plates, then add the dumplings, drizzle over the gravy with the winkles. Finally, add the broccoli purée. The chef suggests serving this dish with sweetbreads, mushrooms and some watercress (see page 6).

Serves 4

For the hogget or lamb stock
1kg hogget or lamb bones
1 white onion, peeled and chopped
2 carrots, peeled and chopped
1 celery stick, chopped
2 garlic cloves, peeled and crushed
3 plum tomatoes, chopped
Splash of olive oil
Sprig of thyme
Sprig of rosemary
1 bay leaf
1 tsp whole black peppercorns
100ml red wine

For the dumplings
15g suet
25g self-raising flour
Grated zest of 1/2 unwaxed lemon
Pinch of chopped rosemary
Pinch of chopped parsley

For the gravy
30g carrot, peeled and diced
15g diced white onion
10g diced celery
2g chopped garlic
1 tsp olive oil
Pinch of ras al hanout spice

For the winkles
200g winkles
Sprig of rosemary
Sprig of thyme
1/2 garlic clove
80ml blackberry or red wine
2 tbsp sherry vinegar
Salt and freshly ground black pepper

For the broccoli purée
400ml light chicken stock
130g broccoli tips, green tips shaved off
40g unsalted butter

For the lamb
2 boneless lamb loin fillets, trimmed
1 tbsp olive oil

A winter-warmer that will satisfy the heartiest of appetites.

BACON-WRAPPED LOIN OF LAMB with pumpkin & potato mash & jus

Tina Bricknell-Webb

A 130-acre organic farm in Devon is home to Tina Bricknell-Webb's idyllic country hotel, Percy's, where the emphasis lies firmly on home produce and zero food miles. With several orchards, six fish ponds, her own flock of sheep (and a racehorse called Yes Chef), Tina's daily harvests dictate the ever-changing dishes on her menus, where the variety of the day's doorstep-reared offerings leads to enterprising, skilled cooking.

Serves 4

For the lamb
180g rindless streaky bacon
Handful of summer savory or thyme,
    rosemary or lavender
1–2 tsp garlic purée
Freshly ground white pepper
2 lamb loins, about 400g each
100g rendered lamb fat, dripping or
    olive oil

For the jus
500ml chicken stock
500ml lamb stock
Handful of summer savory or thyme,
    rosemary or lavender
1 tsp cornflour

For the pumpkin and potato mash
450g peeled Crown Prince pumpkin
    or butternut squash, chopped
450g floury potatoes, preferably
    Toluca, Kind Edward or Rooster,
    peeled and chopped
Handful of summer savory or thyme,
    lavender or rosemary
Sea salt
50–100g unsalted butter

For the spinach
Knob of butter
1 tsp garlic purée
400g spinach

To serve
4 tsp redcurrant jelly
Celery leaves

1   **For the lamb,** lay the bacon on cling film with the
    pieces just overlapping, and beat gently and evenly
    until they form a sheet of bacon large enough to
    wrap around the two pieces of lamb when one piece
    is sitting on the other. Remove the leaves from the
    stalks of the summer savory or other herbs and set the
    stalks aside. Spread the garlic purée on the beaten
    bacon, followed by some white pepper and a generous
    sprinkling of the herb leaves.

2   Place one of the loin pieces on the sheet of bacon and
    place the other loin on top, ensuring that the thickness
    of the meat is even. Carefully wrap the cylinder of lamb
    with the bacon as tightly as possible, then tie the wrapped
    lamb with thin pieces of string every 2–3cm as tightly as
    possible to allow for shrinkage when cooking.

3   Preheat the oven to 200°C (Gas 6). Heat the lamb fat in
    a flat-bottomed wok and, when hot (but not smoking),
    carefully add the wrapped, tied loin and seal evenly on
    all sides, turning frequently in order not to over-brown.

4   Remove the lamb from the fat, place in a roasting tin and
    rest for 8 minutes. Turn the loin over and place in the oven
    for 4–5 minutes. Remove the lamb from the oven, turn the
    meat over and rest for 8 minutes. Turn over once more and return to the oven for a
    further 4–5 minutes. Rest for 8 minutes and then check the core temperature, which
    should be 49°C. If the lamb needs more cooking, repeat the cook-and-rest process.

5   **To make the jus,** combine the two stocks in a pan together with the summer savory.
    Boil hard until it has reduced by three-quarters. Strain, add the cornflour and taste,
    adjusting the seasoning with pepper if necessary. Check the consistency (boil further
    if needed) and keep warm.

6   **For the pumpkin and potato mash,** put the pumpkin or squash and potatoes
    in a pan with the summer savory or other herb and some sea salt. Boil for about
    20 minutes until soft then drain, reserving the cooking liquid. Mash thoroughly
    and add butter, salt and pepper. Mix thoroughly, adding some of the cooking liquid
    to achieve a smooth finish. Set aside.

7   **To cook the spinach,** heat the butter in a large heavy-based pan. Add the garlic purée and
    stir until golden brown. Add the spinach and cook quickly until just wilted. Remove the pan
    from the heat and set aside.

8   **To serve,** place some of the mash in the centre of warmed plates and put some spinach
    on top. Carve the lamb into slices about 6cm thick and place on top of the spinach,
    cut-side uppermost. Ladle some of the jus over the lamb, add a spoonful of redcurrant jelly
    and garnish with celery leaves. The chef suggests serving this dish with roasted beetroot,
    courgettes, French beans, garlic purée and homemade redcurrant jelly (see page 6).

Enhance your
vegetables by
cooking them
with herbs,
then save
the cooking
liquid to make
delicious soups.

SLOW-POACHED CONFIT OF LAMB SHOULDER
with a potato cake
Dave Vale

In the village of Llandybie, Carmarthenshire, Valans is the epitome of the neighbourhood restaurant everyone wants on their doorstep. Head chef and owner Dave Vale has built a menu of stylish dishes based on premium local produce. Although classically trained, Dave calls himself a 'simple chef, who likes to do things well', guaranteeing that, from sauces to ice creams, every component on the plate will be '100 per cent Valans made'.

Serves 4

For the confit of lamb shoulder
2 garlic cloves, peeled
Sprig of rosemary
1kg lamb shoulder, on the bone
Salt and freshly ground white pepper
1 tbsp olive oil

For the redcurrant gravy
1 small celery stick, trimmed and roughly chopped
1 small leek, trimmed and roughly chopped
1 small carrot, peeled and roughly chopped
1 bay leaf
25g redcurrant jelly
Handful of redcurrants

For the potato cakes
300g potatoes, preferably Maris Piper, peeled
½ onion, peeled and thinly sliced
2 garlic cloves, peeled and chopped
Dash of extra-virgin olive oil
50ml whipping cream

1 **For the confit of lamb shoulder,** bring a large pan of water to the boil. Add the garlic, rosemary and lamb shoulder and bring back up to the boil. Reduce the heat and simmer for about 2 hours, skimming occasionally to remove the fat, until the meat is falling off the bone. Remove the lamb from the pan and leave to cool until lukewarm.

2 Remove the meat from the bone, ensuring no gristle, sinew and bones remain. Reserve the bones and any juices for the gravy. Season with salt and pepper. Lay a 50cm-long piece of cling film on a work surface and place the lamb along the centre, shaping it into a rough cylinder 3–4cm in diameter and as long as the lamb will allow.

3 Roll the lamb tightly in the cling film, ensuring that no cling film is wrapped in the meat. Then roll the lamb cylinder by holding the tapered ends of the cling film and continuing to roll it until the cling film has tightened around the meat. Prick the cling film to remove any air bubbles. Place the cylinder on a piece of foil about 40cm long. Trim any trailing ends of cling film, then roll the cylinder in the foil and tighten it by turning the ends of foil against each other. Chill in the fridge for about 2 hours.

4   Cut the cylinder into four and remove the foil and cling film. Heat the oil in a pan and cook the lamb for 4 minutes on each side until golden. Remove from the pan and set aside.

A new twist on a classic Sunday lunch combo – lamb gets lively with a tart redcurrant gravy.

5   **To make the redcurrant gravy,** put the reserved lamb bone and any juices in a pan. Pour over enough water to cover the bone, then bring to the boil and skim to remove any fat. Add the celery, leek, carrot and bay leaf and boil rapidly for 25–30 minutes until reduced by half. Strain the stock through a muslin cloth and return to a clean pan, then add the redcurrant jelly and bring to the boil. Skim any froth that rises to the surface. Add the redcurrants and simmer for 4–5 minutes. Set aside and keep warm.

6   **For the potato cakes,** preheat the oven to 190°C (Gas 5). Grate or shred the potatoes on a mandoline and mix with the onion and garlic. Season with salt and pepper.

7   Heat a large ovenproof pan over a medium heat. Place four 6cm-diameter ring moulds in the pan and drizzle a little oil into each one. Fill the moulds with the potato mixture and cook for 2–3 minutes until brown. Remove the pan from the heat and gently push the mixture down into the moulds with a spoon or spatula. Divide the cream equally between the four rings and leave to soak in. Then turn the potato cakes, gently pushing the mixture down again. A little cream may escape. Transfer the pan to the oven and bake the cakes for 12–15 minutes until they are cooked through.

8   **To serve,** place a potato cake in the centre of each plate and place the slices of lamb confit alongside. Drizzle over the redcurrant gravy, dotting the redcurrants around the plate. The chef suggests serving this dish with an oven-roasted cannon of lamb and a pan-fried topside of lamb escalope, together with stuffed carrots, steamed cabbage and a herb dressing (see page 6).

GOAT KANDHA MASALEDAR
Alun Sperring

Alun Sperring's love of travelling led to his fascination with international cuisine, and with Indian food in particular. The first chef of English descent to be crowned the 'Curry King of Britain', Alun's authentic Indian cuisine emphasises local ingredients at Brighton's the Chilli Pickle. There, as chef-proprietor, Alun labours over the perfect chutneys and flamboyant dishes for which he is known. His goat Kandha masaledar is designed as a feast and is big on impact and big on flavour.

1 **For the goat marinade,** mix the ginger garlic paste with the lime juice and coat the goat shoulder with the marinade. Leave to marinate for a minimum of 4 hours. Mix together the remaining ingredients in a bowl, coat the goat shoulder once again and leave to marinate for a further 4 hours.

2 Preheat the oven to 220°C (Gas 7). Put the goat shoulder in a roasting tin, complete with the marinade, and cook in the oven for 15 minutes. Reduce the oven temperature to 110°C (Gas ¼), cover the goat shoulder with foil and cook for a further 4¼ hours, basting every 30 minutes. Remove from the oven and carefully remove the blade bone. It should come out easily when twisted. Increase the oven temperature to 180°C (Gas 4).

3 **To make the beetroot raita,** place the beetroot in a pan with the beetroot juice, sugar and vinegar. Bring slowly to the boil over a low heat, then drain the beetroot and leave to cool – do not rinse. Peel and finely chop the beetroot, tip into a bowl and add the yogurt, salt and cumin seeds. Stir to an even colour.

4 **For the Kashmiri pilau rice,** heat the oil in a large heavy-based ovenproof pan. Add the onion and cook until golden brown, then add 900ml of water, bring to the boil and add the saffron, cumin, coriander, garam masala, chilli powder and dried limes together with the whole garam masala and the salt, followed by the rice.

5 Bring the rice back up to the boil and simmer for about 5 minutes until the water has evaporated. Cover the rice with a muslin cloth and a lid and place in the oven for 15 minutes. Remove from the oven and fork through to prevent further cooking. Take off the cloth and pick out the dried lime pieces and discard. Add the kewra water (if using) and stir in the remaining ingredients.

6 **To serve,** divide the goat meat and Kashmiri rice between warmed plates. Place a spoonful of beetroot raita to one side and put three roasted almonds on top of the goat. The chef suggests serving this dish with smoked aubergine and lacha paratha (see page 6).

Serves 6–8

For the goat marinade
30g ginger garlic paste
Juice of 1 lime
1 small shoulder of goat
1 tsp salt
150g plain yogurt
1 tsp ground mace
1 tsp ground cloves
1 tsp ground cassia bark
1 tsp ground cumin seeds
2 tsp ground coriander
2 tsp chilli powder
60g crispy onion paste (flourless)
60ml vegetable oil

For the beetroot raita
150g raw beetroot
400ml beetroot juice
1 tsp caster sugar
15ml white wine vinegar
100g plain yogurt
Pinch of sea salt
½ tsp cumin seeds, roasted and
  crushed

For the Kashmiri pilau rice
50ml vegetable oil
1 onion, peeled and sliced
Pinch of saffron threads
1 tsp ground cumin
1 tsp ground coriander
1 tsp garam masala
½ tsp chilli powder
1½ dried limes
Whole garam masala (see the tip,
  below)
1 tsp salt
400g basmati rice
1 tsp kewra water (optional)
50ml ghee
1 eating apple, peeled, cored and
  finely diced
10g glacé cherries, chopped
15g roasted cashew nuts

To serve
18–24 roasted almonds

To make your own whole garam masala, tie 2 blades of mace, 6 green cardamom pods, 6 cloves and 10g cassia bark in a muslin cloth.

BELLY OF PORK
with carrots, celeriac rémoulade & watercress purée
Richard Davies

The stunning surrounds of a 14th-century Manor House hotel in Castle Combe provide a gracious setting for Richard's celebrated, resourceful modern British repertoire. A racing-bike enthusiast and former Ramsay protégé, the Bybrook Restaurant's head chef thrives on adrenaline. Working part-time in the kitchen while still at school, Richard fell in love with the boisterous world of professional cooking. He extols the virtue of 'using simple ingredients to create beautiful dishes – it is the mark of a top chef.'

Serves 4

For the pork belly
50g salt
50g caster sugar
2 tsp smoked paprika
500g pork belly
500g duck fat
Sprig of thyme
1 bay leaf
Splash of olive oil

For the celeriac rémoulade
2 egg yolks
1 tsp white wine vinegar
1 tsp Dijon mustard
Sea salt and freshly ground white
   pepper
300ml rapeseed oil
½ head of celeriac
1 tsp wholegrain mustard
1 tsp finely chopped chives

For the watercress purée
150g watercress
150ml double cream

For the carrots
250g baby carrots, plus an optional
   200g for juicing
2 tbsp white wine vinegar
120ml olive oil

To garnish
Baby watercress shoots
Drizzle of extra-virgin olive oil

1   **For the pork belly,** combine the salt, sugar and paprika in a small bowl and mix thoroughly. Use this to season the pork well on both sides and then leave it to cure for 24 hours.

2   When you are ready to roast the pork, preheat the oven to 150°C (Gas 2). Wash the salt off in cold running water and dry well. Put the pork into a deep roasting tin with the duck fat, thyme and bay leaf and roast for about 4 hours or until you can insert a knife into it with no resistance. Remove from the oven and transfer to a baking sheet lined with baking parchment. Place more paper and another baking sheet plus a 3kg weight on top. Leave in the fridge for at least 6 hours and preferably overnight.

3   **For the celeriac rémoulade,** first make some mayonnaise. Place the egg yolks in a food processor. Add the vinegar, mustard and a pinch of salt. Pulse once or twice to blend. Turn the processor on fully and, with the motor running, add the oil in a thin, steady stream through the top of the lid. After a minute or two, the mixture will change consistency and emulsify into a thick, rich sauce. Stop adding oil when the mayonnaise has reached the desired consistency (you may not need to use all the oil). Taste,

adjust the flavouring by adding more vinegar or mustard, if desired, and season with pepper and a little more salt.

4   Peel the celeriac and thinly slice with a mandoline. Pile four of the slices together and cut into thin julienne strips. Season with a pinch of salt and put in the fridge for 20 minutes. Then squeeze any excess water from the julienne and add the mayonnaise, mustard and chives, and season with salt again, if necessary. Cover and set aside.

5   For the crackling, preheat the oven to 180°C (Gas 4). Heat a non-stick pan over a medium heat and place a sheet of greaseproof paper in the bottom of the pan. Add the oil, slice the pork belly into four portions and trim off the skin. Season with salt and pepper and caramelise in the pan for about 8 minutes or until golden. Cut the skin into strips and put in the oven between two pieces of greaseproof paper for 12–15 minutes or until crisp.

A winter salad of celeriac rémoulade adds a fresh, crisp note to succulent pork belly.

6   **To make the watercress purée,** blanch the watercress leaves in boiling water for about 30 seconds. Then put into iced water to refresh. Boil the cream, add the watercress and blend with a hand-held blender until smooth. Season with salt and pepper and keep warm.

7   **For the carrots,** peel 150g of the carrots, trim into cone-like shapes and place in a small pan. Juice 200g of the carrots in a juicer (if using). Add to the carrots, or add 70ml of water if not using carrot juice. Season with a pinch of salt, bring to the boil, then reduce the heat and simmer for 4–6 minutes until cooked.

8   Slice the remaining 100g of carrots wafer thin using a mandoline. Whisk together the vinegar and olive oil and add a pinch of salt. Toss a teaspoon of this vinaigrette over the shaved carrots.

9   **To serve,** spread a thin layer of watercress purée across warmed plates. Add a pile of rémoulade in the middle of the plates and place the pork on top together with some shaved carrots and crackling. Dot the cooked carrots around the plates and garnish with the watercress shoots and a drizzle of extra-virgin olive oil. The chef suggests serving this dish with pig's cheeks, crayfish and a rich crayfish sauce (see page 6).

PORK LOIN & CRACKLING
with hock & smoked eel lasagne
Jon Howe

Jon Howe's school friends might have ribbed him for doing a 'girls' course' by studying home economics, but there's no doubt that he has had the last laugh. Chef-proprietor at Cheltenham's Lumière, Jon has trained under top chefs including John Campbell and Heston Blumenthal, a background that has seen him develop a cutting-edge culinary style where traditional dishes are ingeniously reconfigured to bring them firmly into the 21st century.

1   **To prepare the loin of pork,** remove the skin from the pork and set the meat aside. Preheat the oven to 160°C (Gas 3). Trim off any excess fat from the pork skin, cut it into long thin strips and season with salt and pepper and a touch of the oil. Lay the strips between two pieces of greaseproof paper with a baking sheet above and below. Bake for 45–50 minutes until the crackling is crisp – you may need to increase the oven temperature. If so, once the crackling is ready, turn the oven back down to 160°C (Gas 3) for the rest of the method.

2   **To cook the beetroot,** peel the beetroot and scoop out balls from the flesh with a melon baller, aiming for 6–8 balls per beetroot. Wrap the beetroot balls in foil with the butter and thyme and bake for 35–40 minutes.

3   **To cook the loin of pork,** heat a splash of the oil in a hot ovenproof pan. Season the meat with salt and pepper, place it in the pan and colour on all sides. Add the butter, garlic and sage to the pan and place it in the oven for 20–25 minutes, basting every 5 minutes with the butter. Remove the meat from the oven and place it on a plate. Cover with foil and leave it to rest for 5–10 minutes.

4   **For the hock and smoked eel lasagne,** sweat the vegetables in the oil. Add the chicken stock, boil to reduce by half, then add the cream and reduce by half again. Add the ham, smoked eel, parsley and mustard to the cream reduction and mix together.

5   Cut the pasta sheets into 12 circles the same size as four individual ovenproof dishes, then layer with the hock mix in the dishes. Grate over the Parmesan cheese and cook in the oven for about 20 minutes until it is piping hot. Finish under the grill, set to high, to brown the top.

6   **To cook the cavolo nero,** sweat the bacon and shallot in a pan with the oil. Add the butter and then the cavolo nero along with the sage, garlic and wine and cover the pan with a lid. Steam for 1–2 minutes and season with salt and pepper.

7   **To serve,** unwrap the beetroot and place in a baking tin, season with salt and pepper and reheat in the oven for 2–3 minutes. Remove the foil from the pork and cut it into 12 equal slices. Season with a little more salt and pepper. Peel and slice the apple into matchstick-sized strips. Divide the cavolo nero between warmed plates and top with the meat and crackling. Add the lasagne dishes or transfer their contents to the plates, then add the beetroot balls and apple sticks. The chef suggests serving this dish with onion purée and watercress oil; you may also wish to make your own pasta and cook a ham hock for the meat in the lasagne, using its cooking liquid in place of the chicken stock (see page 6).

Serves 4

For the loin of pork
1 short loin of pork weighing about 800g
Salt and freshly ground black pepper
Splash of vegetable oil
100g unsalted butter, softened
1 garlic clove, peeled and sliced
Sprig of sage, leaves only

For the beetroot
2 beetroot
25g unsalted butter, softened
Sprig of thyme

For the hock and smoked eel lasagne
2 large banana shallots, peeled and finely diced
1/2 carrot, peeled and finely diced
1/2 leek, trimmed and finely diced
1/2 garlic clove, peeled and finely diced
Splash of vegetable oil
200ml chicken stock
200ml double cream
150g cooked ham, chopped
100g skinned smoked eel fillet, diced
Bunch of flat-leaf parsley, finely chopped
25g wholegrain mustard
4 sheets of fresh pasta
50g Parmesan cheese

For the cavolo nero
2 rashers of streaky bacon, cut into pieces
1 large banana shallot, peeled and sliced
Splash of vegetable oil
50g butter, diced
4 large leaves of cavolo nero, sliced
Sprig of sage
1/2 garlic clove
20ml white wine

To serve
1 eating apple

A stand-out dish that more than repays the effort – irresistibly moreish crackling brings together pork and eel in an ensemble that demands attention.

CASSOULET OF PIG'S CHEEK
with creamed Savoy cabbage
Tom Ilic

'It seems like the whole world stops when you're cooking,' says Tom Ilic, south London hero and chef-proprietor of his self-named restaurant, where gutsy meat cooking and intriguing pairings of texture and flavour garner rave reviews. Born in Yugoslavia, Tom grew up surrounded by food: 'It was just part of life – we grew everything in our garden. You ate a tomato when it was supposed to be there.'

1. **For the braised pig's cheeks,** first marinate the pig's cheeks in the wine overnight.

2. **For the cassoulet,** soak the haricot beans in a bowl of water overnight.

3. Preheat the oven to 150°C (Gas 2). Drain the pig's cheeks, reserving the liquid in a small pan, and pat the cheeks thoroughly dry. Heat half the butter in a separate large heavy-based pan and brown the pig's cheeks all over for 5–10 minutes. Remove and set aside. Heat the remaining butter and brown the mirepoix in the same pan and then return the meat. Reduce the reserved red wine liquid by half and add to the pig's cheeks together with the port and stock, then braise in the oven for 1¹/₂ hours. Remove from the oven and set aside. Increase the oven temperature to 180°C (Gas 4).

4. **To make the cassoulet,** drain the haricot beans, put them in a pan with the bouquet garni and most of the chicken stock and bring to the boil. Reduce the heat, cover with a lid and simmer for 30–40 minutes, checking regularly to make sure it doesn't dry out. If it does, add more stock. Meanwhile, sauté the garlic, onion, carrot and tomato in a little oil just until the flavours are released. Take off the heat and set aside.

5. Once the beans are cooked, drain (reserving the liquid) and add the beans to the vegetables with most of the parsley. Add 50ml of the bean cooking liquid and juices from the braised pig's cheeks. Stir through and season with salt and pepper. Transfer the mix into four individual ovenproof dishes and top each with breadcrumbs. Bake in the oven for 10–15 minutes and finish under a grill for 2–3 minutes before serving.

6. **To make the creamed Savoy cabbage,** blanch the cabbage in boiling water for 3–4 minutes, drain well and set aside. Pour the cream into a pan and heat to reduce by half, then add the Gruyère cheese and season with salt and pepper. Finally, add the cabbage and stir through.

7. **To serve,** warm the pig's cheeks in the remaining braising liquid. Put each cassoulet onto a warmed serving plate and add some creamed cabbage topped with half a pig's cheek. The chef suggests serving this dish with a crépinette of pork fillet, pork belly and caramelised apple (see page 6).

Serves 4

For the braised pig's cheeks
2 pig's cheeks
150ml red wine
120g butter
200g mirepoix of finely chopped celery, carrot and onion
150ml port
150ml veal stock
Sea salt and freshly ground white pepper

For the cassoulet
100g dried haricot beans
Bouquet garni (1 bay leaf, sprigs of rosemary and thyme and 1 peeled garlic clove in a muslin cloth tied up with string)
400–600ml chicken stock
2 garlic cloves, peeled and crushed
1 small onion, peeled and diced
1 carrot, peeled and diced
1 ripe tomato, diced
Splash of olive oil
Small bunch of parsley, chopped
2 tbsp cooking juices, reserved from braised pig's cheeks
50g breadcrumbs

For the creamed Savoy cabbage
¹/₂ head of Savoy cabbage, shredded
100ml double cream
100g Gruyère cheese

Marinating the pig's cheeks overnight helps to get rid of any impurities and also tenderises the meat so it is beautifully soft.

ROAST LOIN OF PORK
with buttery mash & crackling
Lawrence Keogh

Restaurants don't come more patriotic than renowned chef Lawrence Keogh's Roast, where his all-British menus draw in the crowds at London's historic Borough Market. From coronation chicken to steamed puddings, Lawrence celebrates our national dishes; and having cooked for dignitaries such as the late Queen Mother, it's only fitting that his take on the great British roast dinner makes an appearance here.

Serves 8

For the sauce
350ml beef stock
350ml chicken stock
2 tbsp tomato juice
2 garlic cloves, peeled
1 bay leaf
Sprig of thyme
40g very finely chopped shallots
160ml red wine
Salt and freshly ground black pepper

For the roast loin of pork
2.5kg loin of pork, boned
Juice of 1 lemon
2 tsp salt

For the crust
75g wholegrain mustard
Grated zest of $^{1}/_{2}$ orange
1 tsp chopped parsley
1 tsp chopped sage leaves
1 tsp chopped rosemary
1 tsp chopped thyme

For the buttery mash
500g potatoes, preferably Maris Piper,
   peeled and halved
80ml full-fat milk
100g unsalted butter
Freshly ground white pepper

To garnish
50g tendril pea shoots

1   **To make the sauce,** put the beef and chicken stocks in a large pan and bring to the boil. Reduce the heat and simmer with the tomato juice, garlic, bay leaf and thyme for about 30 minutes, skimming regularly, until the sauce is dark and rich and slightly thickened.

2   Meanwhile, put the shallots and red wine in a separate pan and bring to the boil. Reduce the heat and simmer until almost all of the wine has evaporated and the shallots are a deep burgundy colour.

3   Pass the reduced sauce through a sieve to remove the bay leaf and thyme, and add the cooked shallots to the pan. Cook for a further 3 minutes. Season with salt and pepper and keep warm.

4   **For the roast loin of pork,** preheat the oven to 230°C (Gas 8). Using a sharp knife, score the pork skin, down towards you, each cut about 1cm apart. Rub the pork with lemon juice and leave for a few minutes to soak in; this will aid the crackling's crispiness. Then sprinkle the salt evenly over the skin and rub it in thoroughly.

5   Stand the pork in a roasting tin and put it in the oven for 35 minutes. Reduce the temperature to 180°C (Gas 4) and roast for a further 20–30 minutes until cooked through. Take the pork out of the oven and gently remove the crackling. Then place the loin back in the oven and cook for a further 15–20 minutes to render the fat further. Remove from the oven and leave to cool.

6   **To make the crust,** mix together the mustard, orange zest and herbs in a bowl and spread this mixture evenly over the pork to create a smooth crust. Leave the pork to rest for 10–15 minutes.

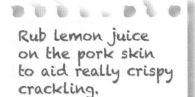

Rub lemon juice on the pork skin to aid really crispy crackling.

7   **For the buttery mash,** put the potatoes in a large pan of water over a high heat. Add a pinch of salt and bring to the boil. Reduce to a simmer and cook for about 20 minutes until tender. Drain the potatoes in a colander and set them aside until the steam has evaporated.

8   Put the milk and butter in a small pan and warm through. Then transfer the potatoes to a large bowl and mash them with a potato masher. Once you're sure there are no more lumps in the potatoes, add some of the warm buttery milk and mash it in. Once it has melted into the mash, add a little more, mash again and check the consistency, adding more milk if necessary. Season with salt and white pepper.

9   **To serve,** place the mash in a piping bag and pipe it in swirls onto warmed plates. Carve the pork and arrange on the plates next to the mash. Gently pull the crackling apart and lay pieces over the pork and mash, as in the photo opposite. Pour the gravy around the pork and sprinkle with pea shoots. The chef suggests serving this dish with apple purée (see page 6).

BRAISED PORK
with black peas & apple sauce
Mary-Ellen McTague

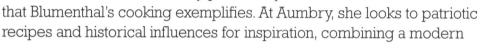

Mary-Ellen McTague's 'shabby-chic' cottage-restaurant in the heart of Prestwich village may look unassuming, but there's nothing ordinary about the precision cooking that has made Aumbry a culinary destination. Previously at the Fat Duck, Mary-Ellen embraces the mix of creativity, practicality and science that Blumenthal's cooking exemplifies. At Aumbry, she looks to patriotic recipes and historical influences for inspiration, combining a modern outlook with an affinity for the much-loved dishes of the past.

Serves 4

For the loin of pork
500g loin of pork
Olive oil

For the pork stock sauce
800ml pork stock
1 blade of mace
125g unsalted butter
Sprig of sage

For the crackling
250g piece of pork skin
Juice of ½ lemon
1 tsp salt
500ml vegetable oil

For the black peas
250g black peas, soaked overnight
20g piece of smoked bacon
¼ onion, peeled
½ carrot
½ celery stick
1 tsp bicarbonate of soda
80g butter, diced
120g grilled smoked streaky bacon, finely diced
Salt and freshly ground black pepper
2 tsp finely chopped mint

For the apple sauce
2 eating apples, preferably Granny Smith
Citric acid or lemon juice

1. **For the loin of pork,** preheat the oven to 60°C (Gas ¼) or as close as possible. Brush the outside of the loin with the oil then roll in baking parchment and tie with string to create a cylindrical shape. Wrap in foil then put in a roasting tin in the oven. Check the temperature of the meat after 40 minutes. For medium rare, the meat should reach 52°C in the centre. Depending on the particular oven and the thickness of the piece of meat, this could take from 40 minutes to over an hour, so check every 5 minutes or so until the correct temperature is reached. Remove from the oven and set aside. Increase the oven temperature to 120°C (Gas ½).

2. **For the pork stock sauce,** pour the the pork stock into a pan, bring to the boil and reduce to around 160ml; it should be intense and meaty flavoured. Add the mace to infuse for 10–15 minutes and set aside.

3. Meanwhile, make a sage beurre noisette to give added flavour to the sauce. Put the butter into a small pan and heat for a few minutes until it turns a dark brown. Remove from the heat and set aside until it has cooled slightly. Add the sage, leave to infuse for 5–10 minutes, then strain the butter through a sieve. Add the sage beurre noisette to the reduced pork stock, to taste, then strain through a muslin cloth.

4   **For the crackling,** score the pork skin, place in a roasting tin, skin-side down, and pour boiling water over the top. Leave to soak for 5 minutes. Remove the skin from the water, pat dry with kitchen paper, then cover with lemon juice and salt. Line a baking sheet with greaseproof paper and place the skin on top. Cover the skin with another piece of greaseproof paper and top it with a second baking sheet. Place a minimum 2kg weight on top of the sheet then cook in the oven for 2 hours.

5   Remove from the oven, trim the fat and turn the baking sheet through 180 degrees. Return it to the oven for another 2 hours, then remove and check the skin is completely cooked through and brittle. Scrape off any remaining fat while the skin is still hot. Heat the vegetable oil to 190°C in a large pan or a deep fryer. Break the crackling into shards and fry for 30–60 seconds until they are puffed up and crisp. Remove and drain on kitchen paper.

6   **To cook the black peas,** drain the peas and then put into a heavy-based pan. Cover with water, add the smoked bacon, onion, carrot and celery stick and bring to the boil. Reduce the heat, add the bicarbonate of soda and simmer the peas for 1–2 hours until a thick purée. Stir regularly to prevent catching as the pea purée thickens and reduces. Push through a sieve to remove any bits of skin. Add the butter and bacon and season with salt and pepper. Add the mint just before serving so the mint flavour is as fresh as possible.

7   **To make the apple sauce,** first peel, core and roughly chop the apples. Put in a pan with 30ml of water and cook gently for about 8 minutes until beginning to soften. Transfer to a food processor and blend until smooth. Push through a sieve then add citric acid or lemon juice to taste. The sauce should be very tangy.

8   Just before serving, sear the loin in a preheated griddle pan for 5–10 seconds, then set aside to keep warm (but not hot or the meat will dry out). Season with salt and pepper.

9   **To serve,** place a spoonful of the apple sauce on each of the warmed plates, followed by the black peas, pressed into and then turned out of a mould. Add the pork loin to the side, add the pork stock sauce and finish with a curl of crackling. The chef suggests serving this dish with vinegar jelly beignets to put in the top of the black peas (see page 6).

SLOW ROAST COLLAR OF PORK
with crispy ham hough bonbons
Geoffrey Smeddle

Six miles out of St Andrews, Geoffrey Smeddle is intent on giving his diners memories to cherish in his elegant restaurant with rooms, the Peat Inn. Geoffrey worked in London, Prague and Chicago before settling in Scotland, where his graceful modern European cooking and respectful approach to pedigree local ingredients have led to great acclaim. His roast collar of pork with crispy ham hough bonbons showcases this stylish chef's consummate attention to detail.

1   **To make the ham hough (for the bonbons),** place all the vegetables in a large stock pot, then wrap the ham hough in a muslin cloth and place in the pan. Cover with water and add the remaining ingredients, but do not add salt. Bring to a simmer and then skim any scum from the surface. Continue poaching the ham for 2–2½ hours, adding more water if necessary, until cooked thoroughly and the meat easily comes away from the bone.

2   Once cooked, leave the meat in the liquid for about 30 minutes, then remove. Allow the ham to cool enough so that it can be handled, then pick the meat from the ham hough bone, discarding any sinew and fat. Strain the cooking liquid into a clean pan and boil to reduce by half. Then strain again and set aside.

3   **To cook the collar of pork,** heat the oil in a frying pan over a medium heat. Add the steaks and seal on all sides, then add the butter. Reduce the heat and continue frying gently for about 30 minutes, turning regularly, until the meat is caramelised on the outside and just done in the middle. Leave it to rest in the warm pan, off the heat.

4   **For the crackling,** preheat the oven to 180°C (Gas 4). Take half the pork skin and cut it into thin fingers, each about 5mm wide and 8–10cm long. Press between two baking sheets and cook in the oven for about 15 minutes until golden brown and crisp. At the same time, cook the remaining piece of pork skin in a baking tin for about 15 minutes until golden and crisp. Remove from the oven, blitz to a powder in a food processor then mix into the breadcrumbs. Keep the oven switched on.

5   **To make the crispy ham hough bonbons,** mix 120g of the cooked ham with the mustard and parsley together with 2 tbsp of the reserved cooking liquid. Roll into walnut-sized balls, then pass through the flour, eggs and breadcrumb mixture twice for a good coating. Heat the oil to 180°C in a large pan or a deep fryer and add the balls. Cook for about 4 minutes until golden brown on the outside and hot in the centre, then finish in the oven for a further 5 minutes.

6   **To serve,** place each pork steak in the centre of a warmed plate together with a bonbon and a couple of pieces of crackling. The chef suggests serving this dish with cauliflower cheese, crushed swede, apple purée and baby fennel (see page 6).

Serves 4

For the ham hough
1 carrot, peeled and sliced
1 onion, peeled and sliced
2 garlic cloves, peeled
About 900g smoked ham hough
1 tsp chopped thyme
Large sprig of rosemary
Small bunch of parsley stalks
1 tsp whole black peppercorns

For the collar of pork
Splash of rapeseed oil
4 pork steaks from the eye
  of the collar
20–30g butter

For the crackling
20 x 35cm sheet of pork skin
200g Panko breadcrumbs

For the crispy ham hough bonbons
1 tsp Arran or wholegrain mustard
1 tsp chopped parsley
200g plain flour
2 eggs, beaten
500ml vegetable oil

Wrapping the ham hough in muslin prevents the vegetables and spices getting caught and stuck on the meat and therefore makes the ham much easier to pick from the bone when it's cooked.

BEEF FILLET WRAPPED IN DRY-CURED COPPA
with polenta & cavolo nero
Andy Appleton

Overlooking the surfing mecca at Watergate Bay, Fifteen Cornwall is home to the southwest arm of Jamie Oliver's legendary training programme. From this beachside address, head chef Andy Appleton leads his team of chefs and apprentices in creating Italian-inspired dishes from Cornish ingredients; and no one is more passionate about showcasing the county's produce. Andy refers to polenta as 'poor man's food, but cooked well and paired with rustic beef fillet there is nothing quite like it.'

Serves 4

For the polenta
375ml full-fat milk
100g polenta, not instant
20g unsalted butter
20g Parmesan cheese
Sea salt and freshly ground black pepper

For the fillet of beef
Sprig of rosemary, leaves finely chopped
1 tsp Dijon mustard
600g fillet of beef
20 slices of dry-cured ham, such as coppa

For the cavolo nero
Splash of olive oil, plus extra to serve
1 banana shallot, peeled and sliced
1 garlic clove, peeled and chopped
Pinch of dry chilli
2 anchovy fillets, salted in oil
Bunch of cavolo nero or curly kale
250ml white wine

1 **For the polenta,** mix the milk in a large pan with 375ml of water and bring to the boil. Add the polenta, reduce the heat to a gentle simmer and cook for at least 45 minutes, stirring often, until the polenta is a smooth consistency. Add the butter and Parmesan and season with salt and pepper.

2 **For the fillet of beef,** while you are cooking the polenta, place a roasting tin in the oven and preheat to 220°C (Gas 7). Make a paste with the rosemary and mustard and rub it over the beef fillet. Lay the slices of ham onto enough baking parchment to cover the beef fillet. Place them side by side and slightly overlapping.

3 Lay the fillet on top, season with salt and pepper and wrap it in the ham and paper. Roll the paper like a parcel and tie with string. Roast to your liking (about 15 minutes for rare, depending on the thickness of the

A hugely satisfying, rustic dish with robust savoury notes.

fillet). Remove from the oven and leave for a good 10 minutes to rest – this is really important because you will want to use the resting juices later.

4   **To cook the cavolo nero,** heat the oil in a large pan over a medium heat. Add the shallot, garlic, chilli and anchovies and sweat for about 5 minutes until soft. Stir in the cavolo nero or kale, add the white wine, cover with a lid and cook, stirring occasionally, for about 4 minutes until the leaves are tender. Season with salt and pepper.

5   **To serve,** make a bed of polenta on each warmed plate and add the cavolo nero or kale. Unwrap the beef, cut into slices and place on top. Pour over the pan juices and finish with a drizzle of oil. The chef suggests serving this dish with pan-fried mushrooms (see page 6).

POACHED, FRIED & BRAISED BEEF
with girolles & duck fat chips
Carson Hill

An Oxford institution, the enchanting Cherwell Boathouse graces the banks of the slow-moving and peaceful river. Inside, head chef Carson Hill thrills to the pull of cutting-edge techniques with which to deliver of-the-moment modern British cooking, be it innovative new dishes or simpler classics. Carson cites Thomas Keller's 'amazing food philosophy' as his inspiration, and this take on 'steak and chips' is an example of this adventurous chef's commitment to perfection.

1   **For the braised beef medallions,** preheat the oven to 150°C (Gas 2). Heat the oil in a roasting tin and fry the carrot and celery for 5–10 minutes to soften. Then add the thyme, followed by the beef shin. Sear the shin on each side, then add the bay leaves, port and beef stock and bring to the boil. Cover with foil and cook in the oven for 4 hours until the meat is cooked through and tender. Remove from the oven and shred the meat. Reserve the stock.

2   Put a long piece of cling film on a work surface and spread the meat over it in a thick layer. Sprinkle the protein powder over the beef (to help the meat stick together), season with salt and pepper and then roll into a sausage shape using the cling film. Twist the ends firmly to seal and leave the meat in the fridge for 2 hours until it is firm.

3   Make a sauce by passing the reserved stock through a sieve, then return it to the pan and reduce by two-thirds on a rapid heat over about 20 minutes, taking care not to over-reduce or burn.

4   **For the poached fillet of beef,** wrap the fillet in two layers of cling film. Bring a large pan of water to the boil, then turn off the heat and after 5 minutes add the beef. Leave it in the water for 10 minutes, then drain it, cut into thick slices and set aside.

5   **To make the duck fat chips,** peel and chop the potatoes into large chunky chips about 10cm long. Heat the duck fat in a large pan over a medium heat until it is hot and fry the chips for 10–15 minutes until they become soft but hold their shape. Drain the chips and pat dry with kitchen paper. Then heat the oil to 200°C in a large pan or a deep fryer and cook the chips for 7–9 minutes until they are golden and crisp. Drain again and pat dry with kitchen paper, then season with salt and pepper.

6   **To finish the three types of beef,** remove the braised shin roll from the cling film and slice the meat into medallions. Season the poached fillet of beef slices and the sirloin with salt and pepper. Heat the oil and butter in a pan on a medium-high heat until hot, then add the braised medallions, poached fillet slices, the sirloin and the girolles. Cook all of them on one side for 3–4 minutes until a nice nutty brown, then turn over, remove from the heat and leave to rest for 5–10 minutes.

7   **To serve,** put a slice of each type of beef on a warmed plate, scatter the girolles over the top and drizzle the sauce over and around the meat. Serve the chips on the side. The chef suggests serving this dish with caramelised truffled onion purée (see page 6).

Serves 4

For the braised beef medallions
1 tbsp olive oil
1 large carrot, peeled and chopped
2 celery sticks, trimmed and chopped
2 sprigs of thyme
2 shin steaks of beef, about 215g each
2 bay leaves
100ml port
500ml beef stock
50g protein powder, unflavoured
Sea salt and freshly ground black pepper

For the poached fillet of beef
350–400g fillet of beef, trimmed and with any sinews removed (you can ask your butcher to do this)

For the duck fat chips
4 large potatoes, preferably King Edward
500g can of duck fat
1 litre vegetable oil

For the fried sirloin of beef
400g sirloin of beef, trimmed and with any sinews removed (you can ask your butcher to do this)
1 tbsp olive oil
Knob of unsalted butter
200g girolles, cut in half if necessary

An improvement on perfection – steak and chips, anyone?

AGED FILLET STEAK
with foie gras & wild mushroom lasagnette
Michael Nadra

A degree in naval architecture is far from typical on a top chef's CV, but the chef-patron of Restaurant Michael Nadra followed his studies with jobs in some of the country's finest dining establishments, including Pétrus and Chez Bruce. He likes to think of his French-influenced, modern European food as 'friendly fine-dining', and his stylish neighbourhood restaurant in west London perfectly reflects Michael's elegant, accomplished cooking.

Served in a luxurious red wine jus, a dish of pure indulgence.

1   **To make the veal stock,** preheat the oven to 200°C (Gas 6). Put the veal bones in a roasting tin and cook in the oven for about 20 minutes until golden. Transfer the bones to a stock pot using a slotted spoon to drain away any oil. Dispose of the oil from the tin safely then deglaze the tin with a small amount of water and add to the liquid in the pot. Add enough water to cover the bones and bring to the boil. Reduce the heat to a very gentle simmer and leave for 1 hour, regularly skimming any scum from the liquid.

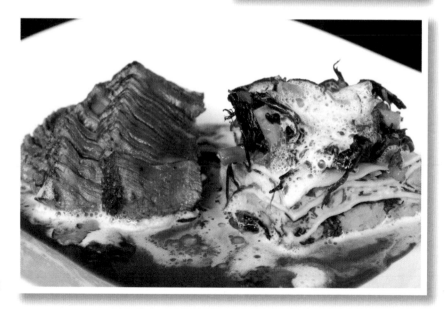

2   Add the vegetables, tomato purée and herbs. Leave to gently simmer for 24 hours. Strain the stock and place it back on the heat to reduce by a third.

3   **For the red wine reduction,** put all the ingredients except the Madeira wine into a pan over a medium heat. Bring to the boil, then lower the heat and simmer to reduce by half. Add the wine reduction to the veal stock and reduce over a high heat, skimming regularly, until it has thickened into a sauce. This all takes about an hour. Pass the sauce through a sieve and set aside.

4   **For the mushroom lasagnette,** first make the chicken mousse. Put the chicken in a chilled food processor and add salt and pepper. Blend the chicken and then add the egg yolk before slowly pouring in the cream and blending to combine. Transfer to a bowl and chill in the fridge until needed.

5   Season the foie gras with salt and pepper, then sauté in a very hot pan for about 30 seconds on each side to colour. Transfer to a bowl and chill in the fridge until needed.

6   Put the sweetbreads in a pan, cover with water and bring to the boil. As soon as the water boils, drain the sweetbreads, remove the membranes and season with curry powder and a pinch of salt. Sauté the sweetbreads in the butter until golden. Next, season and sauté the wild mushrooms in a little more butter until all the excess liquid evaporates.

7   Dice the sweetbreads, foie gras and a third of the sautéed wild mushrooms and, together with the chopped herbs, mix with the chicken mousse.

8   Lay out the pasta sheets and cut out sixteen 7.5cm squares, four for each serving. Lay one pasta square per serving in a steamer. Add some chicken mousse mix, then layer another pasta sheet on top before adding another spoonful of chicken mousse mix. Repeat until you have three layers of mousse mix and then top with the last pieces of pasta. Steam for 6 minutes.

9   **For the aged fillets of beef,** preheat the oven to 200°C (Gas 6). Sear the beef in a hot pan with the oil, then transfer to a roasting tin and cook for 5 minutes. Remove from the oven and leave to rest for about 5 minutes.

10   Bring the red wine jus to the boil and add the Madeira to finish.

11   **To serve,** carve the beef, season with a pinch of sea salt and then place on warmed plates. Add the lasagnette with the rest of the wild mushrooms and spoon over the Madeira jus. The chef suggests serving this dish with mushroom and truffle cream and sautéed spinach together with a garnish of sliced black truffles; you could make your own saffron pasta, too (see page 6).

Serves 4

For the veal stock
1kg veal marrow bones
1 large onion, peeled and roughly chopped
¼ head of celery, trimmed and roughly chopped
2 large carrots, peeled and roughly chopped
1 leek, trimmed and roughly chopped
1 garlic bulb, peeled and roughly chopped
1 tsp tomato purée
Sprig of thyme
Sprig of rosemary

For the red wine reduction
250ml red wine
½ onion, peeled and sliced
Sprig of thyme
Sprig of rosemary
1 tsp redcurrant jelly
25ml Madeira wine

For the mushroom lasagnette
1 skinless chicken breast (weighing about 150g), diced
Salt and freshly ground black pepper
1 egg yolk
150ml double cream
100g foie gras
100g sweetbreads
Pinch of mild curry powder
Knob of unsalted butter, plus extra for the mushrooms
250g wild mushrooms, such as ceps, trompettes, girolles and oyster
Bunch of mixed herbs, such as chives, parsley and tarragon, finely chopped
4 sheets of fresh pasta

For the aged fillets of beef
4 aged fillets of beef, about 200g each, trimmed to remove any sinew
1 tbsp olive oil

BRAISED AND PAN-FRIED BEEF
with potato purée, baby carrots & Swiss chard
Rupert Rowley

Rupert Rowley's career has scaled many heights. He kicked off at Raymond Blanc's Le Manoir aux Quat'Saisons, and has worked at both L'Ortolan in Reading and Restaurant Gordon Ramsay in Chelsea. Now at Fischer's Baslow Hall in Derbyshire, Rupert's sensational modern British cuisine is driven by impeccable sourcing, stunning invention and an abundance of flavour.

1 **For the braised beef,** heat the oil and butter in a large pan over a medium heat. Add the shallots and cook for about 8 minutes to caramelise. Add the beef and, in the same pan, seal on each side, then pour in 300ml of the stock and add the thyme. Cover with a lid and braise on the lowest heat setting for about 3½ hours, topping up with more stock if necessary, until the meat is cooked through.

2 Remove the meat from the stock and set aside. Add the wine and port to the stock, bring to the boil and reduce by half. Then add the remaining stock and reduce once again by half. Pass through a sieve into a clean pan, return the meat to the stock and glaze with the sauce. Set the meat and sauce aside.

3 **To make the potato purée,** first put the potatoes into a pan of cold salted water and bring to the boil. Reduce the heat and simmer for about 20 minutes until just cooked. Remove the potatoes from the water and peel while still hot.

4 Push the potatoes through a ricer (or mash by hand) and then place the mashed potatoes in a pan on a gentle heat. Add the butter and mix well. When all the butter is incorporated, the mix should have a slightly oily look. Pass through a sieve and put into a clean pan. Add enough milk to make a purée, mix in thoroughly and then set aside.

5 **For the pan-fried beef,** season the meat with salt and pepper. Heat the butter in a pan over a medium heat and pan fry the steaks for 4–5 minutes on each side.

6 **For the vegetables,** put the carrots in a pan, barely cover them with water and add a knob of the butter. Season with salt and sugar, then simmer for about 5 minutes until tender. Gently wilt the Swiss chard leaves in a separate pan in a little butter, and warm the nasturtium seeds (if using) in a little butter and water.

7 **To serve,** remove the braised beef from the bone and divide between warmed plates. Add the vegetables and potato purée and place a steak to one side. Finish with a little of the sauce. The chef suggests serving this dish with nasturtium purée and, if you have a spaghetti machine, you may wish to make potato cannelloni to encase the potato purée (see page 6).

> An alternative way to cook the baby carrots is to braise them in carrot juice. This will reduce to a sticky glaze, which coats the carrots.

Serves 2

For the braised beef
1 dessertspoon vegetable oil
Knob of unsalted butter
2 shallots, peeled and finely sliced
1 Jacob's ladder cut of beef, on the bone
400ml beef stock
Small sprig of thyme
200ml red wine
100ml port

For the potato purée
200g potatoes, preferably King Edward, skins on and roughly chopped
60g unsalted butter, softened
60ml full-fat milk

For the pan-fried beef
2 fillets of steak, about 100g each
Sea salt and freshly ground black pepper
10g unsalted butter

For the vegetables
2 baby carrots
Unsalted butter
Pinch of caster sugar
4 large Swiss chard leaves
10 pickled nasturtium seeds (optional)

BEEF ROSSINI 'POT AU FEU'
Luigi Vespero

At Galvin Bistrot de Luxe in London, Luigi Vespero applies his classic French cooking to exemplary renditions of bistro classics. Originally from Italy, Luigi recalls how his grandmother introduced him to the stunning simplicity of certain flavour combinations. 'It blew my mind,' he says of his first mouthful of garlic, tomato and basil. Arriving in London with only a pocket English dictionary for company, Luigi has nevertheless achieved his professional ambition of becoming a head chef by the age of thirty.

1   **For the Madeira beef bouillon,** preheat the oven to 180°C (Gas 4). Put the bones in a roasting tin and place in the oven. Do the same with the chicken wings. Roast for 45–50 minutes until browned and then transfer the bones to a stock pot with the shin of beef. Cover with water and bring to the boil. With a slotted spoon remove any foam that forms on the surface. Add the fresh vegetables and herbs and leave to simmer for about 5 hours over a low heat, skimming the surface occasionally.

2   Pass the liquid through a sieve or muslin cloth into a smaller pot (and chill or freeze half the liquid for use another time). Add the Madeira wine, bring back up to the boil, then remove from the heat. Add the mushrooms, cover with cling film and leave for about 30 minutes to allow the flavours to infuse. Strain the stock again, season with salt and pepper, and keep in the fridge for later.

3   **To make the tortellini,** first make the pasta dough. Put the flour in a mixing bowl and make a well in the centre. Add the 4 whole eggs with the egg yolks, oil, a pinch of salt and a splash of water. Start to knead the mix, slowly incorporating the flour into the wet ingredients until it forms a dough. Knead until all the ingredients are well combined and the dough is smooth. Wrap in cling film and allow to rest in the fridge for 20 minutes.

4   Roll out the pasta using a pasta machine. Start at the highest setting point, pushing the pasta through and folding it in half. Repeat on the same setting. Work your way down the settings, folding between each roll until you reach a setting of 1.5. If the pasta starts to stick to the machine, dust the pasta with a little flour.

5   To make the tortellini, lay out the rolled pasta and cut out sixteen 5cm-diameter discs. Brush each disc on the edge of one half of the circle with egg wash. Place 1–2 tsp of diced foie gras in the centre of each disc, then fold the discs in half, pushing out as much air from the middle as possible, and seal the ends to make a semicircle. Take the two ends and pull them round to meet, sealing with more egg wash.

6   **For the fillets of beef,** season the meat with salt and pepper, then sear in a hot pan with the oil and butter for 2–3 minutes on each side until coloured all over. Transfer to a cooling rack, cover with foil and leave to rest for about 5 minutes.

7   **For the sautéed vegetables,** while the meat is cooking, sauté the vegetables in a hot pan with some oil. Finish with the butter and about 2 tbsp of water to emulsify. Add the watercress at the end to wilt it and then drain off the excess liquid.

8   **To serve,** bring 350ml of the bouillon up to the boil and then add the chopped herbs and a drizzle of truffle oil (if using). Blanch the pasta in salted boiling water for about 3 minutes, or until the tortellini float to the surface. Lift from the pan using a slotted spoon and place in warmed bowls. Place the sautéed vegetables in a ring in the middle of each bowl. Cut each fillet in half and place on top of the vegetables and then sprinkle with the truffle shavings (if using). Garnish the plates with some picked chervil on top of the tortellini and add the bouillon.

Serves 4

For the Madeira beef bouillon
1kg veal or beef bones
500g chicken wings
500g shin of beef
3 carrots, peeled and chopped
1 large onion, peeled and chopped
½ head of celery, trimmed and chopped
1 leek, trimmed and chopped
½ head of garlic
2 bay leaves
5 sprigs of thyme
100ml Madeira wine
25g dried ceps
Salt and freshly ground black pepper

For the tortellini
450g '00' pasta flour
5 eggs, 1 beaten for an egg wash
4 egg yolks
25ml extra-virgin olive oil
150g foie gras, diced

For the fillets of beef
4 fillets of beef, about 170g each
Splash of olive oil
25g unsalted butter

For the sautéed vegetables
2 courgettes, cut into julienne strips
2 carrots, peeled and cut into julienne strips
2 leeks, trimmed and cut into julienne strips
Splash of olive oil
25g unsalted butter
400g watercress

To garnish
20g mixed chopped chives and chervil, plus extra chervil to serve
Drizzle of truffle oil (optional)
20g autumn black truffle, finely chopped (optional)

Foie gras tortellini add a luxurious twist to sumptuous fillets of beef.

FILLET OF CHAR-GRILLED BEEF
with a confit of wild mushrooms & crushed potatoes
Grant Williams

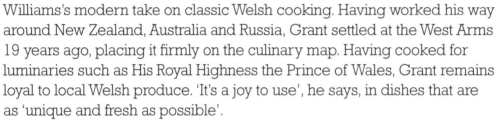

A romantic 16th-century inn in the Denbighshire countryside, the West Arms Hotel is home to Grant Williams's modern take on classic Welsh cooking. Having worked his way around New Zealand, Australia and Russia, Grant settled at the West Arms 19 years ago, placing it firmly on the culinary map. Having cooked for luminaries such as His Royal Highness the Prince of Wales, Grant remains loyal to local Welsh produce. 'It's a joy to use', he says, in dishes that are as 'unique and fresh as possible'.

1   **For the roasted tomato purée,** preheat the oven to 160°C (Gas 3). Put all the ingredients in a food processor and blend to a purée. Pass the mixture through a sieve and then spoon onto a sheet of foil, seal and then place on a baking sheet and cook for 20 minutes. Remove from the oven and set aside. Reduce the oven temperature to 120°C (Gas ½).

> Dark, sumptuous steak with a buttery tarragon sauce.

2   **For the confit of wild mushrooms,** heat the goose fat and butter in a pan. Add the shallots and cook over a low heat for 10 minutes until softened. Remove from the heat, add both types of mushroom, together with the thyme sprigs and diced pears and season with the peppercorns and salt. Spoon the mixture onto a sheet of foil, seal and then place on a baking sheet and cook for 20 minutes. Remove from the oven and leave to cool. Keep the oven switched on.

3   **For the crushed potatoes,** bring a pan of salted water to the boil. Add the potatoes and cook for 10–12 minutes until tender. Remove from the heat, drain and return to the pan and then crush with a fork. Add the oil, olives, horseradish sauce, tomatoes and rocket, season with salt and pepper and keep warm.

4   **For the tarragon butter sauce,** whisk the vinegar into the melted butter. Then stir in the tarragon leaves and set aside.

5   **For the fillets of char-grilled beef,** make an incision in the side of each fillet and place a spoonful of the cooled mushroom confit into each pocket, reserving some mushroom confit for serving. Wrap one slice of ham around each fillet steak, then put the meat in a shallow

dish and pour over the tarragon butter. Marinate for
8 minutes on each side, basting the steak with the butter.

6   Place a griddle pan over a medium-high heat. Add the steaks,
    reserving the tarragon butter, and cook for 4–6 minutes on
    each side to medium rare. Transfer the steaks to an ovenproof
    plate and place in the oven for 8–10 minutes to rest.

7   Heat 2 tbsp of the tarragon butter in a pan. Add the leek,
    carrot, celery and onion and cook over a low heat for about
    3 minutes until soft. Add the roasted tomato purée and the
    wine, bring to the boil, then lower the heat and simmer until
    reduced by half. Add 200ml of the beef stock and bring to the
    boil. Pass through a sieve into the pan the steak was cooked
    in and whisk in knobs of the remaining tarragon butter. Pass
    through a sieve into a clean pan and keep warm.

8   **To serve,** place some crushed potato on each warmed plate
    together with a steak. Add the confit of wild mushrooms and
    dress the plates with the tarragon butter sauce. The chef
    suggests serving this dish with a filo basket filled with creamed
    radish; you might also choose to make your own beef stock for
    the tarragon butter sauce (see page 6).

Serves 4

For the roasted tomato purée
12 plum tomatoes, roughly chopped
3 sprigs of basil
5 shallots, peeled and chopped
Pinch of paprika
Drizzle of olive oil

For the confit of wild mushrooms
60g goose fat
125g unsalted butter, diced
4 shallots, peeled and finely chopped
125g chanterelles, trimmed and
    chopped
125g oyster mushrooms, trimmed and
    chopped
3 sprigs of thyme
2 pears, preferably Comice, peeled
    and diced
2g whole pink peppercorns
Sea salt

For the crushed potatoes
Sea salt and freshly ground black
    pepper
500g new potatoes
Drizzle of olive oil
10 black olives, finely chopped
4 tsp horseradish sauce
2 firm tomatoes, peeled, deseeded
    and finely chopped
Bunch of rocket

For the tarragon butter sauce
1 tsp white wine vinegar
60g unsalted butter, melted
1 sprig of tarragon, leaves only
½ leek, trimmed and white parts only
    chopped
1 carrot, peeled and chopped
1 celery stick, trimmed and chopped
½ onion, peeled and finely chopped
400ml red wine
1½ beef stock cubes dissolved in
    200ml water

For the fillets of char-grilled beef
4 fillet steaks of beef, about 225g
    each, trimmed of sinew and skin
4 slices of ham

BEEF FILLET & SNAIL RAVIOLI
with parsnip purée & potato rösti
Daniel Woodhouse

The only boy in his year to do a home economics A Level, Daniel Woodhouse's youthful commitment to cooking has paid impressive dividends. Now head chef at Maidenhead's Boulters Riverside Brasserie, known for its gorgeous views of the Thames, Daniel keeps his menu local and simple, serving dishes that are beautifully crafted, thoughtful and impeccably sourced.

1   **To make the pasta,** put the flour, eggs and 1½ tsp of salt in a food processor and pulse until the mixture forms small yellow balls of dough that can easily be pressed into one piece once removed from the bowl. The dough should have a firm, smooth, slightly sticky texture. If it seems wet, add a little extra flour. Wrap in cling film and leave in the fridge until ready to use.

2   **For the parsnip purée,** put the potatoes, parsnips and bay leaf in a pan and add enough cream and milk to cover them. Simmer for about 20 minutes until the flesh has softened. Remove from the heat, discard the bay leaf and, using a hand-held blender, purée the mixture until smooth. Season with celery salt and pepper.

3   **For the snail ravioli filling,** heat the oil in a pan over a medium heat. Add the carrot, followed by the onion and then the celery and leek. Finally, add the thyme, bay leaf and garlic and cook for 5–8 minutes until the vegetables are caramelised. Add the beef demi glace or stocks and the bone marrow to the pan and simmer for 20 minutes to reduce by half. Remove the marrow from the bones and put into a bowl. Add the prepared snails and parsley, season with salt and pepper and mix together thoroughly. Discard the bones and reserve the reduced demi glace or stocks.

4   To make the ravioli, take one ball of the pasta dough and feed it through a pasta machine, gradually reducing the settings. Roll it out as thinly as possible, into a sheet about 12cm wide and 60cm long. Using an 8cm-diameter cutter, cut out circles from the pasta and put 1 heaped tsp of the snail filling in every other circle. Brush a little water around each pile of filling, place an empty pasta circle on top and seal the edges, ensuring as little air as possible is trapped inside. Trim the edges with a sharp knife and set aside.

5   **To make the potato rösti,** squeeze any excess liquid out of the grated potatoes and pat dry with a clean tea towel. Salt the potatoes, add the onion seeds and fry in butter in a small frying

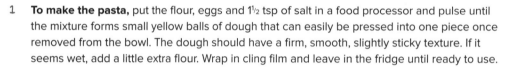

Resting the beef in duck fat helps keep the meat moist and warm.

Serves 4

For the pasta
275g '00' pasta flour
3 eggs, beaten
Salt and freshly ground black pepper

For the parsnip purée
375g parsnips, peeled and diced
60g potatoes, peeled and diced
1 bay leaf
About 150ml double cream
About 150ml full-fat milk
Pinch of celery salt

For the snail ravioli filling
25ml olive oil
½ carrot, peeled and chopped
½ onion, peeled and chopped
1 small celery stick, trimmed and
  chopped
½ small leek, trimmed and chopped
Small bunch of thyme
1 bay leaf
2 garlic cloves, peeled and sliced in
  half
125ml beef demi glace (or 125ml beef
  stock and 1 tsp jelly beef stock)
125g bone marrow in the bone, cut
  into 5cm pieces (ask your butcher
  to do this for you)
25g cooked and shelled snails
Small bunch of parsley, leaves
  chopped

For the potato rösti
2 large potatoes, peeled and grated
1 tsp black onion seeds
50g unsalted butter, diced

For the fillet of beef
1 tbsp olive oil
Sprig of thyme, leaves chopped
600g fillet of beef

For the sauce
20g beef dripping
Small bunch of parsley, leaves
  chopped

pan for 4–5 minutes, stirring continuously, until the potatoes are browned. Allow the potatoes to set in the pan for about 2 minutes until golden, then turn over and cook the other side for about 2 minutes.

6   **For the fillet of beef,** preheat the oven to 180°C (Gas 4). Heat the oil in a pan. Add the thyme and then the beef and seal on all sides. Transfer to a rack in a roasting tin and roast the fillet for 6 minutes. Remove from the tin and leave to rest.

7   **To cook the ravioli,** bring a large pan of salted water to the boil, add the ravioli and simmer for 3–5 minutes until al dente.

8   **For the sauce,** put the beef demi glace or stocks into a pan, bring to the boil and then reduce by half. Add the dripping and parsley and season with salt and pepper.

9   **To serve,** divide the potato rösti between warmed plates. Slice and add the fillet. Drain the pasta and put 1–2 ravioli on top of the beef. Reheat the parsnip purée, add it to the plates and then drizzle the sauce over and around the meat. The chef suggests serving this dish with spinach and parsnip crisps and, for even more flavourful beef, resting it in infused duck fat after cooking (see page 6).

ROAST GROUSE & SHOULDER OF LAMB
with bilberry mead
Frances Atkins

An historic 18th-century coaching house in the Yorkshire Dales, the Yorke Arms is now home to Frances Atkins's famed restaurant-with-rooms; one of the region's finest dining experiences. One of the country's top female chefs, Frances runs what she describes as a 'grown-up' kitchen where, with a brigade of five chefs, she transforms locally sourced raw ingredients into memory-searing dishes. This grouse and lamb main course pays homage to the ethos of 'terroir'; in Frances's kitchen the meat would be imbued with the flavours of the Yorkshire moorland.

1   **To prepare the shoulder of lamb,** cut it in half. Remove the bone and lay the meat flat. Reserve the bones and trimmings for the stock.

2   **To make the lamb stock,** brown the lamb bones and trimmings together with the chopped vegetables, peppercorns and stalks from the herbs (reserve the leaves for serving) in the oil in a large stock pot. Cover with water and bring to the boil, then reduce the heat and simmer, uncovered, for about 1 hour. Strain the stock back into a clean pan, reduce by half and season with salt and pepper.

3   **To cook the shoulder of lamb,** preheat the oven to 200°C (Gas 6). Remove the skin from the meat and place it between two pieces of cling film. Use a rolling pin to firmly flatten the skin. Put half the meat into a food processor, then add the cream and egg white and blend to bring the mixture together.

4   Melt the butter in a pan over a low heat, add the Madeira wine and half the shallots and reduce until dry, allowing the shallots to absorb the Madeira. Chop the rest of the meat and put it in a bowl. Add the remaining shallots and the reduced Madeira liquid and stir to combine. Mix the two meats together, remove the cling film from the lamb skin and spread the meat onto the lamb skin. Roll up and secure with string then cook on the bed of root vegetables in a roasting tin for about 30 minutes.

5   **For the grouse stock and roast grouse,** remove the legs and the breast from the birds and put them in a pan with enough water to cover. Bring to the boil, then reduce the heat and simmer for 30 minutes, skimming the surface occasionally.

6   Wrap the crowns of each grouse in foil and add a slice of pancetta across each breast. Rub over some oil and season with salt and pepper. Put the birds in the oven with foil around the base of the grouse, slightly exposing the breast and pancetta, and cook with the lamb for 8–10 minutes until cooked through. Remove from the oven and allow to rest for 5 minutes.

7   **To make the bilberry mead,** heat 50ml of the grouse stock with the whisky and verjus (if using) in a pan and reduce by half. Add the honey and bilberries or blueberries, let the liquid thicken and then pass through a sieve. Add the extra bilberries or blueberries.

8   **To serve,** slice the lamb and glaze it with the lamb stock. Remove the pancetta and carve the grouse breasts and place both on the lamb. Garnish with the vegetables, mini capers and bilberry mead.

Serves 4

For the shoulder of lamb
1.4kg shoulder of lamb
2 tbsp double cream
1 egg white
30g unsalted butter, diced
50ml Madeira wine
4 shallots, peeled and roughly chopped
2 small carrots, peeled and roughly chopped
1 celery stick, trimmed and roughly chopped
1 leek, trimmed and roughly chopped

For the lamb stock
Handful of chopped carrot, onion, leek and celery
4 whole black peppercorns
Handful of mixed herbs, such as thyme, rosemary and heather flowers
Splash of olive oil
Salt and freshly ground black pepper

For the grouse stock and roast grouse
2 young oven-ready grouse
2 slices of pancetta
Olive oil

For the bilberry mead
50ml peaty malt whisky
50ml verjus (optional)
2 dessertspoons runny honey
60g bilberries or blueberries, plus a few extra to garnish

To garnish
1 tsp mini capers

A tender and intensely flavourful dish of best British meat and game.

GROUSE & DUCK LIVER PIE
with celeriac purée
Kevin Tew

Kevin Tew's childhood ambition to be 'the man repairing the holes in the road' was quickly displaced by his talent for cooking. After spells in some of London's most famous kitchens, including Claridge's and Galvin at Windows, he moved to Corrigan's Mayfair, a restaurant that celebrates quintessential British cuisine with full-bodied flavours and impeccable ingredients. Creative and passionate, Kevin's zest for his craft is driven by 'seeing a full restaurant and people enjoying themselves … it's the little rewards that mean a lot.'

1   **For the pastry,** preheat the oven to 180°C (Gas 4). Mix the flour, butter, water, thyme, 1 tsp of salt and ½ tsp pepper in a bowl to form a dough. Wrap the dough in cling film and leave to rest in the fridge for 1 hour. Roll out the pastry on a lightly floured work surface and line four 8cm-diameter ring moulds. Cut four pie lids from the pastry and set aside. Line the pastry cases with cling film and fill with baking beans, then bake blind for 12 minutes. Remove the cases from the oven and brush with the egg yolks three times, returning to the oven to dry for 1–2 minutes between each coating. Keep the oven switched on and set the remaining egg wash to one side.

Line the pastry case with cling film instead of greaseproof paper as it holds the baking beans in place better.

2   **For the pie filling,** remove the grouse breasts from the carcasses and put the bones into a roasting tin. Roast in the oven for 5–6 minutes. Remove the skin from the grouse breasts and sear the breasts and duck livers in half the oil in a pan for about 5 minutes. Remove from the pan and place on a plate. Cover with cling film and chill in the fridge until needed.

3   **To make the sauce,** put the carrots and onion into a pan with the oil and cook over a medium heat for about 8 minutes to caramelise. Add the roasted bones, red wine and veal stock and cook on a high heat for about 30 minutes.

4   **Meanwhile, for the filling,** blanch the button onions in boiling water for 2–3 minutes, then caramelise them in the remaining oil and the sugar for 4–5 minutes until golden.

5   **To assemble the pie,** layer the chilled grouse and livers with the caramelised carrots and onions and the shredded cabbage inside the pie cases. Pour in the sauce and place a pastry lid on top of each one. Brush the pastry lids with the remaining egg wash, scatter with thyme and bake for about 15 minutes until golden.

6   **To make the celeriac purée,** put the celeriac and milk in a pan, season with salt and white pepper and bring to the boil. Reduce the heat and simmer for about 10 minutes until soft. Transfer to a food processor and blend to a purée.

7   **To serve,** remove the pies from the moulds, place on warmed plates and add the celeriac purée. The chef suggests serving this dish with dressed beetroot and walnuts (see page 6).

Serves 6

For the pastry
500g plain flour
250g unsalted butter, softened
150ml iced water
1 tbsp chopped thyme
Salt and freshly ground black pepper
2 egg yolks, beaten

For the pie filling
3 whole grouse
150g duck livers
2 tbsp olive oil
375g whole button onions, peeled
30g caster sugar
3 Savoy cabbage leaves, shredded
Bunch of thyme, leaves chopped

For the sauce
2 carrots, peeled and chopped
½ Spanish onion, peeled and sliced
1 tbsp vegetable oil
375ml red wine
750ml veal stock

For the celeriac purée
375g celeriac, peeled and diced
375ml full-fat milk
Freshly ground white pepper

A BOWL OF DUCK
with duck tea, chard, butternut squash & broad beans
Paul Bloxham

Local-food champion Paul Bloxham's full-blooded British classics have seen the Tilbury, nestled in the heart of the picturesque village of Datchworth in Hertfordshire, become a central part of the community. His culinary mantra, 'the simplest things when done properly, with superb ingredients, can be truly outstanding', is the bedrock of a menu that celebrates local and regional produce.

1. **To prepare the duck,** debone the thighs and remove the sinew and fat from the breast meat. Cut up the remaining meat so that you have 200g skinless and fat-free meat, including some breast meat, heart and gizzard for the duck tea.

2. **To make the duck tea,** mince the 200g meat and put it in a large bowl with the vegetables, herbs, seasoning, dried mushrooms and the egg whites. Blend together well with your hands. Whisk in the duck stock, soy sauce and veal glace or beef consommé and transfer the mixture to a stock pot.

3. Add the mirin and slowly bring to the boil over about 10 minutes, stirring continuously. Stop stirring when the tea starts frothing on top, and watch for bubbles from the stock. As soon as they start appearing, reduce the heat and wait for the meat to form a solid crust on the surface of the tea. Break a small hole in the crust with a ladle to allow the steam to escape and prevent the crust from breaking up. Simmer the tea for at least 40 minutes or until it has clarified and the flavour has developed.

4. Line a sieve with a muslin cloth and pour the clarified tea through the ventilation hole in the crust (or remove the crust with a slotted spoon) into a clean pan. Leave a small amount of tea to prevent any crust from seeping into the decanted liquid. Adjust the seasoning with salt, pepper and lime juice and set aside, simmering, until ready to serve.

5. **To cook the duck thighs,** melt the duck fat in a heavy-based pan, add the thighs and leave to simmer for 30 minutes or until tender. Remove the thighs from the duck fat and crisp them up in a pan.

6. **To cook the vegetables,** bring a pan of water to the boil. Add the chard, butternut squash and broad beans and blanch for 2 minutes. Drain and remove the skins from the broad beans.

7. **To serve,** slice the duck breast very thinly and shred the meat from the thighs. Place the chard leaves at the bottom of warmed bowls, then add the chard batons, shredded duck thighs and slices of breast, squash and broad beans. Top with the coriander, basil shoots and chilli and serve with a pot of simmering duck tea for the diners to pour over the contents of the bowls. The chef suggests serving this dish with foie gras bonbons and you may wish to make your own duck stock (see page 6).

Serves 2

For the duck
1 farm duck

For the duck tea
2 carrots, peeled and finely diced
1 leek, trimmed and finely chopped
4 spring onions, trimmed and finely chopped
1 celery stick, trimmed and chopped
2 tomatoes, coarsely chopped
2 garlic cloves, peeled and crushed
25g fresh root ginger, peeled and grated
Sprig of lemon thyme, chopped
Pinch of Sichuan pepper
15g dried shiitake mushrooms
5 egg whites
800ml duck stock
2 tbsp dark soy sauce
125ml veal glace, heated until just melted, or 400g can of beef consommé, reduced to 125ml
125ml mirin
Salt and freshly ground black pepper
Lime juice, to taste

For the duck thighs
200g duck fat

For the vegetables
300g rainbow chard, ribs cut into batons and leaves finely shredded
200g peeled butternut squash, diced
200g podded broad beans

To serve
Small bunch of micro coriander
Small bunch of baby basil shoots
1 large red chilli, deseeded and finely sliced

Redolent with Eastern flavours – fresh, fragrant, and oh-so-pretty.

PHEASANT KIEV
with a pheasant Scotch egg
Ross Pike

When Ross Pike set up the British Larder website with his partner, Maddy, they quickly gained an international audience for their inspiring recipe hub, designed to bring like-minded foodies together. Now Ross and Maddy have brought that early vision to glorious life with the opening of their traditional British pub in Bromeswell, where generous-hearted, big-flavoured regional dishes get the run of the menus – with Suffolk produce leading the pack, naturally.

Serves 4

For the pheasant legs
4 pheasant legs
2 heads of garlic, cloves peeled and lightly bashed
Sprig of thyme
300g duck fat

For the pheasant Scotch eggs
4 pheasant's or hen's eggs
200g Cumberland sausagemeat
2 garlic cloves, peeled and crushed
2 tsp ground fennel seeds
4 tbsp finely chopped mixed herbs, such as parsley, chives and chervil
Sea salt and freshly ground black pepper
100g seasoned plain flour
2 eggs, beaten
400g Panko breadcrumbs
500ml vegetable oil

For the pheasant Kiev
4 pheasant breasts, skin removed
2 heads of garlic, peeled
200g unsalted butter, softened, plus extra for frying
60g flat-leaf parsley, chopped
120g seasoned plain flour
2 eggs, beaten
200g Panko breadcrumbs mixed with grated zest of ½ unwaxed lemon
Rapeseed oil
100g curly kale, stalks removed

For the cress salad
1 tsp Dijon mustard
85ml vegetable oil
2 tbsp white wine vinegar
40g mixed cress salad

1 **For the pheasant legs,** preheat the oven to 160°C (Gas 3). Submerge the pheasant legs, garlic and thyme in the duck fat in a roasting tin and cook in the oven for 4–5 hours. Flake the meat off the bone and separate into 100g for the Scotch eggs and 50g for the cress salad. Store in the fridge until needed.

2 **To make the pheasant Scotch eggs,** soft boil the eggs by placing them in a pan of cold water, bringing to the boil and simmering for 6 minutes for pheasant eggs and 7 minutes for hen. Mix the flaked pheasant leg meat with the sausagemeat, garlic, fennel seeds, herbs and seasoning.

3 Plunge the eggs into iced water to stop cooking and ensure a soft boil. Carefully peel the soft boiled eggs and then pack the meat around them and shape into a ball. Leave in the fridge for 15–20 minutes to set.

4 **To make the pheasant Kiev,** take each pheasant breast and, without breaking through the flesh, use a boning knife to make an incision though the fattest part of the meat under the inner fillet. Use a pestle and mortar to crush the garlic with a pinch of sea salt and a pinch of pepper. Mix with the softened butter and chopped

parsley and transfer to a disposable piping bag. Pipe the butter into the cavity of each pheasant breast and chill in the fridge for 30 minutes.

5   Preheat the oven to 180°C (Gas 4). Dip the pheasant breasts in the flour, then in the beaten egg and, lastly, press into the breadcrumbs with lemon zest. Chill in the fridge for 10 minutes. Pan fry the pheasant breasts in a dash of the oil and a knob of butter for 1–2 minutes on each side or until golden all over. Transfer to the oven and cook for 8 minutes. Blanch the kale in boiling salted water, and then refresh in iced water. Dress with rapeseed oil and season with salt and pepper. Keep the oven switched on.

6   **For the cress salad,** make a vinaigrette by whisking the mustard, oil and vinegar together with 40ml of water. Season with salt and pepper.

7   **Just before serving,** roll the Scotch eggs in the seasoned flour, then the beaten egg and finally the breadcrumbs. Heat the oil to 160°C in a large pan or a deep fryer, then deep fry the eggs for 2–3 minutes until golden brown and transfer to the oven for 4 minutes to finish.

8   **To serve,** dress the mixed cress salad and divide between warmed plates together with the curly kale. Cut each Kiev in half and place on the kale. Then cut the Scotch eggs in half, season the yolk with salt and pepper and place on top of the salad. The chef suggests serving this dish with roasted parsnips, a warm truffled spelt salad and, to use up more of the pheasant meat, pheasant, prune and smoked bacon rolls (see page 6).

WOOD PIGEON
with beetroot mash, crab apple fritter & mushrooms
James Golding

The Pig's walled kitchen garden and on-site smokery all help to make head chef James Golding's dream of self-sufficiency a reality in this boutique restaurant-with-rooms. Food that is 'home-grown with clarity of flavour, true to the micro seasons and influenced by the forest' is showcased by this passionate chef, whose wood pigeon dish takes inspiration from the restaurant's New Forest surroundings.

Serves 4

For the beetroot mash
2 large beetroot
2 tbsp olive oil
4 sprigs of thyme
1 garlic clove, peeled and crushed
Sea salt and freshly ground white pepper
1 tsp coriander seeds
4 potatoes, preferably Maris Piper, peeled
100ml double cream
25g unsalted butter, softened

For the wood pigeon
2 wood pigeon
Splash of vegetable oil

For the crab apple fritters
2 crab apples
200g cornflour
200g strong flour, plus 2 tbsp
2 tsp bicarbonate of soda
500ml vegetable oil
8 sage leaves

For the penny bun mushroom with sloe dressing
1 garlic clove, peeled and crushed
125g unsalted butter, softened
50g sloes
50g caster sugar
Splash of olive oil
1 large penny bun mushroom or other fleshy mushroom, thickly sliced
Sprinkle of chopped parsley

1   **For the beetroot mash,** first cook the beetroot. Preheat the oven to 180°C (Gas 4). Chop the beetroot and put it on a baking tray with the oil, thyme and garlic and season with salt, pepper and the coriander seeds. Cook in the oven for 1½–2 hours until tender. Keep the oven switched on.

2   Cook the potatoes in boiling salted water for 20–25 minutes until soft. Purée with the cooked beetroot in a food processor and pass both ingredients through a sieve. Place in a bowl and beat in the cream, butter and season with salt and pepper. Cover and keep warm.

3   **To cook the wood pigeon,** season the birds with salt and pepper. Heat the oil in a pan and when it is hot, sear the birds, colouring all over. Transfer to a roasting tin and cook in the oven for about 12 minutes. Remove from the oven and leave to rest for a further 6 minutes in a warm place.

4   **For the crab apple fritters,** first peel and core the crab apples, then cut into 1cm-thick rings. Sift the cornflour, 200g of flour and bicarbonate of soda into a mixing bowl. Add 200ml of iced water, mix together to make the batter and leave it to rest for 10 minutes. Heat the oil to 180°C in a large pan or deep fryer. Dip the apple rings in the 2 tbsp of flour, then dip them in

the batter and deep fry for 2–3 minutes until they are golden and crispy. Fry the sage at the same time for only a few seconds. Drain the apple and sage on kitchen paper.

5 **For the penny bun mushroom with sloe dressing,** mix the garlic and 1 tsp of salt into the butter in a bowl, then place the garlic butter in the fridge until needed. Put the sloes and sugar into a small pan and cook over a medium heat for 20–25 minutes until the fruit has broken down. Pass through a sieve.

6 In a pan, heat the oil and shallow fry the mushroom slices until they are golden brown. Add a couple of knobs of the garlic butter and the parsley with a small drizzle of the sloe reduction. Stir together until the butter has melted.

7 **To serve,** carve each pigeon, taking off the breasts and carving each into three pieces. Put one large quenelle of beetroot mash on each warmed plate and lean an apple fritter against the mash. Thread a piece of fried sage through each fritter. Top with the slices of pigeon and mushrooms and drizzle around the sloe dressing.

Warm up your winter days with the earthy flavours of the forest.

WILD RABBIT & CRAYFISH MOUSSE
with pumpkin purée
John Abbey

'You don't need fancy equipment to cook good food,' says John Abbey of Oxfordshire's gorgeous riverside restaurant, Leatherne Bottel. Working as an engineer after graduating in engineering mathematics, John had an epiphany in the mid-eighties after being 'blown away' by his experience at Raymond Blanc's Le Manoir. Now, with over 100 varieties of herbs grown on the premises and an abundance of rabbits in neighbouring fields, John's enterprising, modern European menus make full use of the Thameside store-cupboard, as exemplified in this high-impact dish of poached rabbit and crayfish mousse.

1   **For the crayfish mousse,** blanch the live crayfish for 1 minute in boiling water and refresh in iced water. Remove the shells from the tails and the digestive tract from the tail meat. Then put the tail meat into a food processor, add the remaining ingredients and blend to a purée. Push through a sieve. Divide the mixture between two pieces of cling film and roll into two 2cm-diameter by 12.5cm-long sausages, taking care not to catch the cling film in the mousse. Wrap in cling film again to secure each sausage, then poach for 6 minutes in simmering water. Transfer to iced water to cool.

2   **For the pumpkin purée,** melt the butter over a low heat in a pan and add the pumpkin or butternut squash. Cook gently for about 15 minutes until soft. Transfer to a food processor, add the cream and blend to a purée, adding the nutmeg and some salt and pepper. Strain through a sieve then set aside, keeping the purée warm.

3   **For the stuffed rabbit loins,** butterfly the loins by slicing them down the centre, cover each loin with cling film and roll out slightly. Remove the cling film. Season the insides with salt and pepper, then roll each one around half the crayfish mousse. Wrap in the Parma ham and roll in two layers of cling film to make two firm sausages, twisting the ends to keep them compact. Poach in simmering water for about 4 minutes, turning occasionally to check they are still intact, until the centre is piping hot. To test this, insert a sharp knife into the centre of one roll, remove and test the temperature of the blade on the back of your wrist. Remove from the water and rest in a warm place.

4   **For the roasted rabbit saddles,** preheat the oven to 200°C (Gas 6). Heat a pan and add the oil and butter. Briefly colour the saddles then roast them in the oven for 3 minutes. Leave to rest in a warm place.

5   **For the rabbit kidneys,** season the kidneys with salt and pepper then sauté for 30 seconds on each side in butter and oil. Keep warm.

6   **For the mushrooms,** heat the butter in a pan and sauté the mushrooms with the shallots and garlic for 2–3 minutes. Season with salt and pepper and, at the last minute, add a squeeze of lemon juice.

7   **To serve,** remove the cling film from the poached loins and carve at an angle to reveal the crayfish mousse. Carve the saddles into cutlets. Cut the kidneys in half and arrange on the plate with the loin slices and saddle cutlets. Scoop quenelles of the pumpkin purée onto the plates and garnish with sautéed mushrooms. The chef suggests serving this dish with beignets made from the rabbit legs. For extra flavour in the crayfish mousse and to make two sauces, you may also wish to make crayfish and rabbit stocks; and you could confit the leg meat for greater tenderness (see page 6).

Serves 2

For the crayfish mousse
500g live freshwater crayfish
50g white fish, such as turbot
2 pinches of salt
Pinch of white pepper
Small pinch of cayenne pepper
1 egg yolk
25ml double cream
Juice of ½ lemon

For the pumpkin purée
50g butter, softened
200g chopped pumpkin or butternut squash
50ml double cream
Pinch of nutmeg
Salt and freshly ground white pepper

For the stuffed rabbit loins
2 whole rabbits, each boned and prepared into loin, saddle, legs, liver and kidneys (ask your butcher to prepare them for you)
4 slices of Parma ham

For the roasted rabbit saddles
1 tbsp olive oil
25g unsalted butter, diced
2 rabbit saddles

For the rabbit kidneys
2 rabbit kidneys
Knob of unsalted butter
1 tsp olive oil

For the mushrooms
50g butter, diced
200g mixed wild mushrooms, such as girolles, trompettes, pieds bleu
2 small shallots, peeled and finely diced
2 garlic cloves, peeled and crushed
Squeeze of lemon juice

RABBIT 'DUO MODI'
with porcini purée
Davide Degiovanni

'Italian fare with English style' is the menu del giorno at the lavish Amaranto in the Four Seasons Hotel, where head chef Davide Degiovanni draws on recipes from every region of his homeland to serve up 'a taste of the whole of Italy'. Davide sources produce direct from Italy (his mother sends the cheese from local Italian farms) and cooks prestige regional ingredients using modern techniques. A childhood memory of preparing rabbit with his mother inspired this very special dish.

1 **To make the porcini purée,** slice the mushroom heads into 1cm-thick pieces and cut the stalks into 1cm cubes. Set aside the sliced heads and cubed stalks for later and reserve all the trimmings. Melt the butter in a pan and sauté the trimmings before adding the vegetable stock, parsley and some salt and pepper. Using a hand-held blender, blend the mix to a smooth and shiny purée.

2 **For the rabbit belly,** cut the liver, heart and kidneys into small cubes and set aside. Then cut the rabbit belly into small cubes. Brown the onion and carrot in a pan with the butter and oil. Add the chopped belly and 100ml of the white wine. Leave the wine to evaporate and then add the thyme, vegetable stock and season with salt and pepper. Continue to cook at a very low temperature for 20 minutes until the belly is soft.

3 Towards the end of the cooking time, increase the heat to high, add the liver, heart and kidneys and cook for a few minutes with some more oil, salt and pepper. Remove the pan from the heat, add 80g of the reserved porcini stalk cubes and leave to rest for 15–20 minutes until soft. Gently reheat before serving, adding the grapes and parsley.

4 **For the rabbit loin, fillet and rack,** preheat the oven to 180°C (Gas 4). Carefully lay the loin on top of the fillet and wrap them with the speck. Heat the oil and butter in an ovenproof pan until foaming and then sauté the loin and rack for about 2 minutes. Add the sage leaves, transfer to the oven and cook for a further 5 minutes (any longer than this and there is the risk of the meat drying out). Remove from the oven and rest for 4–5 minutes.

5 **For the grilled porcini,** mix together a marinade of the oil and parsley and season with salt and pepper. Grill the reserved sliced heads of porcini on a griddle pan and keep warm in the marinade.

6 **To serve,** place a spoonful of the porcini purée onto the middle of warmed plates. From left to right place the loin, the rack and, in a small ring mould, the rabbit belly and finish with the sautéed porcini and 1 tsp of the cugna jam or apple/pear jam with nuts. The chef suggests serving this dish with stuffed rabbit legs, grapes, toasted hazelnuts and celery leaves; you might also choose to make your own cugna jam (see page 6).

Serves 4

For the porcini purée
300g porcini
Knob of unsalted butter
2 tbsp vegetable stock
Pinch of chopped parsley
Sea salt and freshly ground white pepper

For the rabbit belly
1 whole farmed rabbit, butchered so you have the loin, belly, legs, fillet, liver, kidneys, heart and rack (ask your butcher to prepare it for you)
½ onion, peeled and finely diced
1 carrot, peeled and finely diced
Knob of unsalted butter
Splash of extra-virgin olive oil
200ml white wine
5 sprigs of thyme, tips only
2 tbsp vegetable stock
75g mixed seedless white and red grapes, finely diced
Pinch of chopped parsley

For the rabbit loin, fillet and rack
8 slices of speck, thinly sliced
Splash of extra-virgin olive oil
Knob of unsalted butter
4 sage leaves

For the grilled porcini
2 tbsp extra virgin olive oil
Pinch of chopped parsley

To serve
90g cugna jam or use apple or pear jam and add some chopped walnuts and hazelnuts

Rabbit gets the Italian treatment with porcini mushrooms and deliciously tasty speck.

ROLLED LOIN OF RABBIT with confit of leg & potato purée
Craig Dunn

Executive head chef at Michael Caines at ABode, Exeter, Craig Dunn is a committed champion of the restaurant's philosophy that 'good food is inclusive, not exclusive, and must be accessible to all'. Previously at London's Dorchester hotel, Craig then travelled the world as sous chef on the *QEII* before being embraced by the Caines empire, where he devises robust menus around premium local produce. This dish of roast loin of rabbit is a fine testament to the full-flavoured, award-winning cooking on which Craig has built an enviable reputation.

1   **For the confit of leg,** lightly season the rabbit legs with salt and pepper and leave to marinate for 4 hours. Wash off the salt and pepper and dry with a cloth. Preheat the oven to 130°C (Gas ½). Place the legs in an ovenproof pan, cover with duck fat and bring to a slow simmer for 15 minutes, then cover with foil and cook in the oven for 4 hours.

2   Remove from the oven and increase the temperature to 180°C (Gas 4). Allow the legs to cool in the fat before finely shredding and adding a little duck fat to moisten if desired. Add the mushrooms, tarragon, mustard and vinegar to the leg meat, then roll out between two sheets of greaseproof paper to about 5mm thick and leave in the fridge for about 1 hour to set.

3   **For the sauce,** roast the rabbit bones in a flameproof roasting tin for about 15 minutes until lightly browned. Dust with five-spice powder and roast in the oven for about 10 minutes. Remove from the oven and put the tin on a medium heat on the hob, add the onion rings, garlic, thyme and peppercorns and continue cooking for about 5 minutes until the onions are soft. Deglaze the roasting tin with the chicken stock, then add the veal stock and cream and strain the sauce into a clean pan.

4   Put the honey into a small pan and gently reduce until it goes dark. Also reduce the vinegar in another pan by a third. Mix the honey and vinegar together and stir into the sauce. Bring the sauce to the boil, then reduce the heat and simmer for 30 minutes. Pass through a sieve and reduce once more; this time to a syrupy sauce. Just before serving, add the tarragon and season with salt.

> When making mashed potatoes, cook the potatoes whole with skin on in the oven. You will get a better mash, because there will be less water content. Once cooked, scoop out the contents and then pass through a sieve before finishing.

Serves 2–3

For the confit of leg

2 whole farmed rabbits, butchered
   so you have the legs, loins and
   bones (ask your butcher to prepare
   it for you)
Salt and freshly ground black pepper
A little duck fat
20g cooked mixed wild mushrooms,
   chopped
Few sprigs of tarragon, chopped
½ tsp wholegrain mustard
1 tsp sherry vinegar

For the sauce

All the bones from the rabbit, except
   the leg bones
Pinch of five-spice powder
½ onion, peeled and sliced into rings
1 garlic clove, peeled and chopped
2 sprigs of thyme, leaves only
Few whole black peppercorns
200ml chicken stock
100ml veal stock
20ml double cream
40g runny honey
20ml sherry vinegar
3 sprigs of tarragon

For the rolled loins of rabbit

8 slices of pancetta
2 loins of rabbit, boned
4 tbsp olive oil
2 tbsp unsalted butter

For the potato purée

250g potatoes, preferably Maris Piper,
   peeled and chopped
100ml double cream
50ml full-fat milk
25g unsalted butter, diced
2–3 drops of hickory smoked essence
   (optional)

5   **For the rolled loins of rabbit,** put a piece of cling film onto
the work surface. Place four of the pancetta slices on the cling
film, overlapping each other to make a single sheet. Lay one
of the rabbit loins on the pancetta and season with pepper.
Then tightly roll the rabbit in the cling film and tie the ends.
Repeat with the remaining pancetta and other loin. Bring
a pan of water to a gentle simmer, place the rolled loins
in the water and cook for 20 minutes. Drain the rolls and
carefully remove the cling film. Heat the oil in a pan, add
the rolled loins and colour evenly all over, adding the butter
to finish cooking.

6   **For the potato purée,** bring the potatoes to the boil in a pan
of salted water and cook for 25–30 minutes. When soft, drain
into a colander. Allow to cool slightly and then pass through
a potato ricer or mash thoroughly by hand. Bring the cream, milk and butter to the boil and
reduce by a third, then add the liquid to the potatoes until you get a smooth purée, and finish
with a few drops of hickory smoked essence (if using).

7   **To serve,** cut out rectangles from the confit of leg and place on plates to warm under the grill
or in the oven. Cut the ends off each of the rolled loins, slice each in half and, removing the
plates from the grill or oven, place the loins on the confit of leg. Drizzle over some sauce and
serve with the potato purée. The chef suggests serving this dish with Jerusalem artichokes
and a vinegar gastrique (see page 6).

ASSIETTE OF HARE
with a juniper jus
Thomas Halford

At Albert Roux's prompting, Thomas Halford trained in France, earning him the nickname 'the roast beef' as well as standing him in good stead for his role as head chef at Le Vacherin. Creating authentic Parisian bistro cuisine in west London's Chiswick, Thomas is particularly passionate about butchery and filleting; with his assiette of hare, he wants the home cook really to understand the animal and how the dish works at every level.

1 **For the juniper jus,** put the sugar, vinegar and jam into a pan and cook on a gentle heat for about 5 minutes until they caramelise. Add the Madeira wine, stirring to prevent sticking, and reduce a little before adding the stock. Leave to simmer very slowly for about 30 minutes until you have a sticky sauce with caramel-jam flavour. Just before serving, add the port and blueberries.

2 **To make the hare pie filling,** season the hare shoulders with salt and pepper and sear in a hot pan with the oil until coloured on both sides. Add half of the garlic, a quarter of the shallots and all the thyme and cook for 2–3 minutes until soft. Add the port, red wine and enough hare stock to cover the shoulders. Cover with a lid and, stirring occasionally, leave to simmer for 30–40 minutes until the meat is soft and starting to fall away from the bone. Remove it from the stock and leave to cool for a few minutes. Pick all the meat from the bone with a fork, ensuring there are no bits of cartilage in it. Reserve the stock.

3 Sauté the rest of the vegetables in a pan together with the butter, stirring occasionally, for 4–5 minutes until softened. Add the meat and sweat together for 2 minutes. Pass the reserved stock through a sieve, add to the meat and vegetable mixture and then simmer slowly for 5–6 minutes, letting the sauce reduce slightly and thicken. Adjust the seasoning, add the parsley and keep warm.

4 **For the pie lid,** put the flour, butter and a pinch of salt into a food processor and blend until the mixture resembles breadcrumbs. Transfer to a bowl and mix in the parsley and cumin seeds. Then add the eggs to bind the mixture and combine to form a dough. If it seems too dry, add a splash of water, and if too wet, add a little more flour. Wrap in cling film and leave to rest in the fridge for 20 minutes.

5 Preheat the oven to 180°C (Gas 4). Roll out the pastry on a lightly floured surface to 5mm in thickness, cut four 12cm-diameter pastry lids and drape them over well-greased round moulds, such as ovenproof upside-down bowls. Trim the edges and brush with the beaten egg yolk, then chill in the fridge for 2 minutes before baking for 10–15 minutes until golden. Divide the hare filling between four 10cm-diameter ramekins.

6   **To cook the cutlets of hare,** seal the hare fillets in a hot pan with the oil for 1 minute. Then add the hare cutlets and seal together with the fillets for a further minute. Turn the fillets and cutlets over, add the butter and seal for another 2 minutes. Remove from the pan and leave to rest.

7   **For the vegetables,** sauté the mushrooms with the garlic, shallot and parsley in the fat in the pan the hare cutlets were cooked in for about 5 minutes until softened. Season with salt and pepper. Blanch the remaining vegetables in boiling water, drain and season with salt.

8   **To serve,** divide the hare cutlets and fillets between warmed plates, then add the hare pies and cover each with a lid. Place the blanched vegetables and mushrooms around the plates and dress with the juniper jus. The chef suggests serving this with a celeriac and Vacherin cheese brûlée and juniper oil; you may also want to use up the rest of the hare by making hare stock and some faggots (see page 6).

Serves 4

For the juniper jus
1 tbsp demerara sugar
2 tbsp white wine vinegar
2 tbsp blueberry jam
125ml Madeira wine
1 litre chicken or beef stock
25ml port
40g blueberries

For the hare pie filling
2 shoulders of hare
Salt and freshly ground black pepper
Splash of olive oil
2 garlic cloves, peeled and chopped
4 shallots, peeled and chopped
1 tsp chopped thyme
200ml port
200ml red wine
400ml hare, chicken or beef stock
50g diced celeriac
50g diced celery
50g diced carrots
50g diced leeks
Knob of butter
10g chopped parsley

For the pie lid
220g strong flour, sifted
70g unsalted butter, diced
20g parsley, finely chopped
Pinch of cumin seeds
2 eggs
1 egg yolk, beaten

For the cutlets of hare
2 fillets of hare
Splash of olive oil
8 cutlets of hare
100g butter

For the vegetables
12 girolles or mushroom of your choice
1 tsp chopped garlic
15g chopped shallot
1 tsp chopped parsley
8 baby carrots
8 baby leeks
8 baby beetroot

VENISON MIXED GRILL
with baby beets
Anthony McNamara

Head chef Anthony McNamara's exquisite Mill Tea & Dining Room occupies a 17th-century mill building on the banks of the river Lym, in Lyme Regis. After working as a private chef at Downing Street cooking for luminaries such as Tony Blair, Gordon Brown, Nelson Mandela and President Clinton, Anthony now favours 'straight down the line' English food, a modest description that belies the bold flavours and technical flair of his cooking, as shown in this glorious venison mixed grill.

Serves 4

For the roast venison fillet
500g trimmed venison fillet
Knob of unsalted butter

For the venison liver
300g venison liver, sliced
1 tbsp olive oil

For the faggots
1 venison heart
1 venison kidney
250g shallots, peeled and finely sliced
Sea salt and freshly ground black pepper
Sprig of rosemary, chopped
Bunch of chives, chopped
Bunch of flat-leaf parsley, chopped
2 sprigs of thyme, chopped
100g Panko breadcrumbs
250g caul fat

For the venison brain
1 venison brain, soaked in acidulated water for 15 minutes
6 whole black peppercorns
6 cloves
1 garlic clove, peeled
½ shallot, peeled and chopped
1 carrot, peeled and chopped
2 bay leaves
Sprig of thyme
Dash of white wine vinegar
Small bunch of parsley, chopped
100g plain flour
2 eggs, lightly beaten
100g Panko breadcrumbs
500ml vegetable oil

For the baby beets
12 baby beets
Splash of olive oil, to garnish

For the blackberry wine jus
400ml blackberry wine or any full-bodied fruity red wine
750ml chicken stock
8 blackberries

1. **To prepare the venison fillet and liver,** trim the fillet and liver, retaining the trim. Set the meat aside.

2. **For the faggots,** double mince the heart, kidney, fillet trim, liver trim and the shallots. Season with salt and pepper and add the herbs and breadcrumbs. Roll into small balls, wrap in the caul fat and leave to rest in the fridge for 10 minutes before browning in a hot pan.

3. **To prepare the venison brain,** place the soaked brain in a small pan of cold water with the peppercorns, cloves, garlic, shallot, carrot, herbs and vinegar. Bring to the boil and then take off the heat and leave to cool. Peel the membrane from the brain and pat dry. Divide into four, and roll in the parsley, then roll in the flour, eggs and breadcrumbs. Roll again in the eggs and breadcrumbs and chill until needed.

4. **To cook the baby beets,** boil the beetroot in a pan of lightly salted water for 10–15 minutes until tender. Drain and set aside.

5. **For the blackberry wine jus,** deglaze the faggots' pan with the blackberry or other red wine and reduce for 5–6 minutes to 2 tbsp. Add the chicken stock and reduce to half. Add the faggots and cook for 3 minutes, then add the blackberries and remove from the heat.

6. **To cook the roast venison fillet,** preheat the oven to 190°C (Gas 5). Season the venison and heat the butter in an ovenproof pan. Add the venison and turn frequently for 2–3 minutes until browned all over. Transfer to the oven for 8–10 minutes until cooked to your liking. Remove from the oven (but keep the oven switched on) and set aside to rest for 5 minutes.

7. **To cook the venison liver,** season the sliced liver with salt and pepper. Heat the oil in an ovenproof pan and sear the liver for 1–2 minutes on each side. Transfer to the oven and cook for a further 4–5 minutes.

8. **To finish the venison brain,** heat the oil to 180°C in a large pan or a deep fryer. Deep fry the brain for 30 seconds, remove from the fat and drain on kitchen paper.

9. **To serve,** arrange a piece of roast fillet, a slice of grilled liver, a single braised faggot and a piece of deep-fried brain on each warmed plate. Peel the baby beets, scatter around the plates and garnish with the oil. Finally, drizzle over the jus. The chef suggests serving this dish with pickled cherries and parsnip purée together with some toasted sourdough bread to place beneath the venison brain, and a garnish of wood sorrel leaves (see page 6).

LOIN OF ROE DEER & GAME BRIDIE

with root vegetables & port & blackberry sauce
Neil Forbes

'Keep it simple … let the humble flavours speak for themselves,' says Neil Forbes of his cooking at Cafe St Honoré, a delightfully unaffected French brasserie tucked away down an Edinburgh cobbled street. Previously head chef on the Royal Scotsman train, Neil is a fervent champion of slow-food philosophy and local British produce. Here, his roe deer dish showcases his consummate knowledge of traditional skills and commitment to top-quality seasonal ingredients.

Serves 4

For the venison stock
Rib bones from 1 roe deer
2 tbsp rapeseed oil
1 carrot, peeled and roughly chopped
1 onion, peeled and roughly chopped
1 celery stick, trimmed and chopped
1 bay leaf
Sprig of thyme

For the game bridie
150g plain flour
Sea salt and freshly ground black
  pepper
100g pheasant breast, diced
100g deer trimmings, diced
25g suet
1 onion, peeled and finely chopped

For the port and blackberry sauce
200ml reserve port
2 sprigs of thyme
Handful of blackberries

For the root vegetables
2 carrots, peeled and diced
2 parsnips, peeled and diced
1 squash or ½ swede or turnip, peeled
  and diced
200ml rapeseed oil
200g unsalted butter
Small bunch of thyme

For the loin of roe deer
100ml rapeseed oil
700g loin of roe deer
100g butter
Sprig of thyme

1   **To make the venison stock,** preheat the oven to 180°C
    (Gas 4). Put the bones in a roasting tin and roast for
    15–20 minutes until golden brown. Heat the oil in a
    large heavy-based pan over a medium heat, add the
    carrot, onion, celery, bay leaf and thyme and cook for
    about 4 minutes to soften. Add the bones and cover
    with 1–1.5 litres of water. Bring to the boil, then reduce
    the heat and simmer for 8–12 hours. Pass through a
    sieve and heat again to reduce the liquid to 500ml.

2   **For the game bridie,** put the flour, 100ml of cold water,
    a large pinch of salt and some pepper in a bowl and
    mix to a stiff dough. Divide into four and roll out each
    piece into an oval shape. Cover half of each oval with
    a quarter of the diced meat, suet and a little chopped
    onion and season with salt and pepper. Wet the edges
    of each piece of dough with water and fold over and
    crimp. Make a hole in the middle, transfer to a baking
    sheet and cook for about 30 minutes until golden.

3   **To make the port and blackberry sauce,** reduce the
    port in a hot pan with the thyme until it has a jam-like
    consistency. Then add enough of the venison stock (about 500ml) until it is thick enough
    to coat the back of a spoon. Add the blackberries, check the seasoning and set aside.

4   **Cook the root vegetables** by blanching them in boiling salted water for about 4 minutes until
    just tender. Heat the oil and butter in a wide pan and, when hot, add the vegetables with the
    thyme and seasoning and cook for 12–15 minutes until golden.

5   **For the loin of roe deer,** in a separate ovenproof pan, heat the oil. Season the loin of roe
    deer and fry until golden brown, adding the butter after 1 minute. Add the thyme and transfer
    to the oven for 5–7 minutes to cook until pink. Remove from the oven and leave the meat to
    rest for 4–5 minutes.

6   **To serve,** arrange the cooked vegetables on warmed plates. Slice the roe deer and add next
    to the vegetables, followed by the game bridie. Trickle over the sauce and the blackberries.

HAY-SMOKED VENISON
with parsnip purée & port sauce
Matt Weedon

In a restful corner of the Cotswolds you'll find Lords of the Manor, an idyllic 17th-century former rectory and home to chef Matt Weedon. Matt describes his modern take on French classics as 'French-style food with all the fat and cream taken out'. His cooking is famed for its intricacy and attention to detail, exemplified in this venison dish, which utilises a host of different techniques. 'All parts of the deer can be used,' Matt is keen to remind us, with the loin, liver and leg of the animal all featuring in this elegant dish.

1   **For the port sauce,** preheat the oven to 190°C (Gas 5). Put the bones in a roasting tin and cook in the oven for about 25 minutes until darkly caramelised. Drain in a metal colander and set aside. Heat the oil in a large pan over a medium heat. Roughly chop the mirepoix vegetables, add them to the pan with the juniper berries and thyme and cook for 5–10 minutes until caramelised. Pour in the vinegar and then the port and wine. Bring to the boil, add the bones and then the stock. Bring the sauce back up to the boil once again and cook slowly for 1½ hours. Strain the stock into a clean pan, bring to the boil and reduce for about 20 minutes until it has thickened to a sauce consistency. Pass the sauce through a sieve and keep warm.

2   **For the venison leg,** preheat the oven to 160°C (Gas 3). Heat the oil in a pan over a high heat and caramelise the venison leg on all sides for about 5 minutes. Reserve the pan for later. Transfer to a roasting tin and cook in the oven for about 30 minutes for medium rare. Set aside.

3   **To make the parsnip purée,** peel the parsnips and take 12 shavings to deep fry later. With the remaining parsnips, discard the core, cut into 1.5cm pieces and put in a pan. Cover with equal quantities of cream and water, then season with salt and pepper and add the vanilla seeds and butter. Cook over a medium heat for about 10 minutes until the parsnips are soft, checking regularly and adding a splash more water and cream if necessary. Transfer to a food processor and blend until smooth. Cover in cling film and set aside in a warm place.

4   **For the hay-smoked venison loin and liver,** if you are smoking the meat, get the hay smouldering in a stove-top smoking box on a low heat and with the lid on. Season the flour with salt and pepper and coat the liver in the flour.

5   In the same pan used for cooking the leg piece, caramelise the loin and liver in foaming butter and rapeseed oil for 3–5 minutes, then season with salt and pepper. Transfer the loin to the smoking box (if using) for 6–8 minutes and after 3 minutes add the liver. Alternatively, continue to pan fry the meat for about 8 minutes for the loin and 5 minutes for the liver.

6   **To cook the vegetables,** put a pan of salted water on to boil. For the parsnip crisps, heat the oil to 150°C in a large pan or a deep fryer. Deep fry the parsnip shavings for about 30 seconds until they are crisp and then drain on kitchen paper. Boil the cauliflower for about 5 minutes until tender and, when ready to serve, add the spinach and remove both vegetables from the pan after 10 seconds. Drain on a tea towel.

7   **To serve,** add the blackcurrants to the port sauce and check the seasoning. Slice the loin, liver and leg, seasoning with salt and pepper. Place the spinach on warmed plates and add the slices of loin, liver and leg topped with parsnip crisps and a drizzle of the sauce. Add the remaining vegetables and some parsnip purée. The chef suggests serving this dish with salt baked beetroot and braised red cabbage (see page 6).

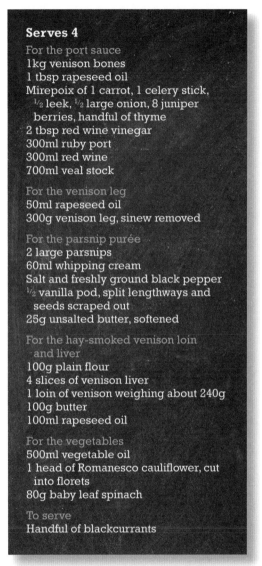

Serves 4

For the port sauce
1kg venison bones
1 tbsp rapeseed oil
Mirepoix of 1 carrot, 1 celery stick,
  1/2 leek, 1/2 large onion, 8 juniper
  berries, handful of thyme
2 tbsp red wine vinegar
300ml ruby port
300ml red wine
700ml veal stock

For the venison leg
50ml rapeseed oil
300g venison leg, sinew removed

For the parsnip purée
2 large parsnips
60ml whipping cream
Salt and freshly ground black pepper
1/2 vanilla pod, split lengthways and
  seeds scraped out
25g unsalted butter, softened

For the hay-smoked venison loin
  and liver
100g plain flour
4 slices of venison liver
1 loin of venison weighing about 240g
100g butter
100ml rapeseed oil

For the vegetables
500ml vegetable oil
1 head of Romanesco cauliflower, cut
  into florets
80g baby leaf spinach

To serve
Handful of blackcurrants

Spoons will scrape plates for this ruby-red port sauce, infused with an intensely meaty, savoury tang.

VENISON LOIN, HAM & HAUNCH
with garden roots & thyme-roasted buckwheat
Simon Crannage

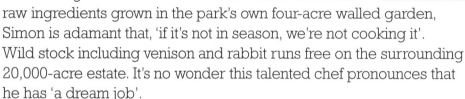

A chef who 'wants to be in the kitchen, not walking around with a clipboard,' Simon Crannage has the pick of premium Yorkshire produce for his exhilarating menus at Samuel's at Swinton Park. With raw ingredients grown in the park's own four-acre walled garden, Simon is adamant that, 'if it's not in season, we're not cooking it'. Wild stock including venison and rabbit runs free on the surrounding 20,000-acre estate. It's no wonder this talented chef pronounces that he has 'a dream job'.

1 **For the braised haunch of venison,** preheat the oven to 140°C (Gas 1). Heat the vegetable oil in a large ovenproof pan over a medium heat and sauté the chopped vegetables (keeping back the dice), garlic and rosemary for 8–10 minutes until caramelised. Add the venison and pour in the wine. Bring to the boil and reduce by half, then add the chicken stock. Cover and cook in the oven for around 2 hours until the meat can be pulled off the bone. Remove all the meat and flake into the cooking juices before leaving to cool for an hour to room temperature. Strain the juices into a clean pan and reduce over a high heat until they form a rich dark sauce. Increase the oven to 180°C (Gas 4).

2 While the venison is cooking, blanch the pearl barley in boiling salted water until tender and refresh in cold water. Sauté the finely diced carrots, celery and shallots in the butter until just soft, then add the pearl barley to this mix and season well with salt and pepper. Add the shredded venison haunch and mix well.

3 Lay a slice of venison ham on cling film and add a quarter of the haunch mix along one edge of the slice. Then roll the ham in the cling film to form a long roll and tie at both ends. Repeat with the remaining mix and slices of ham to create four rolls of braised haunch. Chill in the fridge to set.

4 **For the garden roots,** wrap the beetroot in foil and roast them for 25 minutes. Then peel the beetroot while they are still warm.

5 Peel the parsnips and cut into fondant, barrel-shaped pieces. Bring a pan of water to the boil and add half the butter followed by the parsnips. Reduce the heat and simmer for 8–10 minutes until soft. Heat the remaining butter in a pan and colour the bases of the parsnips. Cover with a butter wrapper or greaseproof paper to keep them warm and moist.

6 **For the kale,** blanch the leaves in salted boiling water for 30 seconds. Season with salt and pepper and keep warm until ready to serve.

7 **For the thyme-roasted buckwheat,** blanch the buckwheat in boiling salted water for 2 minutes and refresh in cold running water. Then sauté the buckwheat in hot butter for 3–5 minutes until golden and crispy and add the thyme. Spread out onto kitchen paper to remove the butter residue.

8 **To finish,** place the venison haunch rolls in a pan of hot water to reheat. Remove when hot and keep warm. In a very hot pan, seal the venison loin in some oil. When the loin is starting to colour, add a knob of butter and baste the venison with the foaming butter for 5–8 minutes until cooked to medium rare. Remove from the heat and leave to rest in a warm place for about 4 minutes.

9 **To serve,** arrange the roots and kale across each warmed plate. Unwrap the cling film from the venison rolls, slice off the ends and place on a piece of parsnip. Slice the loin into thick slices and arrange on the kale. Garnish the plate with the cocoa nibs and the crunchy buckwheat, then pour on the rich venison sauce and grate over some dark chocolate. The chef suggests serving this dish with lemon caramel squash purée (see page 6).

Serves 4

For the braised haunch of venison
Splash of vegetable oil
3 carrots, peeled and chopped, plus 20g very finely diced
2 celery sticks, trimmed and chopped, plus 20g very finely diced
1 large onion, peeled and chopped
1/2 garlic bulb, peeled
Sprig of rosemary
1kg whole haunch of venison, on the bone
250ml red wine
2 litres dark chicken stock
50g pearl barley, prepared as on the packet's instructions
2 banana shallots, peeled and very finely diced
Knob of unsalted butter
Salt and freshly ground black pepper
4 slices of venison ham

For the garden roots
12 baby beetroot (small)
4 parsnips
25g unsalted butter, diced

For the kale
50g kale, stalks removed and leaves finely shredded

For the thyme-roasted buckwheat
50g buckwheat
Knob of unsalted butter
5g finely chopped thyme leaves

To finish and serve
400g loin of venison, fat and sinew removed
Splash of vegetable oil
Knob of unsalted butter
20g cocoa nibs
Dark chocolate (70% cocoa solids)

Basting small cuts of meat with foaming butter gives a great finish and a big roast flavour.

KANGAROO COTTAGE PIE
with kangaroo rump & beetroot carpaccio
Ruth Hurren

Darcy's eclectic, suave brand of modern European cuisine with Pacific Rim accents makes this smart restaurant the hot ticket in historic St Albans. Australian chef Ruth Hurren favours big flavours and classy cooking over pretentious cuisine, presenting fresh, innovative food – with the occasional challenge for the more adventurous palate. Ruth's kangaroo combination showcases the possibilities of this meat, introducing a favourite Aussie ingredient to classic British dishes.

1. **To make the cottage pie filling,** heat half the oil in a large pan and fry the mince until browned, in batches if necessary. Remove from the pan and set aside. Heat the remaining oil in the same pan. Add the carrot, celery and shallots and cook on a gentle heat for about 10 minutes until soft. Then add the garlic, flour and tomato purée, increase the heat and cook for a few more minutes.

2. Return the mince to the pan, add the red wine and Madeira and reduce by half before adding the stock. Add the Worcestershire sauce, bush spices or star anise and the myrtle leaves, bring to a simmer and cook, uncovered, for about 30 minutes until the gravy is thick and coating the meat. If a lot of liquid is remaining, increase the heat slightly to reduce the gravy. Season well with salt and pepper and remove and discard the myrtle leaves.

3. **For the cottage pie topping,** preheat the oven to 200°C (Gas 6). Put the potatoes in a pan of cold water over a high heat. Add a pinch of salt, bring to the boil and then reduce the heat and simmer for about 10 minutes until tender. Drain the potatoes in a colander and leave for 3–4 minutes until the steam has evaporated. Transfer to a large bowl and mash with a potato masher. Add the butter and mash, and then add a splash of cream. Mash again and check the consistency, adding more cream if necessary. Season with salt and pepper, then add the cheese.

4. Spoon three-quarters of the meat into four ovenproof tea cups, pipe the mash to cover the mince, glaze with the egg yolk and bake for about 10 minutes until the topping is golden.

5. **For the jus,** heat the oil in a large pan, then add the shallots, pepper berries or peppercorns, thyme, garlic and bay leaf and

Kangaroo should only be cooked rare or medium/ rare. Cook it well done and it tastes like boot leather as it is 98 per cent fat free.

For the cottage pie filling
2 tbsp olive oil
500g kangaroo, beef or venison mince
1 large carrot, peeled and chopped
1 celery stick, trimmed and chopped
4 shallots, peeled and chopped
1 garlic clove, peeled and roughly chopped
1 tbsp plain flour
1 tsp tomato purée
150ml red wine
80ml Madeira wine
500ml jellied veal or beef stock
2 tbsp Worcestershire sauce
1 tbsp bush spices (wattle seed, bush tomato, mountain pepper) or star anise
3 lemon myrtle leaves
Sea salt and freshly ground black pepper

For the cottage pie topping
500g potatoes, peeled and chopped
50g unsalted butter
25ml double cream
50g mature Cheddar cheese, grated
1 egg yolk, beaten

For the jus
1 tbsp olive oil
2 shallots, peeled and thinly sliced
6 black pepper berries or whole black peppercorns
4 sprigs of thyme
1 garlic clove, peeled and bruised
1 bay leaf
80ml port
200ml red wine
500ml jellied veal or beef stock
500ml jellied chicken stock

For the beetroot carpaccio
1 golden beetroot
1 beetroot
50ml white wine vinegar

For the rump steak
½ tsp Jimmy's saté paste
2 sprigs of thyme
1 tbsp olive oil
400g kangaroo or beef rump steak, trimmed

season with salt. Cook on a medium heat for about 5 minutes, stirring regularly, until the shallots are golden. Add the port and red wine and reduce by two-thirds, then add both of the stocks. Bring to the boil and skim away any scum or impurities that rise to the surface. Reduce the heat to a gentle simmer, cover with a lid, and cook for 30 minutes or until thickened to a sauce consistency. Season with salt and pepper.

6   **For the beetroot carpaccio,** put the two types of beetroot in a pan of salted water with the vinegar. Bring to the boil, then turn down the heat and simmer for 30–40 minutes until tender. Drain and set aside to cool before peeling. Slice finely on a mandoline and set aside.

7   **To cook the rump steak,** mix together the saté paste and thyme and rub over the meat. Heat the oil on a griddle pan until hot and then sear the steak for about 2 minutes on each side. Set aside to rest for 5 minutes in a warm place or wrapped in foil.

8   **To serve,** layer the beetroot in the middle of each warmed plate and top with the sliced steak. Add a cup and saucer of the cottage pie and then drizzle jus around the meat. The chef suggests serving this dish with a fillet Wellington, black pepper toffee bark for the sliced steak and some salsa verde (see page 6).

PAN-ROASTED OSTRICH FILLET
with cauliflower custard & blueberry sauce
Ivano de Serio

With five years of training in southern Italy under his belt, Ivano de Serio wields his continental know-how at the Old Bakery in Lincoln, employing a medley of European flavours in his repertoire of dishes that impress with their inventiveness. Ivano names renowned Italian chef Gaultiero Marchesi as a key influence. 'He was like an artist,' he says. And artistry is more than evident in this dish of ostrich fillet and cauliflower, a symphony of contrast, texture and flavour that brings genuine excitement to the plate.

Serves 4

For the pan-roasted fillet of ostrich
90g pistachio nuts, shelled, peeled
    and finely chopped
100ml rapeseed oil
300g fillet of ostrich
Sea salt and freshly ground black
    pepper

For the diced roasted potatoes
2 large baking potatoes
100ml rapeseed oil

For the cauliflower custard
100g butter, softened
100g cauliflower florets
100ml white wine
300ml full-fat milk
70ml whipping cream
2 egg yolks
½ tsp truffle oil (optional)
Freshly ground white pepper
1 small black truffle (optional)

For the blueberry sauce
100g butter
10g juniper berries, crushed
200g blueberries
2 tsp verjus (optional)

1   **For the pan-roasted fillet of ostrich,** first preheat the oven to 180°C (Gas 4). Toast the pistachios in a pan on low heat for 2–3 minutes. Season the fillet of ostrich with salt and pepper and heat the oil in an ovenproof pan over a medium heat. Add the meat, pan fry for 30 seconds on each side and transfer to the oven to roast for 4–5 minutes. Remove the meat from the oven and roll in the toasted pistachios to coat the edge of the fillet.

2   **For the diced roasted potato,** peel and cut the potatoes into 5cm cubes. Then, with a small round cutter, take out the centre of the potato. Soak 6 tbsp of white oak smoking chips in a little water until they are needed. Blanch the potatoes in boiling salted water for about 6 minutes until just soft. Drain and smoke the potatoes in a stove-top smoking box with the smoking chips. To finish, pan fry the potatoes in the oil for about 1 minute on each side until golden.

3   **For the cauliflower custard,** line a container measuring about 14 x 8cm with cling film. Melt the butter in a pan over a medium heat, add the cauliflower florets and cook for 3–5 minutes to soften. Add the wine and milk and cook for 20–25 minutes until soft and reduced. Transfer to a food processor and blend to a purée. Mix the whipping cream with the egg yolks and truffle oil (if using) in a large bowl and season with salt and white pepper. Add the purée to the egg mixture and pour into the prepared container. Cook in a steamer for 20 minutes, or over a pan of simmering water for 25–30 minutes until set in the centre.

4   **To make the blueberry sauce,** first melt the butter in a pan over a low heat, add the crushed juniper berries and cook for 10 minutes. Pass through a sieve into a clean pan and discard the remains. Add the blueberries to the melted juniper butter and cook on a medium heat for 5 minutes. Pour in the verjus (if using) together with a little water and cook for further 8–10 minutes. Blend the blueberries with a hand-held blender.

5   **To serve,** spread the blueberry sauce in the centre of each warmed plate. Cut the fillet of ostrich into thick slices and place in the centre of the sauce. Add a slice of custard cut with a palette knife next to it. Top with truffle shavings (if using) and finish with a cube of potato.

Brush the cooked ostrich with some rapeseed oil at the last minute to make the chopped pistachio stick evenly on the surface, and always cut the fillet against the grain of the meat.

121

Desserts...

WHITE CHOCOLATE & EARL GREY GANACHE
with salted lemon ice cream
Matthew Mason

The Jack in the Green describes its culinary ethos as 'sophisticated simplicity', and it enjoys an enviable reputation for offering some of the best dining in Devon. Head chef Matthew Mason uses premier West Country ingredients in his accomplished modern British dishes, taking inspiration from the Devonshire larder and artisan producers. A passionate chef, he professes to be 'consumed by cooking and the relationship between people, the region and its food'.

1   **For the lemon confit syrup,** first score eight evenly spaced lines down each of the lemons. Blanch for 30 seconds in boiling water, then refresh in iced water. Repeat this process ten times. Meanwhile, make a stock syrup by putting the sugar and 200ml of water in a small heavy-based pan and bring slowly to the boil, stirring to dissolve the sugar. Boil for 2 minutes and leave to cool slightly, then strain into a clean pan, add the lemons and cook them slowly, covered with a lid, at a low simmer for 4 hours. Transfer to a food processor and blend until smooth. Pass through a sieve and store in the fridge.

2   **To make the salted lemon ice cream,** put the cream, milk, trimoline or glucose, sugar, salt and 250ml of water into a pan and bring to the boil, then reduce the heat and simmer for 1 minute. Leave to cool slightly, then add the chocolate and lemon juice and whisk together. Strain through a sieve and leave to cool. Churn in an ice-cream machine until set.

3   **For the ginger cake,** preheat the oven to 140°C (Gas 1) and line a 28 x 22cm baking tin with greaseproof paper. Beat the sugar and eggs together in a large bowl until doubled in volume. Melt the butter in a small pan and add the oil, then gradually incorporate the oily butter into the egg and sugar mix, whisking continuously with an electric hand-held mixer. Reduce the speed, then add the remaining ingredients and mix well.

4   Pour into the baking tin (you only need a thin layer of the cake when it is cooked) and bake for 15–20 minutes until it is firm to the touch. Leave to cool in the fridge for 10 minutes.

> If you can't find trimoline, which is used to stabilise the sugar to ensure a smooth ice cream, glucose would be a suitable replacement. Failing that, use 100g caster sugar in addition to the 20g given in the recipe.

For the lemon confit syrup
2 lemons, preferably Amalfi
200g caster sugar

For the salted lemon ice cream
250ml double cream
100ml full-fat milk
65g trimoline or glucose
20g caster sugar
2 tsp sea salt
150g white chocolate, broken into pieces
80ml lemon juice from 2 lemons, preferably Amalfi

For the ginger cake
65g caster sugar
2 eggs
65g unsalted butter
90ml olive oil
65g ground almonds
65g polenta
65g strong flour
20g ground ginger
$\frac{1}{2}$ tsp cocoa powder
1 tsp baking powder
35g stem ginger, diced
65g molasses

For the white chocolate ganache
200g crème fraîche
2 Earl Grey tea bags
200g white chocolate, broken into pieces

For the brandy snap mix
25g runny honey
30g golden syrup
55g strong flour
55g unsalted butter
110g caster sugar
$\frac{1}{2}$ tsp sesame seeds
$\frac{1}{2}$ tsp poppy seeds

To decorate
Pink grapefruit segments
Lemon balm leaves

5 **To make the white chocolate ganache,** put the crème fraîche and tea bags in a pan and bring to the boil. Reduce the heat and simmer for 3–4 minutes. Pass the mixture through a sieve, then pour it over the chocolate while it is hot and mix well.

6 Using four 5cm-square by 2.5cm-deep metal frames, cut out four pieces of ginger cake. With the frames still in place, top each piece of ginger cake with ganache. Leave to chill in the fridge. About 30 minutes before eating, remove from the fridge to bring it up to room temperature.

7 Using a small amount of trim from the cake, blitz it until it resembles fine breadcrumbs.

8 **For the brandy snap mix,** preheat the oven to 160°C (Gas 3). Put all the ingredients into a food processor and mix until combined. Refrigerate until chilled. Scoop out balls of brandy snap mix each roughly the size of a 50p piece and flatten them on greaseproof paper with the palm of your hand. Bake for 9–10 minutes until golden. Remove from the oven and leave to cool slightly before cutting into eight 5 x 2.5cm rectangles.

9 **To serve,** unmould the ganache pieces by warming the outside of the metal frames slightly with a blow torch (or between warmed hands). Cut in half vertically and top each slice with a brandy snap rectangle. Place on serving plates, add some cake breadcrumbs near the ganache slices and top with a quenelle of ice cream. To finish, dot lemon confit syrup around each plate and decorate with pink grapefruit segments and some lemon balm leaves. The chef suggests serving this dessert with a pink grapefruit and lemon posset (see page 6).

BLACKBERRY CREMEUX IN BLACKBERRY JELLY
with cardamom meringue & poached pear
Michael Wignall

'All I wanted to do was ride BMXs,' says head chef Michael Wignall of his childhood ambitions. Luckily his mother had other ideas for her talented son, who is now head chef at the magnificent Latymer restaurant in Surrey's Pennyhill Park Hotel. Michael's technically refined modern European cooking with classical undertones delivers astonishingly innovative dishes and culinary pyrotechnics that leave his diners struggling for superlatives.

East meets West in a sensational marriage of classic British fruits with aromatic cardamom.

1   **To make the blackberry juice,** put the blackberries in a food processor and blend to a purée. Pass through a sieve and retain the juice.

2   **To make the blackberry crémeux,** cut four 10 x 8cm rectangles from acetate, roll along the long edge and tape each into a cylinder. Put 200ml of the blackberry juice in a pan and heat to reduce by half. Soak the gelatine in a bowl of cold water for about 5 minutes to soften. Meanwhile, in a clean pan combine the reduced juice, egg, egg yolk and caster sugar. Cook on a low heat, stirring continuously, for about 5 minutes or until it thickens. Squeeze the gelatine to drain it, add to the blackberry mix and stir until dissolved. Then gradually add the butter. Transfer the mix into a piping bag fitted with a small nozzle and pipe into the cylindrical moulds. Place them in the fridge for about 1 hour to set.

3   **For the cardamom meringue,** preheat the oven to its lowest setting and line a baking sheet with a silicone mat or baking parchment. Put the egg whites and caster sugar into a bowl and whisk with an electric hand-held mixer until soft peaks form. Slow the mixer speed to the lowest setting and gradually add the icing sugar, cornflour and crushed cardamom seeds. Turn the mixer speed back up to full and whisk the meringue for 10 minutes until velvety and smooth. Spread the meringue 2mm thick onto the prepared baking sheet and cook for about 1 hour to form a pavlova-like crust. Remove from the oven and, while still warm, transfer it to an airtight container.

4   **To poach the pear,** first peel the pear then place in the pan with the remaining ingredients. Cover it with a circle of greaseproof paper with a hole in the middle to stop the pear browning. Gently poach the pear for about 20 minutes until it is soft.

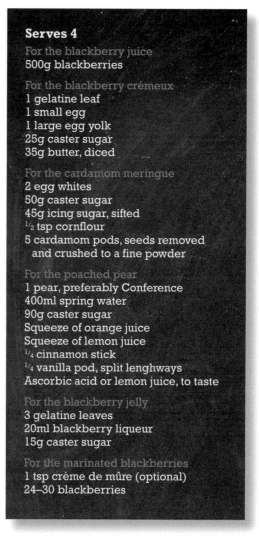

Serves 4

For the blackberry juice
500g blackberries

For the blackberry crémeux
1 gelatine leaf
1 small egg
1 large egg yolk
25g caster sugar
35g butter, diced

For the cardamom meringue
2 egg whites
50g caster sugar
45g icing sugar, sifted
½ tsp cornflour
5 cardamom pods, seeds removed
   and crushed to a fine powder

For the poached pear
1 pear, preferably Conference
400ml spring water
90g caster sugar
Squeeze of orange juice
Squeeze of lemon juice
¼ cinnamon stick
¼ vanilla pod, split lenghways
Ascorbic acid or lemon juice, to taste

For the blackberry jelly
3 gelatine leaves
20ml blackberry liqueur
15g caster sugar

For the marinated blackberries
1 tsp crème de mûre (optional)
24–30 blackberries

5   **For the blackberry jelly,** soak the gelatine in a bowl of cold water for about 5 minutes to soften. Put 150ml of the blackberry juice and 80ml of water in a pan and add the other ingredients. Bring to a simmer, squeeze the gelatine to drain it, add to the pan and stir until dissolved. Pass the mix through a sieve into a large shallow container lined with cling film. Put in the fridge to set.

6   **To marinate the blackberries,** first make a blackberry syrup. Mix together 30ml of the blackberry juice with the crème de mûre (if using), and add the blackberries. Leave to marinate until needed.

7   **To serve,** cut the jelly into four 10 x 8cm rectangles. Carefully remove the moulds from the blackberry crémeux and gently roll the jelly around the crémeux. Place off-centre on large plates. Slice the poached pear and place on the plates with some broken pieces of cardamom meringue. Finish with 3–4 marinated blackberries. The chef suggests serving this dessert with cardamom ice cream, shortbread espuma, beurre noisette crumble, custard, white chocolate namelaka and pear gel (see page 6).

POACHED PEAR
with white chocolate ganache & ale & treacle ice cream
Jonny Davison

Jonny Davison is the head chef at the Bay Tree in Holywood, Northern Ireland, where his unpretentious, home-cooked bistro food has won this self-taught chef numerous plaudits. As a fierce supporter of regional suppliers, Jonny's poached pear with ale and treacle ice cream uses fresh local produce, with the richness of the ganache offering a note of pure indulgence.

1   **To make the ale and treacle ice cream,** pour the black ale into a deep pan and reduce over 10–15 minutes by three-quarters. Add the double cream and milk and bring to the boil with the vanilla pod. Remove from the heat. Whisk the egg yolks and sugar to combine and then add a ladleful of the hot milk and cream mixture, whisking continuously. Pour the egg yolk mixture back into the hot milk and cream and return the mixture to a low heat. Stirring constantly (do not allow the sauce to boil or the mixture will separate), cook for 5–10 minutes until the mixture is thick enough to coat the back of a spoon.

2   Remove from the heat and discard the vanilla pod. Add the black treacle and pass the mixture through a sieve. Mix in the chocolate and allow the mixture to cool to room temperature. Then churn in an ice-cream machine until set.

3   **For the ganache,** pour the double cream and whiskey into a pan and bring up to a gentle simmer. Leave to simmer for 2 minutes, then remove from the heat and let it sit for 2 minutes. Add the white chocolate and mix through to melt. Place in a container and put in the fridge for about 40 minutes to set.

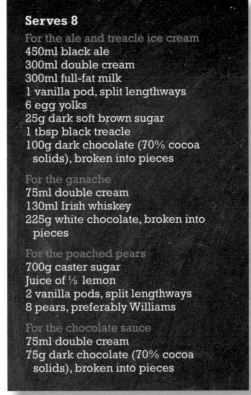

Serves 8

For the ale and treacle ice cream
450ml black ale
300ml double cream
300ml full-fat milk
1 vanilla pod, split lengthways
6 egg yolks
25g dark soft brown sugar
1 tbsp black treacle
100g dark chocolate (70% cocoa solids), broken into pieces

For the ganache
75ml double cream
130ml Irish whiskey
225g white chocolate, broken into pieces

For the poached pears
700g caster sugar
Juice of ½ lemon
2 vanilla pods, split lengthways
8 pears, preferably Williams

For the chocolate sauce
75ml double cream
75g dark chocolate (70% cocoa solids), broken into pieces

4   **For the poached pears,** first make a stock syrup. Put 1 litre of water in a large heavy-based pan with the sugar, lemon juice and vanilla pods. Bring to the boil to allow the sugar to dissolve, and then reduce the temperature to low.

Sleek, sophisticated and utterly grown-up.

5   Peel, halve and core the pears and put them in the syrup, cover and weigh down with a heatproof plate so that all of the pears are kept under the surface of the syrup. Gently poach for 15–20 minutes until you can push a knife through the pear with little resistance. Remove from the heat and set aside.

6   **To make the chocolate sauce,** put the double cream in a small pan and warm through. Remove from the heat, add the dark chocolate and stir to melt. Drain the pears, cut each one in half lengthways and remove the core. Dip the rounded side of each pear into the warm chocolate sauce.

7   **To serve,** using a pastry brush, swipe a layer of chocolate sauce across each plate and place a scoop of ice cream at one end and some ganache at the other. Put 1–2 pear halves next to the ganache. The chef suggests serving this dessert with some hazelnut praline for extra decoration (see page 6).

SEASIDE FAVOURITES
Dameon Clarke

Assiette is Dameon Clarke's first solo venture, offering global modern cooking in a 16th-century setting in historic Stamford, Lincolnshire. Dameon started cooking under Michel Roux Jr in the iconic Le Gavroche, before going on to work with Gary Rhodes in Edinburgh and in the world-famous Tetsuya, Sydney. This fantastically inventive seaside favourites dish is inspired by Dameon's childhood. Despite its quirkiness, each of the components is beautifully balanced, carefully showcasing this chef's meticulous attention to the finer details.

1 **For the lavender cream,** pour the cream into a pan and add the lavender, sugar and gellan gum (if using), and bring slowly to the boil. Remove from the heat and allow to cool, then chill. Pass the mixture through a sieve and pour into a bowl. Whip the cooled cream with a whisk until the mixture reaches ribbon stage and then return to the fridge.

2 **For the honeycomb,** mix the honey and glucose with 100ml of water in a pan and cook over a medium heat for about 10 minutes until caramel in colour. Remove from the heat, add the bicarbonate of soda and mix. Tip out onto a silicone mat or baking parchment, leave to cool and then break into small pieces.

3 **For the chocolate filling,** pour the cream into a pan. Add the butter and bring slowly to the boil. Remove from the heat. Put the chocolate into a glass bowl, then pour the warm cream over it and stir until the chocolate has melted. Leave to cool and then chill in the fridge.

4   **For the lavender and honeycomb cones,** preheat the oven to 180°C (Gas 4). Whisk the egg white in a bowl until soft peaks have formed. Fold in the butter, icing sugar, flour and cocoa powder and mix to a smooth paste. Chill in the fridge for about 20 minutes until firm. Draw two 10cm equilateral triangles with one side curved to look like a cone on some baking parchment. Spread the chilled paste within the lines of the cone shapes and cook for about 6 minutes until golden brown. Remove from the oven and, while still hot, wrap around cone moulds to form two cones. Leave to cool.

5   To assemble the cones, pour 1 tbsp of the chilled chocolate filling into the base of each cone and reserve the remaining filling for the lollipops. Fill the cones halfway up with the lavender cream. Sprinkle over some honeycomb and then fill with the remaining lavender cream. Sprinkle over more honeycomb and place in the freezer.

6   **For the chocolate ice cream,** pour the cream into a pan and slowly bring to the boil. Remove from the heat. Mix the egg yolks, sugar and cocoa powder together in a bowl. Pour the hot cream over the egg mix, stirring continuously, then add the chocolate and stir the egg mix until the chocolate has melted. Pass the mixture through a sieve into a clean pan and cook over a low heat until the mixture is thick enough to coat the back of a spoon. Leave to cool, then churn in an ice-cream machine until it set.

7   For each portion of chocolate ice cream, half fill a lollipop mould with the reserved chocolate filling and freeze. When it is solid, remove it from its mould, half fill the mould once again, but this time with the chocolate ice cream, and push the frozen chocolate filling into the centre. Return to the freezer and leave to set.

8   **For the chocolate and peanut coating,** preheat the oven to 180°C (Gas 4). Melt the chocolate in a bowl over a pan of simmering water. Spread the peanuts out on a baking sheet and roast in the oven for 5 minutes. Remove from the oven, leave to cool and chop into fine pieces.

9   Remove the frozen ice-cream lollipops from their moulds and dip in the melted chocolate to cover. Roll in the chopped roasted peanuts to cover the whole lollipop and return to the freezer.

10   **To serve,** blitz the remaining honeycomb in a blender to a fine powder to resemble sand and form the base of the dish. Stick the cones and lollipops into the 'sand'. The chef suggests serving this dessert with sticks of rock and a chocolate and caramel candyfloss (see page 6).

Serves 2

For the lavender cream
200ml double cream
Bunch of cooking lavender
25g caster sugar
1g gellan gum (optional)

For the honeycomb
100g runny honey
25ml liquid glucose
½ tsp bicarbonate of soda

For the chocolate filling
100ml double cream
1 tsp salted butter
100g dark chocolate (67% cocoa solids), broken into pieces

For the lavender and honeycomb cones
1 egg white
25g butter, melted
25g icing sugar
25g plain flour
1 tsp cocoa powder

For the chocolate ice cream
150ml double cream
3 egg yolks
15g caster sugar
50g cocoa powder
20g dark chocolate (67% cocoa solids), broken into pieces

For the chocolate and peanut coating
50g dark chocolate (67% cocoa solids)
10g salted peanuts

Crispy, crunchy, chocolatey – a host of delectable seaside treats.

A MINI APPLE BRULEE
with an apple & blackberry delice & vanilla tuiles
Gwyn Roberts

At the Kinmel Arms in Abergele, Gwyn Roberts offers up traditional Welsh food 'with a modern pulse', citing Raymond Blanc and Marco Pierre White as key influences. Gwyn's menu at this popular eatery is woven with ingredients from the Kinmel's on-site farm; they rear pigs and sheep, and maintain an abundant herb garden. His cooking displays a warm attention to detail, baking bread, making preserves and presenting his native produce with flair and flavour.

1   **For the apple brûlées,** preheat the oven to 140°C (Gas 1) and divide the diced apple between four 8cm-diameter ramekins. Put the milk, cream and vanilla pod in a pan and bring to the boil. Whisk the egg yolks, sugar and apple brandy in a bowl until thick and creamy. Take the milk and cream off the boil and, continuing to whisk, add to the egg yolk mixture. Pass through a sieve and into the ramekins on top of the apple. Transfer to a baking sheet and cook in the oven for about 30 minutes until set. Leave to cool. Increase the oven to 180°C (Gas 4).

2   **For the blackberry jelly,** warm the juice and sugar in a pan. Soak the gelatine in a bowl of water for about 5 minutes to soften, then squeeze the gelatine to drain it and add to the warm blackberry juice. Pass the mixture through a sieve and set aside.

3   **For the blackberry mousse,** soak the gelatine in a bowl of water for about 5 minutes to soften. Heat the blackberries, both sugars and crème de cassis in a pan until soft. Transfer to a food processor and blend to a purée, then pass through a sieve. Using an electric hand-held mixer, whisk the eggs and elderflower cordial in a glass bowl over a pan of simmering water for about 3 minutes until pale. Squeeze the gelatine to drain it, add to the egg mixture and stir until dissolved. Whip the cream until it is slightly thickened. Fold the blackberry purée and egg mixture together and then gently fold in the cream.

4   **For the vanilla sponge,** line a 15 x 18cm baking tin with baking parchment. Put the eggs, sugar and vanilla seeds into a bowl and whisk until thick. Fold in the flour and pour the sponge mix into the prepared tin and bake for 8–10 minutes. Remove from the oven and, when cool, turn out onto a wire rack.

5   **To assemble the delice,** line a 15cm-diameter ring mould or loose-bottomed cake tin with cling film. Using the cake tin as a template, cut out a 15cm-diameter circle from the sponge and put

Serves 4

For the apple brûlées
1 eating apple, preferably Granny
   Smith, peeled and finely diced
150ml full-fat milk
150ml double cream
1 vanilla pod, split lengthways
4 egg yolks
60g caster sugar
1 tsp apple brandy, such as Calvados
Caster sugar, for dusting

For the blackberry jelly
300ml blackberry juice
50g caster sugar
3 gelatine leaves

For the blackberry mousse
3 gelatine leaves
250g blackberries
80g caster sugar
60g icing sugar
1 tsp crème de cassis
2 eggs
50ml elderflower cordial
200ml double cream

For the vanilla sponge
2 eggs
60g caster sugar
½ vanilla pod, split lengthways and
   seeds scraped out
60g plain flour, sifted

For the vanilla tuiles
3 egg whites
165g icing sugar
115g plain flour, sifted
125g butter, melted

in the bottom of the tin. Top with the blackberry mousse mixture until the tin is two-thirds full and put in the fridge for about 45 minutes to set. Add a layer of the cold blackberry jelly.

6   **For the vanilla tuiles,** preheat the oven to 180°C (Gas 4). Whisk the egg whites, sugar and flour in a bowl to form a paste, then incorporate the butter and chill for about 30 minutes until firm. Lay greaseproof paper on a baking sheet and cut out a narrow rectangular stencil from acetate or card, measuring 10cm x 5mm. Spread a thin layer of the mixture inside the stencil with a palette knife. Remove the stencil and repeat another 3 times or until all of the mixture is used. Place the baking sheet in the oven and bake for about 5 minutes until golden. Remove the tuiles and, while still warm, mould into a spiral around a rolling pin and allow to cool and harden for 2–3 minutes.

7   **To serve,** finish the apple brûlées by dusting the surface with caster sugar and then caramelise them with a blow torch or by putting the ramekins under a preheated grill. Place in the centre of each plate. Cut the delice into triangles, then place a portion next to each brûlée and top with a tuile. The chef suggests serving this dessert with apple jelly, a blackberry ice cream and an apple crisp together with a sugar cage and spring for decoration (see page 6).

> Rich, brandy-laced indulgence makes this sweet treat one for the sophisticates.

SLOE GIN CREME BRULEE
with damson ice cream
Ian Swainson

The White Room at Seaham Hall might see Ian Swainson in the first head chef role of his career, but he brings heavyweight experience to the table after four years working with Will Holland at La Bécasse. With a thoroughly modern take on patriotic British cooking, Ian makes the most of the abundant northeast larder, creating menus that showcase produce from the Northumbrian pastures to the North Sea. All delivered with exciting flair and a terrific sense of fun.

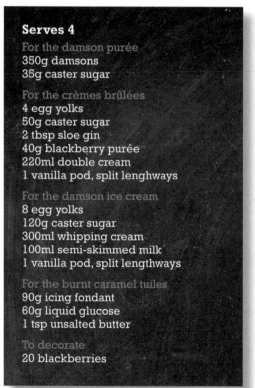

Serves 4

For the damson purée
350g damsons
35g caster sugar

For the crèmes brûlées
4 egg yolks
50g caster sugar
2 tbsp sloe gin
40g blackberry purée
220ml double cream
1 vanilla pod, split lenghways

For the damson ice cream
8 egg yolks
120g caster sugar
300ml whipping cream
100ml semi-skimmed milk
1 vanilla pod, split lengthways

For the burnt caramel tuiles
90g icing fondant
60g liquid glucose
1 tsp unsalted butter

To decorate
20 blackberries

1 **To make the damson purée,** first halve the damsons and remove the stones. Put the damsons into a pan with the sugar and cook over a medium heat for about 20 minutes until the fruit is soft. Drain the damsons, reserving the liquid, then transfer to a food processor and blend to a purée, adding some of the juice if necessary. Pass through a sieve and leave to cool.

2 **For the crèmes brûlées,** preheat the oven to its lowest setting. Whisk together the egg yolks and sugar in a bowl with an electric hand-held mixer until they are creamy. Pour the gin, purée and cream into a pan, add the vanilla pod and bring the mixture to the boil. Then add the egg mixture and stir until all the ingredients are incorporated. Skim off any foam, remove the vanilla pod and pour the mixture into four 7–8cm-diameter ramekins. Cook for about 50 minutes until the crèmes brûlées are set with a slight wobble in the middle. Remove from the oven and leave to cool.

3 **To make the ice cream,** cream together the egg yolks and sugar in a large bowl using a whisk. Put 200g of the damson purée with the whipping cream, milk and vanilla pod into a large pan and bring to the boil. Pour this mixture over the egg mix, then return to the pan and

cook on a low heat, stirring continuously, until the mixture reaches 84°C. Pass it through a sieve and leave to cool. Churn in an ice-cream machine until set.

4   **For the burnt caramel tuiles,** put the fondant and glucose into a pan over a high heat and cook to 155°C. Mix in the butter, then remove the pan from the heat. Pour the caramel in a thin layer onto greaseproof paper, then place another sheet of greaseproof paper over the caramel and roll it out with a rolling pin. Put to one side to set. Remove the tuiles from the greaseproof paper and put onto a baking sheet. Use a blow torch or a grill preheated to high to slightly burn the caramel.

5   **To serve,** put the crèmes brûlées on large plates. Top with a shard of broken caramel and add a scoop of damson ice cream. Finish with a scattering of blackberries. The chef suggests serving this dessert with a biscuit crumble, blackberries in a verbena syrup and, if you have a cream whipper, a blackberry lemongrass espuma (see page 6).

CAMBRIDGE BURNT CREAM
with black pepper shortbread
Kyle Greer

Kyle Greer is a chef at Belfast's on-trend, modern brasserie No 27 Talbot Street. Inspired by his granny's home baking, Kyle cooks with simple, inexpensive ingredients, and is creatively stimulated by the idea of making 'something from nothing'. His Cambridge burnt cream pudding typifies his passion for home-cooked comfort food with a twist; the black pepper in the shortbread adds a flicker of heat.

Serves 6

For the Cambridge burnt cream
450ml whipping cream
1 vanilla pod, split lengthways and seeds scraped out
4 egg yolks
60g caster sugar, plus extra for caramelising the top

For the black pepper shortbread
1 vanilla pod, split lengthways and seeds scraped out
125g plain flour
50g icing sugar
1 tsp freshly ground black pepper, plus extra to decorate
95g unsalted butter, softened
1 egg yolk
Caster sugar, to decorate

1 **To make the Cambridge burnt cream,** preheat the oven to 130°C (Gas ½). Put the cream and vanilla seeds in a heavy-based pan and gently heat to just below boiling point. Remove from the heat and leave for 1–2 minutes for the vanilla to infuse.

2 Meanwhile, put the egg yolks and sugar in a large bowl and whisk gently until the sugar has dissolved. Slowly add the vanilla cream to the egg mixture, whisking continuously. Pass the mixture through a sieve and leave to cool slightly for 5 minutes, skimming any froth that appears on the surface.

3 Place six small coffee cups in a large ovenproof dish and fill them almost to the top with the cream mixture.

4 Pour boiling water into the dish until it comes halfway up the cups, then cover the whole dish with five layers of cling film (to stop any holes appearing in the mixture due to shrinkage). Carefully place the dish in the oven to bake for 25–30 minutes until set. There should just be a little wobble in the middle, like jelly.

5 Take off the cling film and remove the cups from the dish. Place in the freezer for 10 minutes and then in the fridge for at least 30 minutes until set.

When the set cream is cooking in the oven, the cling film may melt slightly, but that won't affect the dessert. If you prefer, use a layer of foil instead.

6   **For the black pepper shortbread,** preheat the oven to 180°C (Gas 4). Put the vanilla seeds, flour, icing sugar and black pepper into a food processor and pulse gently to mix. Add the butter and again pulse until a crumbly biscuit texture is achieved, then add the egg yolk with the machine on full power and blend until a dough is formed. Remove the dough from the food processor, wrap in cling film and chill in the fridge for 30 minutes.

7   Once rested, use a rolling pin to roll the dough until it is about 1cm thick and cut it into 1 x 5cm rectangles. Bake on greaseproof paper for about 12 minutes until lightly golden. Remove from the oven and sprinkle the tops with equal quantities of black pepper and caster sugar mixed together.

8   **To serve,** sprinkle 1 tsp of sugar over the top of each set cream and caramelise with a blow torch or under a medium-hot grill. Serve each cup of set cream with a plate of shortbread biscuits. The chef suggests serving this dish with 'sandwiches' made from Victoria sponge (see page 6).

PEAR & ALMOND PANNA COTTA
with poached blackberries & nut crunch
Bruce Elsworth

Bruce Elsworth's 'modern British dishes with French and Yorkshire nuances' have proved enduringly popular at the charming Angel Inn at Hetton, which was groundbreaking in bringing fine food to the pub landscape. As a child, Bruce was inspired by Marco Pierre White and the Roux brothers, reading their books cover to cover, and that desire to learn drives him to this day: 'Things are never the same,' says Bruce. 'You can't stop learning – things never stand still.'

Serves 8

For the poached pear
200ml medium white wine
200g caster sugar
¼ cinnamon stick
Sprig of thyme
1 pear, preferably Rocha, peeled, cored and cut in half lengthways

For the pear and almond panna cotta
80ml full-fat milk
240ml double cream
20g caster sugar
1½ gelatine leaves
2 tsp amaretto

For the poached blackberries
50g caster sugar
150ml red wine
1 star anise
½ cinnamon stick
2 strips of lemon peel, thinly sliced
¼ vanilla pod, split lengthways
32 blackberries

For the nut crunch
30g shelled pistachio nuts
10g hazelnuts
2 egg whites
40g icing sugar
2 tbsp pistachio nuts, peeled and chopped, optional

To serve
2 tbsp pistachio nuts, peeled and chopped
100g clotted cream

1 **For the poached pear,** put the wine, sugar, cinnamon stick and thyme into a pan together with 150ml of water and bring to the boil. Add the pear and cover the pan with a sheet of greaseproof paper. Reduce the heat and gently simmer for about 25 minutes until the pear is tender. Remove the pan from the heat and allow the pear to cool in the liquid. Drain, transfer the pear to a food processor and blend to a purée.

2 **To make the pear and almond panna cotta,** bring the milk and cream to the boil in a pan. Add the sugar and stir until it dissolves. Soak the gelatine in a bowl of cold water for about 5 minutes to soften, then squeeze the gelatine to drain it and add to the creamy mixture together with the amaretto. Stir until the gelatine is dissolved. Pour the mixture into a bowl over ice cubes and stir occasionally. When it is starting to thicken, mix in the pear purée, leave for 10 minutes and transfer to eight 5cm-diameter dariole moulds. Place in the fridge for at least 1 hour (or overnight, if possible) to set.

3 **For the poached blackberries,** put the sugar, wine, star anise, cinnamon stick, lemon peel and vanilla pod into a pan and slowly bring to the boil. Reduce the heat and simmer for 10 minutes. Remove the whole spices, lemon peel and vanilla pod and allow the mixture to cool a little. Then add the blackberries and leave for about 35 minutes to cool completely. Drain and discard half the liquid from the pan, then remove the blackberries and set aside. Reduce the remaining stock to a syrup.

> If you are short on time when making the panna cotta, add an extra half leaf of gelatine, which will set firmer and allow it to be turned out earlier if required.

4 **For the nut crunch,** preheat the oven to 180°C (Gas 4) and line a baking sheet with a silicone mat or baking parchment. Put the pistachio nuts and hazelnuts into a food processor and blend until they resemble fine breadcrumbs. Add the egg whites and sugar to the blitzed nuts and mix until combined. Spread the mix evenly on the prepared baking sheet and sprinkle with the chopped pistachio nuts (if using). Bake for about 10 minutes, then remove from the oven and use a small round cutter to press out at least 24 circles. Allow to cool before separating out the discs.

5 **To serve,** unmould the panna cottas, place on large plates and top with some pistachio nuts. Layer three discs of the nut crunch with a few of the poached blackberries and top with a scoop of clotted cream and then drizzle some of the syrup around each plate. The chef suggests serving this dessert with plum fool and apple purée (see page 6).

DARK CHOCOLATE FONDANT
with a raspberry wafer
Giancarlo Vatteroni

Taking inspiration from Spain and Italy, Giancarlo Vatteroni's impeccable tapas at central London's buzzy Dehesa emphasises quality ingredients and big flavours. Previously at the Providores, Giancarlo was first inspired by his father's passion for Tuscan produce. 'I love exploring through cooking,' he says. 'So many flavours, combinations of spices – the world coming together on a plate.' And this sumptuous, silky chocolate fondant would surely melt the hearts of sweet-lovers the world over.

1   **To make the chocolate crème anglaise,** first put the milk, cream and vanilla extract in a pan and bring to the boil. In a bowl, beat the yolks and sugar with an electric hand-held mixer until light and creamy. Slowly pour the infused milk into the egg mix, stirring continuously. Return to the pan and gently cook, making sure the mix doesn't come to the boil. Add the chocolate and continue to stir until the custard is thick enough to coat the back of a spoon. Sieve into a container, top with a piece of greaseproof paper cut to the size of the container and chill in the fridge for about 30 minutes.

2   **To make the chocolate sauce,** put all the ingredients into a pan with 50ml cold water and gently simmer, stirring continuously, until you have a smooth sauce. Transfer to a bowl and chill in the fridge for about 20 minutes.

3   **For the chocolate ganache,** melt the chocolate in a glass
    bowl over a pan of simmering water. In a separate bowl, whip
    the cream and sugar until firm. Add the melted chocolate to the
    cream, gently fold through and set aside.

4   **For the chocolate casing,** melt the chocolate in a glass bowl
    over a pan of simmering water. Lightly grease four 7cm-diameter
    and 5cm-deep ring moulds and put them onto a baking sheet
    lined with greaseproof paper. Using a pastry brush, brush the
    melted chocolate around the inside of the moulds, including the
    bottom, to about 1mm in thickness. Put the moulds in the freezer
    for 10 minutes to harden the chocolate. You may need to repeat
    the painting and freezing another two or three times to make
    the coating thick enough.

5   **To assemble the dark chocolate fondants,** take the chocolate
    moulds from the freezer and divide half of the chocolate
    ganache into the bottom of each (reserving the other half for the
    top layer). Chill for 10 minutes in the fridge to set the ganache.
    Remove from the fridge and divide the chocolate sauce equally
    between the moulds then chill for another 10 minutes.

6   Divide the chocolate crème anglaise between the moulds and
    rest in the fridge for a further 10 minutes or until set. Finally, finish
    by topping each with the remaining ganache and smooth the
    tops. Chill in the fridge for a further 20 minutes or until required.

7   **To make the raspberry wafers,** preheat the oven to 140°C (Gas 1)
    and line a baking sheet with a silicone mat or greaseproof paper.
    Gently melt the butter in a pan with the glucose and vinegar. Add
    the sugar, raspberries and pectin and continue to cook over a
    low heat until the sugar dissolves. Remove from the heat, add
    the chocolate and whisk through until the chocolate has melted.
    Pour the mixture onto the prepared baking sheet and bake for
    15–20 minutes until the mixture becomes crisp but not too dark
    in colour (it should resemble a brandy snap). Remove from the
    oven and leave to cool.

8   **To serve,** take the moulds with the chilled chocolate fondants
    from the fridge and warm the rings slightly with a blow torch (or
    between warmed hands). Turn each onto a plate (so the solid
    chocolate bottom is now on the top) and gently push out of
    the moulds. Blast each in the microwave for about 10 seconds
    to soften the centre and make the outer casing glossy. Place
    a quenelle of whipped cream on the top of each chocolate
    fondant and top with two large shards of raspberry wafer. Dust
    with icing sugar. The chef suggests serving this dessert with
    liquid liquorice, coffee syrup and ground hazelnuts (see page 6).

Serves 4

For the chocolate crème anglaise
90ml full-fat milk
60ml double cream
4 drops of vanilla extract
2 egg yolks
50g caster sugar
80g dark chocolate (75% cocoa
 solids), broken into pieces

For the chocolate sauce
40g dark chocolate (75% cocoa
 solids), broken into pieces
1 tsp caster sugar
1 tbsp double cream

For the chocolate ganache
175g dark chocolate (75% cocoa
 solids), broken into pieces
90ml double cream
40g caster sugar

For the chocolate casing
150g dark chocolate (75% cocoa
 solids), broken into pieces

For the raspberry wafers
45g unsalted butter
25ml liquid glucose
20ml muscat wine vinegar
40g caster sugar
8g freeze-dried raspberries
2g pectin
20g white chocolate, broken into
 pieces

To serve
100ml double cream, whipped
Icing sugar, for dusting

To test the temperature
of melting chocolate,
dip a spoon into the
mix and then test it
on your upper lip. It
should never feel hot.
If it does, you are at
risk of splitting the
chocolate as the cocoa
butter will separate
from the solids.

VANILLA CUSTARD IN FILO PASTRY
with a raspberry coulis
George Psarias

George Psarias has been educating his loyal Leeds customers in the Greek classics since the early eighties; much to their unwavering delight. His flagship taverna, the Olive Tree in Rodley, delivers honest Greek cooking enlivened by gems inspired by his library of 600 cookery books. George cites his mother-in-law as a key influence. 'We should go back to the way our grandmothers cooked,' he says. 'Real ingredients, cooked by real people using only the best the season has to offer.'

Serves 6

For the vanilla custard
650ml full-fat milk
Pared rind of ½ unwaxed lemon and grated zest of the other ½
3 egg yolks
100g caster sugar
20g unsalted butter, softened
Pinch of salt
125g fine semolina
½ vanilla pod, split lengthways and seeds scraped out
200g filo pastry
125g unsalted butter, melted

For the syrup
200g caster sugar
Pared rind and juice of ½ unwaxed lemon
1 cinnamon stick
2 cloves
Splash of rose water (optional)

For the coulis
110g raspberries
2 tsp icing sugar
Juice of ½ lemon
2–3 drops of rose water (optional)

To serve
Raspberries
Icing sugar, for dusting

1. **To make the vanilla custard,** preheat the oven to 180°C (Gas 4). Heat the milk with the lemon rind in a small pan to boiling point. Remove from the heat and leave to cool for 10 minutes. Remove the lemon rind and discard. Using an electric hand-held mixer, whisk the egg yolks with the sugar in a bowl until thick and creamy. Add the butter, lemon zest and salt and stir well. Then gradually add the semolina, mixing continuously.

2. Slowly pour in the cooled milk, mixing thoroughly after each addition, and return the mixture to a clean pan. Cook over a low heat for 3–4 minutes, stirring occasionally, until the mixture is thick enough to coat the back of a spoon. Remove the custard from the heat and add the vanilla seeds. Cover the surface with cling film to prevent a skin forming and leave to cool.

3. Butter a 15 x 20cm baking tin and line the base with half the filo pastry, brushing each sheet with melted butter and spreading one on top of the other. Spread the cooled custard evenly with a spatula over the pastry and turn the edges of the pastry over the custard to keep it from oozing out.

4. Cover the surface of the custard with the remaining sheets of filo pastry, each brushed with melted butter.

Brush the top with more melted butter and seal the edges with a little cold water. Score the top layer of pastry with a sharp knife diagonally across the tin about 8cm apart and in both directions to form diamond shapes. Bake in the oven for 30–35 minutes until golden brown. Remove from the oven and allow to cool before cutting into six slices.

5 **For the syrup,** put the sugar, lemon rind, cinnamon and cloves with 150ml of water into a pan. Bring to the boil, reduce the heat and simmer for about 5 minutes. Then add the lemon juice and rose water (if using) and simmer for a further 2–3 minutes. Strain the cinnamon stick, lemon rind and cloves out of the hot syrup before pouring it carefully all over the cold pastry.

6 **To make the coulis,** put the raspberries, icing sugar, lemon juice and rose water (if using) into a blender together with 1 tbsp of water and blend for a few seconds. Pass through a sieve to remove the seeds.

7 **To serve,** place a custard slice in the centre of each plate and drizzle the coulis around it. Decorate with the raspberries and dust with icing sugar.

For the best results, always put cold syrup on to hot filo pastry or hot syrup on to cold filo pastry or the surface of the pastry curls up and softens.

LEMON CURD & RASPBERRY SORBET
with meringue & raspberry compote
Simon Walley

Longevity, atmosphere and classics-with-a-twist are the order of the day at the historic McCoys at the Tontine, where head chef Simon Walley keeps up the fine cooking for which this Cleveland restaurant has long been renowned. Simon worked at the Ritz before moving to Melbourne to work with star chef Shannon Bennett. Known for the visual impact of his dishes, this deconstructed lemon tart is a fascinating elaboration on a classic, combining his twin loves of the traditional and the new.

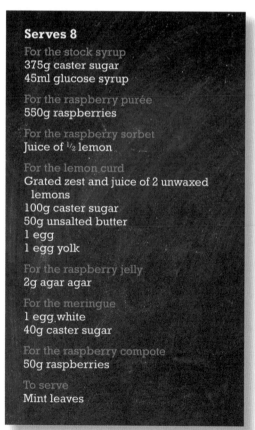

Serves 8

For the stock syrup
375g caster sugar
45ml glucose syrup

For the raspberry purée
550g raspberries

For the raspberry sorbet
Juice of ½ lemon

For the lemon curd
Grated zest and juice of 2 unwaxed
  lemons
100g caster sugar
50g unsalted butter
1 egg
1 egg yolk

For the raspberry jelly
2g agar agar

For the meringue
1 egg white
40g caster sugar

For the raspberry compote
50g raspberries

To serve
Mint leaves

1 **To make the stock syrup,** put the sugar and glucose with 320ml of water in a heavy-based pan and heat gently until the sugar has dissolved. Bring to the boil for 5 minutes. Allow to cool, then strain and transfer to a container with a lid, and place in the fridge until required.

2 **To make the raspberry purée,** put the raspberries in a food processor and blend until smooth. Sieve the mixture to remove any seeds and divide into 300g for the raspberry sorbet, 200g for the raspberry jelly and 25g for the raspberry compote.

3 **To make the sorbet,** heat 250ml of the stock syrup in a pan. Add the 300g of raspberry purée and lemon juice, stir to combine and then leave to cool. Churn in an ice-cream machine until set.

4 **For the lemon curd,** combine the lemon zest and juice with the sugar and butter in a pan. Slowly heat the mixture over a medium heat and, when the butter has melted, whisk the egg and egg yolk and pour into the lemony butter. Mix then cook on a low heat for 8–10 minutes until thick and smooth. Spoon into a container and put in the fridge to cool.

5 **For the raspberry jelly,** line a shallow container with cling film. Put the 200g of raspberry purée into a large

pan and bring to the boil. Add the agar agar and whisk briskly for 20–30 seconds. Remove from the heat and pour into the prepared container, then allow to set in the fridge.

Silky lemon curd stars in this celebration of British fruits and flavours.

6 **To make the meringue,** preheat the oven to 100°C (Gas ¼) and line a baking sheet with a silicone mat or baking parchment. Whisk the egg white in a bowl with an electric hand-held mixer until stiff peaks are formed. Slowly mix in the sugar and, when the mixture is thick and shiny, turn off the mixer and spoon the meringue into a piping bag fitted with a small round nozzle. Pipe eight lines of the mixture 1–2cm thick and 6cm long on the prepared baking sheet, then cook in the oven for 40 minutes. Leave to cool.

7 **To make the raspberry compote,** place the raspberries in a bowl. Bring the remaining 25g of raspberry purée to the boil in a pan and then pour it over the whole raspberries and leave in the fridge for 1 hour to cool.

8 **To serve,** cut the jelly into 1cm squares using a heated knife and place under a hot grill for about 20 seconds. Use a hot tablespoon to scoop the lemon curd into neat ovals and place in the centre of large plates. Do the same with the raspberry sorbet, then add some pieces of raspberry jelly and finish with the raspberry compote topped with chopped meringue batons and mint leaves. The chef suggests serving this dessert with sweet pastry crumbs, raspberry mayonnaise and raspberry powder (see page 6).

SALTED CARAMEL APPLE
with apple mousse
Marcello Tully

Marcello Tully is the chef-director of Kinloch Lodge on the Isle of Skye. Of Brazilian descent, and trained by the Roux brothers, he gives locally produced Scottish ingredients a South American twist, using fruits to season and enhance his cooking. In this recipe he takes a classic British dessert and modernises it in a dish that is all about the delicate balance of flavours.

1   **For the apple base,** first make an apple jelly. Soak the gelatine in cold water for about 5 minutes to soften. Pour the apple juice into a pan and bring to the boil. Add the tea bag, infuse for 1 minute, then remove the pan from the heat and the tea bag from the pan. Squeeze the gelatine to drain it and add to the pan, stirring to combine. Set aside.

2   Put the vanilla seeds and pod into a heavy-based pan with the caster sugar and butter. Peel and finely chop the apples and add to the pan. Over a medium heat, cook the apples for about 15 minutes until the liquid has evaporated and the butter and sugar have turned a golden caramel colour. Remove from the heat, take out the vanilla pod and set aside to cool to room temperature so that the mix does not melt the jelly.

Gently stir the apple jelly with a wooden spoon until it has cooled down and begun to set. This will ensure the mint is evenly distributed throughout the jelly otherwise it will rise to the top.

3   Line eight 10cm-diameter ring moulds with cling film. Place 30g of the apple mix in each mould and add 25g of jelly on top. Put in the fridge to set.

4   **For the apple mousse,** first make a crème anglaise. Boil the milk in a pan with the vanilla pod to release the seeds. In a bowl, cream together 90g of the caster sugar with the egg yolks. Pour the milk and vanilla mix onto the sugar and eggs, whisking as you do so. Return to a clean heavy-based pan, passing through a sieve to remove the vanilla pod, and stir over a low heat for about 5 minutes until the mix thickens, but do not allow it to boil. Leave to chill.

5   Soak the gelatine in cold water for about 5 minutes to soften. Peel and dice the apples and cook with the butter, rest of the sugar and apple juice in a pan over a medium heat for about 15 minutes until the liquid has reduced. Squeeze the gelatine to drain it and add to the pan, stirring to combine.

Serves 8

For the apple base
3½ gelatine leaves
250ml apple juice
1 English Breakfast tea bag
½ vanilla pod, split lengthways and
 seeds scraped out
40g caster sugar
50g butter
300g eating apples, preferably
 Gala Royal

For the apple mousse
250ml full-fat milk
¼ vanilla pod, split lengthways
140g caster sugar
4 egg yolks
2 gelatine leaves
300g eating apples, preferably
 Gala Royal
50g butter
100ml apple juice
250g mascarpone cheese
25ml apple brandy, preferably
 Calvados

For the salted caramel topping
1 gelatine leaf
100g caster sugar
200ml double cream
40g butter
Pinch of coarse sea salt

For the caramelised apples
1 eating apple, preferably Gala Royal
A sprinkling of caster sugar

6 Put the apple mixture with the crème anglaise, Mascarpone cheese and apple brandy in a food processor and blend until smooth. Pour 45g on top of the jelly in each ring mould and place in the fridge for about 1 hour to set.

7 **For the salted caramel topping,** soak the gelatine in cold water for about 5 minutes to soften. Place the sugar in a heavy-based pan and melt over a medium heat for about 5 minutes to make a lightly golden caramel. Remove the pan from the heat, then add the cream and butter to taste. Squeeze the gelatine to drain it and add to the pan, stirring to combine. Allow the mix to cool a little and then sprinkle on the salt. Once the apple mousse has set, pour the cooled caramel on top using a spoon. Return to the fridge once more to allow the caramel topping to set.

8 **To make the caramelised apples,** peel, core and cut the apple into 16 thin wedges. Place the wedges on a baking sheet in eight pairs, each with one slice slightly overlapping the other. Sprinkle the caster sugar over the top and, using a blow torch (or heating under a hot grill), gently caramelise until deep golden brown.

9 **To serve,** gently unmould the mousses using a blow torch around the ring to release the sides (or roll the moulds gently between warmed hands) so that they come out perfectly. Remove the cling film and position on plates. Using a palette knife, arrange the wedges of caramelised apples on top of the mousses. The chef suggests serving this dessert with minted apple jelly (see page 6).

CHOCOLATE, PRALINE & GANACHE MOUSSE

Hans Schweitzer

Few chefs enjoy as impressive a pedigree as Hans Schweitzer, who was awarded the title of maître de cuisine when he was just 25 years old. He trained as a confiseur and chocolatier in Switzerland and Paris, before opening the glorious Midsummer House in Cambridge. Now owner and head chef at Cotto, Hans's cooking wows with deep flavours extracted from simple, seasonal ingredients.

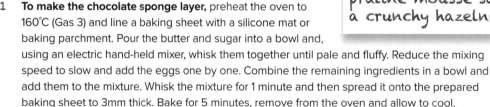

Heaven is a place on earth. Velvety ganache and praline mousse sandwich a crunchy hazelnut crisp.

1   **To make the chocolate sponge layer,** preheat the oven to 160°C (Gas 3) and line a baking sheet with a silicone mat or baking parchment. Pour the butter and sugar into a bowl and, using an electric hand-held mixer, whisk them together until pale and fluffy. Reduce the mixing speed to slow and add the eggs one by one. Combine the remaining ingredients in a bowl and add them to the mixture. Whisk the mixture for 1 minute and then spread it onto the prepared baking sheet to 3mm thick. Bake for 5 minutes, remove from the oven and allow to cool. Cut out four sponge discs using an 8cm-diameter cookie cutter.

2   **For the chocolate praline mousse,** soak the gelatine in a bowl of cold water for about 5 minutes to soften. Melt the milk chocolate in the microwave. Beat the egg yolks, sugar and 2 tbsp of water in a glass bowl over a pan of simmering water until hot and fluffy. Squeeze the gelatine to drain it, add it to the egg and sugar mix and stir until dissolved. Then add the praline or hazelnut spread and melted chocolate and whisk until the mixture reaches a smooth and creamy texture. Allow to cool to room temperature, then whip the cream until stiff and fold into the mixture. Set aside.

3   **For the crunchy roasted hazelnut crisp,** line a baking sheet with a silicone mat or baking parchment. Put the sugar into a small heavy-based pan over a medium heat and let it melt and turn golden brown. Then add the nuts and caramelise quickly. Immediately pour the mixture onto the prepared baking sheet and allow to cool and set. Melt the chocolate in a bowl in the microwave. Crush the nut mix in a food processor until it forms a coarse powder and fold into the melted chocolate. Spread a thin layer of the mixture on to baking parchment and cool for 20 minutes. Using the same 8cm-diameter cutter as for the sponge, cut out four discs and keep them in a cool place.

Serves 4

For the chocolate sponge layer
100g unsalted butter, at room
   temperature, diced
100g caster sugar
2 medium eggs
80g plain flour
20g crushed cocoa beans
1 tsp baking powder
30g cocoa powder

For the chocolate praline mousse
1 gelatine leaf
50g milk chocolate, broken into
   pieces
2 medium egg yolks
1 tsp caster sugar
75g soft praline or hazelnut spread
250ml double cream

For the crunchy roasted hazelnut crisp
15g caster sugar
10g roasted and peeled hazelnuts
50g milk chocolate, broken into
   pieces

For the chocolate ganache mousse
100g dark chocolate (70% cocoa
   solids), broken into pieces
200ml double cream

For the chocolate discs
75g dark chocolate (70% cocoa
   solids), broken into pieces

For the dark chocolate sauce
100g dark chocolate (70% cocoa
   solids), broken into pieces
75ml full-fat milk

To serve
Vanilla ice cream

4   **For the chocolate ganache mousse,** melt the chocolate in a large bowl in the microwave. Whip half of the cream to stiff peaks. Pour the other half of the cream into a pan, then bring to the boil and slowly stir it into the melted chocolate. Allow the mixture to cool and then fold in the whipped cream.

5   **For the chocolate discs,** line a baking sheet with a silicone mat, baking parchment or a chocolate transfer sheet. Melt the chocolate in a bowl in the microwave. Heat in 20-second blasts to check that it's not burning and give it a stir. You will need it to reach 42°C. Then pour the melted chocolate onto the prepared baking sheet. Spread the melted chocolate evenly and place in the fridge to set. Before the chocolate gets too hard, mark out four discs with the same 8cm-diameter cutter as used above. Place the sheet back in the fridge for another 10 minutes until set. Take out and gently lift out the four discs.

6   **To assemble,** place the separate elements into four 8cm-diameter ring moulds. Start with a sponge disc, then add a 1cm layer of the praline mousse, next a crunchy roasted hazelnut crisp, then almost fill each mould with the chocolate ganache mousse and top with a chocolate disc. Place in the fridge for about 3 hours to set.

7   **For the dark chocolate sauce,** melt the chocolate in a bowl in the microwave. Heat the milk in a pan to 85°C and stir into the melted chocolate. Keep warm.

8   **To serve,** take the four desserts out of the fridge, warm the rings slightly with a blow torch (or between warmed hands) and slide onto large plates. Pour over the hot chocolate sauce and top with a scoop of ice cream.

JERUSALEM ARTICHOKE MOUSSE
on hazelnut sponge with blackberry compote
Laurie Gear

Laurie Gear's Buckinghamshire restaurant, Artichoke, has been said by Raymond Blanc to be one of his 'best discoveries in the last five years'; it's stunning recognition for a restaurant that has literally risen from the ashes after fire damage caused a lengthy closure. Laurie has worked at Noma in Denmark, and his subtle but creative modern European dishes receive rapturous reviews on home shores. Here, his Jerusalem artichoke mousse symbolises 'seasonality and originality; the different textures and tastes working in complete harmony.'

Serves 4

For the hazelnut sponge
3 egg whites
70g caster sugar
3 egg yolks
40g strong flour
40g cornflour
170g hazelnuts
Icing sugar, for dusting

For the artichoke mousse
1.5kg Jerusalem artichokes (to make 300g of purée), scrubbed
700ml full-fat milk
200ml double cream
2 gelatine leaves
Cold milk, for soaking

For the Italian meringue
100g caster sugar
1 tsp liquid glucose
3 egg whites
160ml double cream
2 tsp lemon juice

For the blackberry compote
200g blackberries
50g caster sugar
1 tbsp blackberry liqueur, preferably crème de mûre or cassis
1 star anise
1 fresh liquorice root
1 small cinnamon stick
Grated zest of ½ unwaxed lemon
Squeeze of lemon juice

To serve
2 tbsp hazelnut liqueur

1   **To make the hazelnut sponge,** preheat the oven to 200°C (Gas 6). Line a shallow baking tin measuring about 20 x 40cm with baking parchment. Beat the egg whites and sugar together in a bowl until pale and fluffy, adding the sugar a spoonful at a time. In a separate bowl, beat the egg yolks and then fold into the meringue. Sift in the flour and cornflour and carefully fold into the mixture to create a smooth texture.

2   Toast the hazelnuts in a hot pan for about 2 minutes until golden brown and set aside 100g for decoration. Chop the remaining nuts with a sharp knife. Fold the hazelnuts into the meringue mix, pour into the prepared baking tin and smooth the surface with a wet palette knife. Bake for 7–10 minutes until pale golden. Remove from the oven and cool slightly, then dust with a little icing sugar and leave to stand until cool and crisp.

3   **For the artichoke mousse,** first make some artichoke purée. Slice the artichokes thinly with a mandoline. Combine 500ml of the milk with the double cream in a heavy-based pan on a medium heat. Add the slices of artichoke and bring to the boil. Reduce the heat and leave to simmer for 15–20 minutes until

soft. Using a slotted spoon, transfer the artichokes to a food processor and blend until smooth and silky (adding some of the hot milk if necessary) and then pass through a sieve.

4   Soak the gelatine in a small pan of cold milk for about 5 minutes to soften and then warm through slightly, stirring to dissolve the gelatine. Squeeze the gelatine to drain it and add to the artichoke purée, combine well and leave to cool slightly.

5   **To make the Italian meringue,** combine the caster sugar and liquid glucose with 70ml of water in a pan over a gentle heat and stir to dissolve. Increase the heat and bring the syrup to the boil. Reduce the heat and continue to cook for 5 minutes until the temperature reaches 120°C.

6   In a separate large bowl, whisk the egg whites with an electric hand-held mixer until stiff, then trickle in the syrup, whisking continuously, until it is fully incorporated. In another bowl, lightly whip the cream until peaks form and gently fold into the meringue. Gradually add the lemon juice, folding it in lightly.

7   **To assemble the mousse,** cover one end of each of two 7.5cm-square metal frames with cling film to create a base. Gently fold the artichoke purée through the Italian meringue until combined. Divide the mix equally between the moulds and leave in the fridge for 2–3 hours to set.

8   **To make the blackberry compote,** put the blackberries in a pan, sprinkle over the caster sugar and leave to macerate for 10–15 minutes. Add 100ml of water and the liqueur, then simmer for 4 minutes on a gentle heat. Then add the spices, lemon juice and zest and simmer for another 10–12 minutes or until the liquid has reduced a little. Remove from the heat and leave to cool and infuse for 20–25 minutes. Remove all the spices and chill until required.

When making Italian meringue, put a little lemon juice into the bowl first to remove any grease. This ensures the egg whites whisk better.

9   **To serve,** take a spare 7.5cm-square metal frame and cut out two pieces of the sponge and put on a plate. Wet very slightly with some of the hazelnut liqueur. Remove the cling film from the mousse moulds, turn upside down and use a blow torch to gently heat the edges to encourage the mousse to rest on top of the sponge. Repeat with the other mousse. Cut each in half and transfer to plates. Sprinkle the top of the mousse with the reserved hazelnuts. Pick out some of the berries from the compote, arrange around each mousse and dress with a little of the syrup. The chef suggests serving this dish with hazelnut liqueur ice cream and toasted coconut (see page 6).

MIXED-BERRY MOUSSE
with sponge & raspberry granita
Freddy Money

Freddy Money is junior sous chef at The Grill in one of London's most iconic hotels, The Dorchester, serving classic British cuisine with a contemporary twist. Freddy worked with the celebrated chef Rowley Leigh before moving to Spain, where he was introduced to the intricacies of molecular gastronomy at the sister restaurant to the world-famous El Bulli under Paco Roncero. Freddy loves the 'freedom and creativity' in cooking; in his own words, 'you never stop learning.'

Serves 8

For the stock syrup
300g caster sugar

For the mixed-berry purée and consommé
1kg mixed berries

For the raspberry granita
500g raspberries, juiced or 500ml raspberry juice

For the mixed berry gel
3g agar agar

For the mixed berry mousse
2½ gelatine leaves

For the sponge
160g caster sugar
4 egg yolks
160g butter, softened
225g strong flour
15g baking powder
Large pinch of fleur de sel (optional)

To decorate
8 raspberries
8 blackcurrants
8 redcurrants
Lemon balm cress
Edible flowers, such as borage

1   **To make the stock syrup,** put the sugar with 300ml of water in a heavy-based pan and heat gently until the sugar has dissolved. Bring to the boil for 5 minutes, then set aside to cool.

2   **For the mixed-berry purée and consommé,** first make the purée. Put the berries into a pan with enough water to cover and bring to the boil. Remove from the heat and cover with cling film. Leave for 1 hour to infuse, then strain through a muslin cloth. Weigh the purée and mix one-third of its weight (about 125g) with an equal amount of stock syrup to make the consommé. Reserve the remaining purée.

3   **For the raspberry granita,** blitz the raspberries in a food processor and pass them through a sieve into a bowl (or just add the raspberry juice). Add 125g of the stock syrup and freeze, spread out in a baking tin. When set, break up into crystals using a spatula.

4   **For the mixed-berry gel,** mix together 250g of the reserved consommé with the agar agar in a pan on a medium heat. Bring to the boil for 1 minute, whisking continuously by hand, then pour into a large shallow container. Place in the fridge for at least 30 minutes to set.

5   **For the mixed-berry mousse,** soak the gelatine in a bowl of cold water for about 5 minutes to soften. Heat

200g of the stock syrup in a pan. Squeeze the gelatine to drain it, add to the syrup and stir until dissolved. Mix with the reserved purée and put in the fridge to chill.

6 **To make the sponge,** preheat the oven to 160°C (Gas 3). Whisk the sugar and egg yolks until pale and fluffy in a kitchen mixer. Change the whisk attachment to a paddle and slowly add the butter. Once fully incorporated, slowly sift in the flour, baking powder and fleur de sel (if using). Transfer the sponge mix into a piping bag and pipe a 1cm-thick layer into eight 6cm-diameter ring moulds on a baking sheet. Bake for 7 minutes or until golden brown on top. Remove from the oven and leave to cool.

7 **To serve,** divide most of the mixed-berry gel between eight large plates. Place a sponge disc on top of the gel, then top with the granita and the mousse. Decorate the plate with the remaining gel, fresh berries and the lemon balm cress and edible flowers. The chef suggests covering the mousse and granita with a white chocolate dome, and adding raspberry 'rocks' and crystallised raspberries to the decoration (see page 6).

A bushel of berries in the prettiest of sponge and mousse confections.

CHERRY MOUSSE & A COCONUT CHOCOLATE BAR
with a cherry & coconut sorbet
Iain Walker

Iain Walker started cheffing at the tender age of 15, and is now senior sous chef at the iconic Glasgow restaurant Ubiquitous Chip, a 'magical space' that showcases some serious Scottish fine dining. Citing Nick Nairn and David Everitt-Matthias as key culinary influences, Iain revels in the creativity of the chef's role, as exemplified in this playful yet exquisite take on a Bounty bar.

1   **To make the cherry sorbet,** put the sugar, glucose and cherry purée in a pan together with 120ml of water and bring to the boil. Allow to cool and then add the lemon juice. Churn in an ice-cream machine until set. Transfer to a container and leave in the freezer. Reset the ice-cream machine for the coconut sorbet.

2   **To make the coconut sorbet,** put the sugar and glucose in a pan together with 300ml of water and boil for about 15 minutes until thickened. Then add the coconut milk, desiccated coconut and lime juice. Remove from the heat, allow to cool and churn in the ice-cream machine until set.

3   Return the cherry sorbet to the ice-cream machine and mix the two sorbets until a swirled effect is achieved. Or, for a coarser swirl, mix in a large bowl by hand.

4   **To make the cherry mousse,** pour the liqueur into a microwave-proof bowl and add the gelatine. Put the cherry purée and the vanilla seeds in a small pan over a medium heat and bring to a simmer. Whisk in the milk powder. Whisk the egg yolks with 1 tsp of the sugar in a separate bowl. When the purée is simmering, slowly pour half of the purée onto the egg yolks and whisk for 1 minute. Then pour the egg mixture into the warm purée and cook over a medium heat, stirring continuously, until the sauce reaches 80°C. Strain into a bowl and leave to cool slightly.

5   Microwave the liqueur and gelatine for 10–20 seconds to melt the gelatine slightly. Stir it into the purée. Whisk the egg white with 1 tbsp of the sugar until soft peaks form, then add the rest of the sugar and beat to stiff peaks. Whip the cream to medium peaks and fold into the purée and then fold in the egg white mixture. Set in four to eight square or round 5cm moulds and chill for at least 2 hours to set.

6   **For the coconut chocolate bar,** line a shallow flat container with cling film. Put the sugar, glucose, chocolate and 100ml of water into a heavy-based pan and boil to a syrupy consistency. Add the coconut, remove from the heat and stir until all the syrup is absorbed into the coconut. Pour into the prepared container and chill for 30 minutes until it is 'tacky'.

7   **To serve,** unmould the mousses and position on plates. Add a small rectangular piece of the coconut chocolate bar and, using a dessertspoon, scoop out an oval-shaped ball of the sorbet. Decorate with mint tips. The chef suggests serving this dessert with some cherry fluid gel, chocolate tuiles and cocoa sherbet (see page 6).

Serves 4–8

For the cherry sorbet
125g caster sugar
2 tbsp liquid glucose
500g cherry purée
Juice of 1 lemon

For the coconut sorbet
175g caster sugar
2 tbsp liquid glucose
120ml coconut milk
50g desiccated coconut
Juice of ½ lime

For the cherry mousse
25ml cherry liqueur
2 gelatine leaves
170ml cherry purée
½ vanilla pod, split lengthways
   and the seeds scraped out
1 tbsp milk powder
3 egg yolks
30g caster sugar
1 egg white
210ml double cream

For the coconut chocolate bar
100g caster sugar
50ml liquid glucose
50g dark chocolate (53% cocoa
   solids), broken into pieces
160g desiccated coconut

To decorate
Mint tips

When making the cherry mousse, ensure each part is ready before you put them together or various elements will set at different times.

BLACKBERRY SOUFFLE
with blackberry & elderflower granita
Tony Fleming

Executive chef at the capital's impressively stylish Axis at One Aldwych, Tony Fleming has designed a menu that champions uncomplicated, gutsy British food and premium produce – to the delight of his diners in the heart of theatreland. Tony cites Marco Pierre White's iconic book *White Heat* as one of his biggest inspirations; he went on to work with the chef at the Oak Room and Marco remains one of Tony's greatest culinary influences.

1   **For the blackberry purée,** put the blackberries and sugar together with 25ml of water into a pan and bring to the boil. Break the blackberries down with the back of a spoon, then simmer on a low heat for 8–10 minutes until the blackberries are well cooked and mushy. Transfer to a food processor and blend until smooth, then push through a sieve and chill.

2   **To make the blackberry and elderflower granita,** put the blackberries, elderflower cordial and lemon juice into a food processor and blend until smooth. Pass through a sieve and pour into a shallow metal tray, then freeze. Fork through the granita at 30-minute intervals to ensure even freezing.

3   **For the blackberry soufflé base,** put 250g of the blackberry purée into a pan and bring to the boil. Mix the blackberry liqueur and cornflour in a small container and then mix in 1 tbsp of the hot purée. Tip it back into the pan and simmer for 5 minutes until thick. In a separate, very small pan, gently heat the caster sugar with 50ml of water until the sugar has dissolved. Bring to the boil and continue to cook until it reaches 120°C (hardball stage). Pour half of this into the blackberry purée (making smaller quantities of the sugar solution makes it difficult to check the temperature). Combine and chill in the fridge.

4   Preheat the oven to 180°C (Gas 4) and generously butter six 130ml soufflé moulds and line with sugar. Brush the butter in

Soufflés can be kept for a while in the fridge before cooking. If you are having a dinner party and don't want to make them at the last minute, then make the soufflés in the afternoon, store in the fridge and bake when needed. Just add on an extra minute or two to the cooking time.

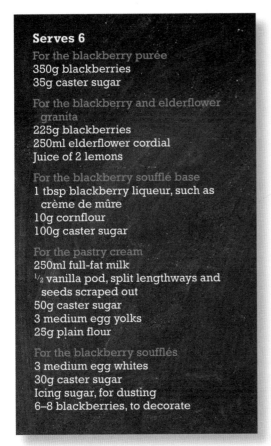

Serves 6

For the blackberry purée
350g blackberries
35g caster sugar

For the blackberry and elderflower
granita
225g blackberries
250ml elderflower cordial
Juice of 2 lemons

For the blackberry soufflé base
1 tbsp blackberry liqueur, such as
crème de mûre
10g cornflour
100g caster sugar

For the pastry cream
250ml full-fat milk
$\frac{1}{2}$ vanilla pod, split lengthways and
seeds scraped out
50g caster sugar
3 medium egg yolks
25g plain flour

For the blackberry soufflés
3 medium egg whites
30g caster sugar
Icing sugar, for dusting
6–8 blackberries, to decorate

an upwards direction from the base of the dish to the rim. This will encourage the soufflés to rise. Chill the moulds in the fridge and, once the butter is hard, paint lines of blackberry purée inside each mould and return to the fridge.

5   **For the pastry cream,** boil the milk with the vanilla pod and seeds and leave to cool slightly. In a bowl, whisk together the sugar, egg yolks and flour. Whisk in the infused milk and return to a clean pan. Remove the vanilla pod and cook gently for 5 minutes until thickened and then chill in the fridge.

6   **To make the soufflés,** whisk the egg whites and caster sugar in a bowl until soft peaks form. In a separate bowl, combine 50g of the blackberry soufflé base with 100g of the pastry cream. Beat in 1 spoonful of the egg whites and then gently fold in the rest. When folding in the last lot of egg whites, do this thoroughly but very carefully so as not to knock out any air.

7   Divide the soufflé mixture evenly between the six moulds; run your thumb around the rims to clean them and this will help the soufflé to rise straight and evenly. Bake for about 6 minutes until risen and golden.

8   **To serve,** remove the soufflés from the oven, dust with icing sugar, place a blackberry on top and put on plates. Add the blackberry and elderflower granita. The chef suggests serving this dessert with cranachan and almond brittle (see page 6).

PEAR SOUFFLE
with poached pear
Chris Gould

First inspired by his grandmother's home baking, Chris Gould describes the cooking process as 'magic before your eyes'. Having kick-started his career at the Hilton in Cardiff, Chris now cooks at the Hardwick outside Abergavenny, where his food balances traditional comfort with thoughtful sophistication. The Hardwick's philosophy is to showcase local seasonal ingredients with a no-fuss approach to presentation. Chris is keen to allow great produce to 'speak for itself', producing classic dishes with flawless technique.

1   **For the mixed-berry stock syrup,** preheat the oven to 180°C (Gas 4). Put the berries in a baking tin and lightly sprinkle with the caster sugar. Roast in the oven for about 15 minutes until soft. Strain into a bowl, squeezing the berries to get as much juice from them as possible, then add 400ml of water and lemon juice to the syrup to taste.

2   **For the pear purée,** cook the pears in a pan with 3 tbsp of water for about 10 minutes until the pears have softened. Transfer to a food processor and blend to a purée then return to the pan and add the sugar. Simmer the mixture until it has reduced by half, then whisk in the cornflour until smooth.

3   **For the poached pears,** put the pears in a pan with the berry stock syrup and cook over a gentle heat for 10–15 minutes until tender. Use a sharp knife to check the centre of each pear (there should be very little resistance). Leave to cool at room temperature.

4   **To make the crème pâtissière,** slowly bring the milk and cream to the boil in a small pan. At the same time, whisk the egg with an electric hand-held mixer, then, continuously mixing, gradually add the caster sugar, followed by the flour and cornflour. When the milk and cream are boiling, add them to the egg mixture. Transfer to a clean pan over a medium heat and cook for about 2 minutes, stirring occasionally, until the mixture is thick enough to coat the back of a spoon. Remove from the heat and pass through a sieve.

5   **For the pear soufflé,** preheat the oven to 180°C (Gas 4) and butter four 9cm-diameter and 7cm-deep ramekins with butter and a sprinkling of caster sugar. Whisk together the egg whites and sugar to form soft peaks. Mix 240g of the pear purée with the crème pâtissière, then gently fold in half of the meringue mix. Once incorporated, add the other half. Divide the mixture between the ramekins and cook in the oven for 8–10 minutes until well risen.

6   **To serve,** place a soufflé to one side of each plate and add a poached pear and drizzle of the remaining pear purée. The chef suggests serving this dessert with honey ice cream, a jug of pear-and-berry sauce and some honeycomb brittle (see page 6).

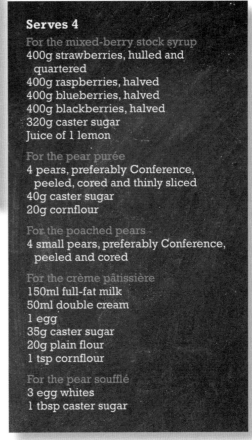

Serves 4

For the mixed-berry stock syrup
400g strawberries, hulled and quartered
400g raspberries, halved
400g blueberries, halved
400g blackberries, halved
320g caster sugar
Juice of 1 lemon

For the pear purée
4 pears, preferably Conference, peeled, cored and thinly sliced
40g caster sugar
20g cornflour

For the poached pears
4 small pears, preferably Conference, peeled and cored

For the crème pâtissière
150ml full-fat milk
50ml double cream
1 egg
35g caster sugar
20g plain flour
1 tsp cornflour

For the pear soufflé
3 egg whites
1 tbsp caster sugar

Delicate and dreamy, a showstopping soufflé that's less tricky than you'd think.

ARMAGNAC PARFAIT & PLUM SORBET
with cobnut praline & plum crisps
Tom van Zeller

One of Yorkshire's most exciting young chefs, Tom van Zeller sets out to deliver innovative, fine dining without pretension in his self-named restaurant – and his credentials are impeccable. Beginning at the world-famous Betty's Tearooms, Tom can name star chefs including Raymond Blanc, Pierre Koffman and Tom Aikens as previous employers. His Armagnac parfait is a modern derivative of the classic tarte Tatin. Tom says, 'It really is autumn on a plate, with fantastic contrasting temperatures, colours and textures.'

1   **To make the plum crisps,** preheat the oven to 95°C (Gas ¼). Put the sugar and 50ml of water in a pan. Bring to the boil, then reduce the heat and simmer for 3–5 minutes until the sugar has dissolved. Remove the pan from the heat.

2   Slice the plums as thinly as possible using a knife or mandoline. Dip the slices in the hot syrup, then drain well and lay inbetween silicone mats or baking parchment on a heavy baking sheet. Place another baking sheet on top and put into the oven to cook for 3–4 hours. Check the crisps after 20 minutes and, if possible, every 10 minutes thereafter. When almost dry, remove the top baking sheet and continue to dry in the oven. Place on a wire rack and then store in an airtight container.

3   **To make the plum sorbet,** soak the gelatine in a bowl of cold water for about 5 minutes to soften. Put 250ml of water with the sugar and glucose in a heavy-based pan. Gently bring the mixture to the boil, then reduce the heat and simmer for 3–5 minutes until the sugar has dissolved. Squeeze the gelatine to drain it, then add to the pan and stir until dissolved. Strain and allow to cool.

4   Put the plums into a food processor and blend until very smooth. Strain through a sieve, then add to the cool syrup and adjust the sweetness with lemon juice. Churn in an ice-cream machine until set.

5   **For the Armagnac parfait,** soak the gelatine in a bowl of cold water for about 5 minutes to soften. Put 160ml of the cream in a bowl, add the brandy and, using an electric hand-held mixer, whip to soft peaks. Put the milk, remaining cream, sugar and vanilla seeds into a heavy-based pan and slowly bring to the

> Heavenly smooth parfait gets a crunch of nutty praline.

boil, then remove from the heat. Squeeze the gelatine to drain it, add to the hot milk and cream and stir until dissolved.

6 Put the egg yolks into a bowl and gradually pour the hot cream mixture onto the yolks, stirring continuously. Place over iced water and whisk continuously until thick. Then fold in the whipped cream.

7 Lay a 20cm length of cling film on a work surface. Using a 75ml ladle, scoop up a level ladleful of the parfait and drop it onto the cling film. Roll it into a cylinder, being careful not to roll the film into the mix as this will spoil the shape later. Secure the ends and freeze for a minimum of 6 hours (preferably overnight). Make eight of these. Alternatively, pour the mixture into a silicone non-stick muffin tray and freeze.

8 **For the nut praline,** preheat the oven to 180°C (Gas 4) and line a baking sheet with a silicone mat or baking parchment. Put the cobnuts or hazelnuts and almonds in a small baking tin and warm in the oven for 5 minutes. Put the sugar with 2 dessertspoons of water into a small pan and heat to a medium caramel, then fold in the hot nuts. Flatten the mix onto the prepared sheet and allow to cool.

9 Dredge a work surface with plenty of icing sugar and roll out the puff pastry as thinly as possible, covering with more icing sugar if needed. Cut into 10cm squares and place them between two layers of baking parchment on a baking sheet and put a heavy baking sheet on top. Bake in the oven for 15–20 minutes until dry, golden and caramelised and leave to cool on a wire rack. Finely chop the nut caramel and puff pastry and combine. Using a spice grinder, blitz a third to a fine powder. Reserve both pralines in airtight containers.

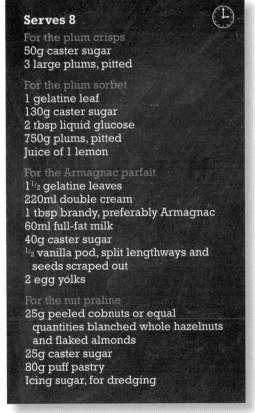

Serves 8

For the plum crisps
50g caster sugar
3 large plums, pitted

For the plum sorbet
1 gelatine leaf
130g caster sugar
2 tbsp liquid glucose
750g plums, pitted
Juice of 1 lemon

For the Armagnac parfait
1½ gelatine leaves
220ml double cream
1 tbsp brandy, preferably Armagnac
60ml full-fat milk
40g caster sugar
½ vanilla pod, split lengthways and seeds scraped out
2 egg yolks

For the nut praline
25g peeled cobnuts or equal quantities blanched whole hazelnuts and flaked almonds
25g caster sugar
80g puff pastry
Icing sugar, for dredging

10 **To serve,** sprinkle the coarse praline in a line across the plates. Put the fine praline onto a baking sheet. Take the frozen parfaits out of the freezer, unwrap (or unmould) them, trim the ends and cut in half diagonally. Roll the parfaits in your hands until tacky, roll in the praline dust and stand them up at regular intervals on the plates. Then add three scoops of sorbet along the line and decorate with plum crisps. The chef suggests serving this dessert with pickled cherries, Lapsang Souchong prunes, Lapsang Souchong jelly and caramelised quince (see page 6).

WHITE CHOCOLATE COLLAR & VANILLA MASCARPONE
with shortbread & a raspberry compote
Christopher Owen

Christopher Owen fell in love with cooking while studying for an NVQ at college. 'Being in the kitchen, surrounded by heat and flames' ignited a passion that inspired him to join the kitchen at Dawson's at the Castle Hotel, Conwy, at just 17 years old. Chris's food embraces the region's stellar produce: Welsh lamb is 'the best in the world', he argues; and that competitive streak runs deep, with Chris winning Junior Chef of Wales in 2007.

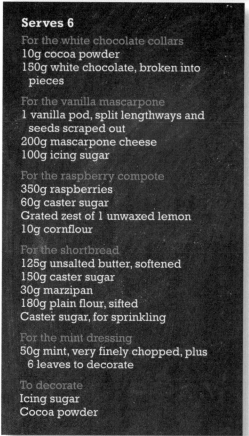

Serves 6

For the white chocolate collars
10g cocoa powder
150g white chocolate, broken into
  pieces

For the vanilla mascarpone
1 vanilla pod, split lengthways and
  seeds scraped out
200g mascarpone cheese
100g icing sugar

For the raspberry compote
350g raspberries
60g caster sugar
Grated zest of 1 unwaxed lemon
10g cornflour

For the shortbread
125g unsalted butter, softened
150g caster sugar
30g marzipan
180g plain flour, sifted
Caster sugar, for sprinkling

For the mint dressing
50g mint, very finely chopped, plus
  6 leaves to decorate

To decorate
Icing sugar
Cocoa powder

1   **For the white chocolate collars,** cut six pieces of acetate, each about 9cm square, and dust lightly with the cocoa powder. Melt the white chocolate in a glass bowl over a pan of simmering water and, using a palette knife, spread the chocolate thickly onto each piece of acetate, over the cocoa powder, leaving a 1cm strip uncovered down one side. When the chocolate loses its shine and is almost ready to set, roll up the acetate to form a hollow cylinder with the chocolate on the inside. Use sticky tape to hold the edges together and store in the fridge for at least 20 minutes to set.

2   **To make the vanilla mascarpone,** put the vanilla seeds and mascarpone in a large bowl. Add the icing sugar to sweeten (you may not need all of it) and mix thoroughly. Transfer to a piping bag, snip off the end and leave in the fridge until needed.

3   **For the raspberry compote,** pour half of the raspberries into a pan and add the sugar, lemon zest and 4 tbsp of water and bring to the boil. Mix the cornflour in a little warm water to dissolve it and then add to the raspberries to thicken the sauce. Push through a sieve and leave the sauce to cool. Mix in the remaining raspberries to make the raspberry compote.

4   **To make the shortbread,** preheat the oven to 180°C (Gas 4) and butter a baking sheet. Put the butter, sugar and marzipan in a bowl and cream together until pale and fluffy, then fold in the flour. Turn out onto a floured work surface and roll out. Cut out circles with a 5cm-diameter cutter and then cut into each of these with a 4cm-diameter cutter to create moon-shaped biscuits. Transfer to the prepared baking sheet and bake for 7–10 minutes until golden brown. Remove from the oven and immediately sprinkle with the caster sugar.

5   **To fill the chocolate collars,** take one collar out of the fridge. Very gently remove the acetate and then pipe the vanilla mascarpone into the collar to a quarter of the way up. Place a teaspoonful of the raspberry compote on top, then add some more mascarpone. Repeat this process until you completely fill the collar, making sure the final layer is mascarpone. Repeat with the remaining collars.

6   **For the mint dressing,** mix together the mint with 25ml of water until it is very smooth.

7   **To serve,** place five raspberries from the compote around a chilled plate. Add a chocolate collar just off-centre, top it with another raspberry from the compote and put a shortbread biscuit next to it. Decorate with a mint leaf, add a few blobs of the mint dressing around the plate and finish with a dusting of icing sugar and cocoa powder. The chef suggests serving this dessert with vanilla ice cream (see page 6).

DARK CHOCOLATE GANACHE with barley ice cream & hazelnut & chocolate cake
Adam Simmonds

Adam Simmonds is one of the most eminent chefs working in the UK today. His self-named dining room in the magnificent Danesfield House is home to modern European dishes lauded for their crystalline flavours and exquisite detailing. An extreme-sports enthusiast, Adam's energy has seen him through stints in the kitchens of Raymond Blanc and Marco Pierre White. 'As chefs,' he says, 'we are constantly pushing the boundaries.'

A chocolate temptation that's quite simply irresistible.

1   **To make the barley ice cream,** preheat the oven to 160°C (Gas 3). Spread the barley across a baking sheet and toast in the oven for about 20 minutes until golden. Warm the cream and milk in a pan to 70°C, then add the barley and leave to infuse overnight.

2   Re-warm the creamy barley mixture in a pan. In a large bowl, whisk together the egg yolk, xylitol and trimoline. Pour the creamy barley over the egg mixture, mix together, then return to the pan and heat to 76°C. Pass through a sieve into a bowl standing over a bowl of ice and leave to cool. Churn in an ice-cream machine until set.

3   **To make the dark chocolate ganache,** soak the gelatine in a bowl of cold water for about 5 minutes to soften. Break the chocolate into a large bowl. Warm the milk and cream in a pan until almost boiling. Squeeze the gelatine to drain it, add to the milk and cream and stir until dissolved. Then pour the milk and cream over the chocolate and stir until the chocolate has melted. Melt the cocoa butter (if using) and also add it to the chocolate. Cover with cling film to stop a skin forming and leave for 15–20 minutes, without stirring, to cool.

4   Put four pieces of cling film at least 15cm long on a work surface. Transfer the ganache into a piping bag, cut a hole 2.5cm wide and pipe a 12cm line of the ganache onto each piece of cling film. Roll into cylinders in the cling film and freeze for about 15 minutes. Trim the edges, unwrap the cling film and leave the cylinders for about 10 minutes to defrost.

5   **For the hazelnut and chocolate cake,** preheat the oven to 180°C (Gas 4) and line a baking tin measuring 17 x 7 x 8cm with greaseproof paper. Melt the chocolate in a glass bowl over a pan

Serves 4

For the barley ice cream
170g barley
165ml UHT cream
280ml full-fat milk
1 egg yolk
40g xylitol
20g trimoline

For the dark chocolate ganache
1½ gelatine leaves
100g dark chocolate (67% cocoa
   solids)
20ml full-fat milk
100ml double cream
6g cocoa butter (optional)

For the hazelnut and chocolate cake
40g dark chocolate (70% cocoa
   solids), broken into pieces
1½ eggs
85ml hazelnut oil
45g plain flour
40g ground hazelnuts
½ tsp baking powder
1 tsp cocoa powder
60g caster sugar
Pinch of bicarbonate of soda

For the hazelnut purée
50g hazelnuts
200–215ml full-fat milk
2–3 tsp hazelnut oil

To serve
Cob nuts, shelled and sliced

of simmering water. Combine the eggs and oil in a large bowl, then stir in the melted chocolate. In a separate bowl, combine the remaining ingredients and mix into the chocolate. Transfer to the prepared baking tin and cook for 35–40 minutes until risen and cooked through. Remove from the oven and transfer the cake to a wire rack. Keep the oven switched on. Preheat the grill to high and when the cake is cool, tear it into bite-sized pieces and place under the grill to crisp slightly.

6   **For the hazelnut purée,** roast the hazelnuts for a few minutes on a baking sheet until golden brown and crush well using a pestle and mortar. Put the hazelnuts into a heavy-based pan and cover with 200ml of the milk. Bring to the boil, reduce the heat and simmer for 20–25 minutes until soft. Transfer to a food processer and blend until smooth. Pour into a bowl and whisk in 2 tsp of the hazelnut oil. Taste and adjust, if required, with the remaining milk and oil.

7   **To serve,** arrange portions of the dark chocolate ganache, hazelnut purée and the chocolate and hazelnut cake, together with a scoop of the barley ice cream, on large plates and add cob nut slices to finish. The chef suggests that this dessert can also be decorated with a hazelnut milk skin and cocoa nib tuiles (see page 6).

APPLE CRUMBLE
with toffee pear & cider granita
Gareth Johns

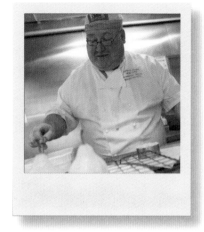

'We have one of the world's great natural larders around us,' says chef-proprietor Gareth Johns of the Wynnstay Hotel in the thriving market town of Machynlleth. Not content with running his own restaurant, Gareth is also a reserve army officer and could be called upon at any time to serve his country, rather than his diners. In the meantime, he continues with his meticulous sourcing and modern take on classic Welsh dishes, as exemplified by this celebration of orchard fruits. 'If you stay close to your roots,' Gareth advises, 'you can't go wrong.'

1   **For the apple crumble,** preheat the oven to 150°C (Gas 2) and line a baking sheet with greaseproof paper. Rub together the flour, oatmeal, 55g of the sugar and 110g of the butter in a bowl to the consistency of breadcrumbs. Transfer to the prepared baking sheet and bake for 10–15 minutes until golden brown. Remove from the oven and allow to cool, then cover with a clean tea towel and crush lightly with a rolling pin to keep the crumble texture. Increase the oven temperature to 180°C (Gas 4).

2 Put the apple in a heavy-based pan on a medium heat and sweat in the remaining butter with a pinch of sugar and mixed spice for 2–3 minutes until soft. Pile the apple into four 10cm-diameter ring moulds and top with a good layer of the crumble mix. Bake in the oven for about 10 minutes until the top is golden.

3 **For the toffee pears,** first make a stock syrup by putting 200g of the sugar and 200ml of water in a heavy-based pan. Bring to the boil, then reduce the heat and simmer for 2 minutes. Peel the pears and put in the stock syrup together with the wine. Cover (see the tip, below) and bring to the boil, then turn off the heat and leave the pears to cool in the poaching liquid.

4 Melt the remaining 115g of sugar with 1 tbsp of water in a heavy-based pan over a high heat until you reach a caramel with a medium golden colour. Keep warm and fluid. When the pears are cooked, dip each one in the warm caramel and set aside on a wire rack to cool. Retain the stock syrup.

5 Use the remaining caramel to make run-outs by drizzling the warm caramel onto greaseproof paper using a spoon. Leave to harden and store in an airtight container if not using straight away.

6 **To make the custard,** pour the milk and cream into a pan and add the vanilla seeds. Bring to the boil, take off the heat and leave to infuse. Meanwhile, whisk together the egg yolks and sugar in a bowl. If you are worried about it splitting, add the cornflour. Pour a quarter of the warm milk and cream onto the eggs and sugar and whisk together to incorporate. Transfer to a clean pan, add the remaining milk and cream, then cook over a gentle heat until the mixture thickens enough to coat the back of a spoon. Stir in the liqueur, then cover and keep the custard warm.

7 **For the cider granita,** pour the apple juice and cider into a pan, bring to the boil over a medium heat and reduce by half so that you end up with approximately 300ml in liquid. Taste and add some stock syrup if it needs to be sweeter. Churn in an ice-cream machine until set.

8 **To serve,** place each crumble in its ring on a large plate. Carefully unmould and then place a toffee pear next to it. Add a ball of granita in a small bowl and then spoon over the custard and decorate with a caramel run-out.

Serves 4

For the apple crumble
225g plain flour
1 tbsp fine oatmeal
55g light soft brown sugar, plus an extra pinch
110g butter, diced, plus ½ dessertspoon
1 firm eating apple, peeled, cored and roughly chopped
Pinch of mixed spice

For the toffee pears
315g caster sugar
4 small pears, such as Williams
300ml sweet white wine

For the custard
200ml full-fat milk
100ml whipping cream
½ vanilla pod, split lengthways and seeds scraped out
2 egg yolks
2 tbsp caster sugar
1 tsp cornflour, if needed
25ml whisky liqueur

For the cider granita
350ml apple juice
250ml dry cider

When poaching the pears, place a saucepan lid or plate slightly smaller in diameter to the pan on top of the pears so they are held down and submerged in the liquid. This will ensure they cook evenly.

APPLE CRUMBLE & CUSTARD
with rosemary ice cream & port wine syrup
Steve Love

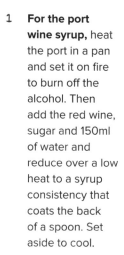

A much-decorated chef and former Roux scholar, Steve Love flies the flag for fine dining in Birmingham's stylish Canal Square. Having trained with Alain Ducasse in Paris and at the Waterside Inn in Bray, Steve brings his classical French training to bear on intricate dishes at his own Loves Restaurant, producing crystal clear flavours in dishes that champion seasonal British produce.

1 **For the port wine syrup,** heat the port in a pan and set it on fire to burn off the alcohol. Then add the red wine, sugar and 150ml of water and reduce over a low heat to a syrup consistency that coats the back of a spoon. Set aside to cool.

2 **For the custard,** bring the milk and double cream to a simmer in a pan. Whisk together the sugar, egg yolk and vanilla seeds in a bowl until pale and pour the hot milk and cream over

the egg and sugar, whisking continuously. Pour the mixture into a clean pan on a low heat, then bring the custard up to 75°C, still continuing to stir. When the custard is thick enough to coat the back of a spoon, remove from the heat and pass it through a sieve. Set aside a small amount for use in the ice cream.

3 **To make the rosemary ice cream,** blanch the rosemary sprigs in boiling water for 10 seconds and refresh in iced water to remove any harshness of flavour. Bring the milk and cream to a simmer in a pan with the sprigs of rosemary. Whisk together the sugar, egg yolks and vanilla seeds and pour the hot milk and cream over the egg and sugar, whisking all the time. Return the mixture to a clean pan and put back on a low heat, then bring the mix up to 75°C, stirring continuously. When the mixture is thick enough to coat the back of a spoon, remove it from the heat and pass through a sieve, then leave to cool.

4 Put the blanched spinach into the small amount of reserved custard so the custard turns green and then return this to the chilled ice-cream mix. Blend it and mix until it all gains a light green colour. Pass through a sieve. Churn in an ice-cream machine until set.

5 **For the crumble mix,** preheat the oven to 180°C (Gas 4). Put the butter, flour and oats into a bowl and rub with your fingers to a crumb-like consistency. Add the sugar and mix through. Spread the mixture onto a baking sheet and cook for 15–20 minutes until it goes a golden-brown colour, mixing occasionally. Remove from the oven. Reduce the temperature to 160°C (Gas 3).

6 **For the crumble filling,** heat the fondant icing with 2 tbsp of water in an ovenproof pan for 8–10 minutes until caramelised and golden. Remove from the heat. Peel, core and quarter the apples and place on top of the caramel. Cover with a lid and bake in the oven for about 20 minutes until soft. Remove the fruit with a slotted spoon, allowing the apple caramel syrup to drain into the pan, and place in a bowl. Transfer the syrup into a clean pan and heat it until it has reduced to a thicker caramel. Fold the caramel into the apples and set aside.

7 **To serve,** warm through the crumble filling and spoon into a jar or glass. Sprinkle a layer of the crumble mix over the top and then add some of the custard. Place each jar or glass on a large plate. Coat the blackberries in the port wine syrup, drain with a slotted spoon and then arrange the blackberries on the plates. Sprinkle over some more crumble mix and add a scoop of rosemary ice cream. Decorate the blackberries with some gold leaf (if using). The chef suggests serving this dessert with blackberry purée, an apple pie and pieces of blackberry crisp to decorate (see page 6).

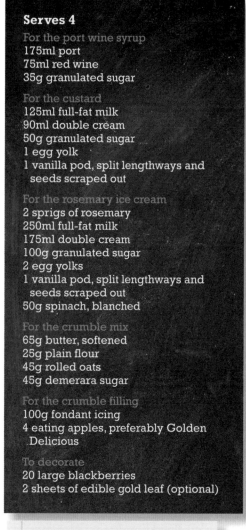

Serves 4

For the port wine syrup
175ml port
75ml red wine
35g granulated sugar

For the custard
125ml full-fat milk
90ml double cream
50g granulated sugar
1 egg yolk
1 vanilla pod, split lengthways and seeds scraped out

For the rosemary ice cream
2 sprigs of rosemary
250ml full-fat milk
175ml double cream
100g granulated sugar
2 egg yolks
1 vanilla pod, split lengthways and seeds scraped out
50g spinach, blanched

For the crumble mix
65g butter, softened
25g plain flour
45g rolled oats
45g demerara sugar

For the crumble filling
100g fondant icing
4 eating apples, preferably Golden Delicious

To decorate
20 large blackberries
2 sheets of edible gold leaf (optional)

Impress your guests with this dinner-party take on a cherished British classic.

APPLE CRUMBLE
with ginger cream tuiles & apple granita
Gerard Virolle

An intimate Regency town house in the heart of London's West End is home to Gauthier Soho, where head chef Gerard Virolle's menus celebrate seasonal ingredients cooked classically, in 'the French way'.

Previously at the internationally renowned Roussillon, where he worked his way up from commis to head chef, Gerard's love of cooking was ignited as a child, where his family's farming background impressed on him the importance of food and communal dining to family life.

Serves 4

For the apple slices
1 eating apple, preferably Granny Smith

For the apple granita
50g caster sugar
150ml apple juice

For the crumble mix
50g unsalted butter, melted
50g ground almonds
50g plain flour
50g caster sugar

For the apple compote
2 cooking apples, preferably Bramley
40g caster sugar
1 cinnamon stick
Juice of 1 lemon
1 tbsp apple liqueur, preferably Calvados

For the sugared apples
4 eating apples, preferably Granny Smiths
150g isomalt sugar

For the ginger cream tuiles
4 sheets of filo pastry
150g unsalted butter, melted
150g icing sugar

For the ginger cream
200ml whipping cream
25g fresh stem ginger, peeled
5 small egg yolks
40g caster sugar

1 **For the apple slices,** preheat the oven to its lowest setting. Peel the apple, cut into thin slices with a mandoline and transfer to a baking sheet. Dry the apple in the oven for about 1 hour. Remove from the oven and increase the temperature to 180°C (Gas 4).

2 **To make the apple granita,** put the sugar into a pan with 150ml of water and heat until the sugar has dissolved. Place in the fridge for about 10 minutes to chill and then add the apple juice. Pour a very thin layer into a baking tin and place in the freezer.

3 **For the crumble mix,** put all the ingredients in a bowl, mix together to a breadcrumb consistency and then spread across a baking sheet. Dry in the oven for 15–20 minutes, then remove and set aside to cool. Keep the oven switched on.

4 **To make the apple compote,** peel, core and slice the apples and put the slices into a pan with the remaining ingredients and cook on a low heat for about 30 minutes. Transfer the apples to a bowl, discard the cinnamon stick, and blitz with a hand-held blender until smooth.

A divine, ginger-infused cream encased in flaky filo accompanies this fabulous take on the humble apple crumble.

5 **For the sugared apples,** peel and core the apples and roll in the isomalt. Put them into a microwave-proof bowl and cook in the microwave on high for 4 minutes. Set aside.

6 **To make the ginger cream tuiles,** cut each filo pastry sheet into a 7cm square and brush it with melted butter. Roll each pastry square carefully around a 1.5cm-diameter metal tube, such as an ovenproof utensil handle, and cook in the oven for about 2 minutes until golden. Remove from the oven and slide off the tubes, then place on a wire rack and sprinkle with the icing sugar.

7 **For the ginger cream,** bring the cream to the boil in a pan. Immediately remove it from the heat and then add the ginger and leave to infuse in the hot cream for about 5 minutes. Mix together the egg yolks and sugar and pass through a sieve, then combine with the ginger-infused cream. Place the bowl over a pan of simmering water for about 5 minutes, stirring occasionally, until the mixture is thick enough to coat the back of a spoon. Pass the ginger cream through a sieve once more and transfer to a piping bag fitted with a narrow nozzle.

8 **To serve,** make a pool of the apple compote to one side of each large plate. Break the cooled crumble mixture into pieces, roll the sugared apples in it and stand them on the compote. Fill the filo pastry tubes with the ginger cream and lay on the plates, balanced against the apple crumble and with an apple slice at each end. Remove the apple granita from the freezer and scrape and crush it with a fork, then press into small moulds and turn out onto the plates.

MILLEFEUILLE OF CIDER-POACHED APPLES
with apple brandy fool
Mark Jordan

Mark Jordan has worked with some of the world's leading chefs, including Keith Floyd and Jean-Christophe Novelli. He fell in love with Jersey on his first visit, joining the Atlantic Hotel as head chef of the Ocean Restaurant in 2004. His high-end, pitch-perfect spin on island produce has put the restaurant firmly on the culinary map. This deconstructed apple crumble is typical of Mark's modernist take on much-loved classics.

1   **For the cider-poached apples,** pour the cider into a pan and add the vanilla pod with the five-spice powder and the sugar. Place on a gentle heat and slowly bring to a simmer. Peel the apples and then, using a melon baller, scoop out the flesh in little balls and put in a bowl – you need about 24 balls of apple per serving. Halve the lemons and squeeze the juice onto the apples. Once the cider mix is simmering, remove from the heat and add the apples to the cider. Cover with a piece of cling film and leave to cool at room temperature.

2   **To make the nougatine,** gently heat a large heavy-based pan and sprinkle the caster sugar into it. Stir the sugar until it has melted and turned golden brown (a splash of water early on may help prevent burning). Gently and carefully pour the mix onto a silicone mat or baking parchment and leave it to set and cool completely. Break up the sugar mix, place it in a food processor and pulse into a fine powder. Put the powder in a sealed, airtight container.

3   Preheat the oven to 150°C (Gas 2) and cut a 10cm-diameter circle from a piece of plastic, such as a plastic lid. Line a baking sheet with baking parchment and, using a sieve, gently sprinkle the nougatine powder over the plastic template. Gently remove the template and repeat until you have 16 discs. Place the baking sheet in the oven for 10–15 seconds or just long enough for the sugar to melt and turn into discs of translucent glass-like sugar. Leave them to cool and then store in an airtight container until required.

4   **For the apple brandy fool,** first make the apple purée. Peel and core the apple and cut it into rough dice. Sauté in a pan with the butter and vanilla pod for about 3 minutes until the apple starts to turn golden. Remove the pan from the heat and add the caster sugar, lemon juice and a dash of water and then allow the mixture to simmer gently for a couple of minutes or until the apples are soft. Transfer the apple mix to a food processor, remove the vanilla pod and blend until the purée is silky smooth. Put it into a plastic container covered with cling film and set aside to cool.

5   Pour the double cream into a bowl and whip to slightly thicken it. Sift the icing sugar into the cream and add 1 tbsp of the apple purée and the brandy. Gently start to whip again, only whipping just enough for the cream to be velvety, shiny and not too firm. Transfer the mix into a piping bag and put in the fridge.

6   **To serve,** drain the apple balls from the cider mix. Place a disc of nougatine on each plate and lay a circle of apples on the discs. In the centre of the apples, pipe a small amount of the apple fool. Place a second disc on top of the apples and add another apple ring and some apple fool. Repeat one more time and top with a fourth disc of nougatine. Drizzle each plate with a little maple syrup and finish with a sprig of mint. The chef suggests serving this dessert with black butter ice cream (see page 6).

Serves 4

For the cider-poached apples
500ml medium cider
1 vanilla pod, split lengthways
1 tsp five-spice powder
250g caster sugar
8 large eating apples, preferably Russet, Cox's or Braeburn
2 lemons

For the nougatine
1kg caster sugar

For the apple brandy fool
1 eating apple, preferably Russet, Cox's or Braeburn
25g unsalted butter
½ vanilla pod, split lengthways
50g caster sugar
Juice of ½ lemon
250ml double cream
1 tbsp icing sugar
25ml apple brandy, preferably Calvados

To serve
Maple syrup
4 sprigs of mint

When making the nougatine, take the sugar off the heat as soon as it reaches golden brown and it will continue to cook in its residual heat. Taking it any further means that it will burn and taste bitter.

APPLE & BLACKBERRY CRUMBLE
with blackberry sorbet & a doughnut
Eddy Rains

The 16th-century Wheatsheaf pub in Somerset is the first head chef role for Eddy Rains, and his modern approach to basic classics and bold flavours has already seen him make his mark. Eddy has travelled widely and trained with some of the world's most celebrated chefs, including Michael Caines and Shaun Rankin. This collection of mini puddings is a fresh take on some delectable, time-honoured favourites.

1   **For the crumble mix,** preheat the oven to 180°C (Gas 4). Lightly rub the butter and flour together in a bowl until breadcrumb-like in texture. Stir in the sugar and oats, spread in a baking tin and cook in the oven for 5–10 minutes until golden brown. Cool and blitz in a food processor to achieve a crumble mix.

2   **For the blackberry sorbet,** combine 250g of the blackberry purée (reserve the rest to make a coulis) and the sugar with 250ml of water in a pan and bring to the boil. Add the glucose and lemon juice and then chill over a bowl of ice. Churn in an ice-cream machine until set.

3   **To make the crumble filling,** peel and finely dice the apple and sweat gently in a small pan with the sugar for 5–10 minutes. Add the blackberries and continue to cook for 2–3 minutes to soften. Put the fruit in a small ovenproof dish, top with the crumble mix, reserving a little for serving, and bake for 5 minutes.

4   **For the doughnuts,** combine the flour, yeast and the sugar in a food processor. Add the melted butter with the egg and milk and mix again, then roll into four balls and leave to prove until doubled in size. Heat the oil to 180°C in a large pan or deep fryer, then deep fry the doughnuts, one at a time, until golden brown. Remove with a slotted spoon and drain on kitchen paper.

5   **For the crème patissière,** whisk together the sugar, yolks, flour and cornflour in a bowl. Put the vanilla seeds and milk into a pan and bring to the boil. Pour a quarter over the egg mixture and then return everything to the pan. Cook for 2 minutes and leave to cool in the fridge before piping into the doughnuts. Finally, roll the doughnuts in extra caster sugar.

6   **To serve,** first make a blackberry coulis. Put the reserved purée and the sugar in a heavy-based pan and heat to reduce gently for 5–10 minutes until it is a syrupy consistency. Paint a swish of coulis across large plates. Place a serving of the crumble on each plate and add a ball of sorbet on some crumble mix. Top the sorbet with a blackberry. Finally, add a doughnut resting on a bed of crème patissière. The chef suggests serving this dessert with a cider and blackberry jelly (see page 6).

Serves 4

For the crumble mix
25g unsalted butter
25g plain flour
25g caster sugar
25g porridge oats

For the blackberry sorbet
300g blackberry purée
125g caster sugar
1 tbsp liquid glucose
1 tbsp lemon juice

For the crumble filling
1 cooking apple, preferably Bramley
25g caster sugar
4 blackberries

For the doughnuts
125g strong flour
10g fresh yeast
20g caster sugar, plus extra for rolling
15g unsalted butter, melted
½ egg
50ml semi-skimmed milk
500ml vegetable oil

For the crème patissière
20g caster sugar
2 egg yolks
1 tsp plain flour
½ tsp cornflour
½ vanilla pod, split lengthways and seeds scraped out
125ml semi-skimmed milk

To serve
25g caster sugar
4 blackberries

TRIO OF BLACKBERRY PUDDINGS

Wayne Carville

The emphasis is firmly on sustainability at Dundrum's Mourne Seafood Bar, where head chef Wayne Carville has his pick of the catch from the local ports. Wayne runs Northern Ireland's only dedicated seafood cookery school, but also turns a skilled hand to thrilling desserts such as this one, which ensures that the full flavour of the fruit is captured.

1 **To make the pastry,** cream together the butter and icing sugar in a bowl until soft and pale. Gradually beat in the vanilla extract and enough egg to make a smooth dropping consistency. Mix in the flour and bring together to form a dough. Knead until the dough is smooth. Wrap in cling film and leave to rest in the fridge for 20 minutes.

2 Preheat the oven to 190°C (Gas 5). Roll out the pastry to line six 5cm-diameter dariole moulds, then line with greaseproof paper and fill with baking beans. Bake blind for 10 minutes. Remove from the oven, take out the paper and beans and return for 5–6 minutes until the middle is cooked. Reduce the oven temperature to 180°C (Gas 4).

3 **For the berry mixture,** put the blackberries into a pan with the sugar and lemon juice. Cook on a high heat for 4–6 minutes until soft.

4 **To make the meringue,** put the sugar in a pan with 35ml of water and boil until the mixture reaches 110°C. Meanwhile, beat the egg white in a large bowl with an electric hand-held mixer until the temperature of the sugar has reached 116°C. Then slowly pour the sugar into the white and continue to beat until they have cooled.

5 **For the curd,** cook 50g of the berry mixture with the egg, sugar, butter and cornflour in a pan over a medium heat for about 5 minutes until well thickened and the cornflour is cooked.

6 **To make the blackberry crumble,** mix the flour with the butter and sugar in a bowl. Set aside a further 50g of the berry mixture and then divide the remaining mixture between another six 5cm-diameter dariole moulds. Top with the crumble and bake in the oven for about 10 minutes until golden.

7 **To make the meringue pie,** remove the pastry cases from their moulds and almost fill with the curd mixture, top with the meringue and toast with a blow torch or put under a hot grill for about 30 seconds.

8 **To make the blackberry mousse,** whip the cream and fold in half of the reserved 50g of the berry mixture. Layer in six shot glasses with the remaining berry mixture and top each with blackberries and a sprig of mint. Pass the remaining berry mixture through a sieve to make a small quantity of coulis.

9 **To serve,** swipe some of the coulis across each plate with a teaspoon, then place each of the three puddings in a line and sprinkle with popping candy and micro herbs (if using).

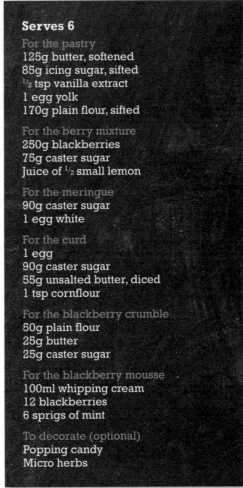

Serves 6

For the pastry
125g butter, softened
85g icing sugar, sifted
1/2 tsp vanilla extract
1 egg yolk
170g plain flour, sifted

For the berry mixture
250g blackberries
75g caster sugar
Juice of 1/2 small lemon

For the meringue
90g caster sugar
1 egg white

For the curd
1 egg
90g caster sugar
55g unsalted butter, diced
1 tsp cornflour

For the blackberry crumble
50g plain flour
25g butter
25g caster sugar

For the blackberry mousse
100ml whipping cream
12 blackberries
6 sprigs of mint

To decorate (optional)
Popping candy
Micro herbs

A gorgeous celebration of blackberry in the shape of a meringue pie, a crumble and a mousse.

BRAMBLE & APPLE BREAD PUDDING
with a light bourbon vanilla cream
Willie Deans

Willie Deans was head chef at some of Scotland's most prestigious establishments before opening his family-run restaurant, Deans @ Let's Eat, near the centre of Perth. Willie specialises in vibrant modern cooking with French accents, his menu led by the best seasonal Scottish produce. Everything, from bread to petits fours, is made in the restaurant, and Willie's bramble and apple bread pudding exemplifies this philosophy, with each element being made from scratch.

1   **To make the apple filling,** peel and core the eating apples and put in cold water with half of the lemon juice. Put the remaining lemon juice and butter into a stainless-steel pan with a tight-fitting lid. Slice the cooking apples into the pan and gently stew for about 5 minutes until tender, then blend in a food processor until smooth. Return to the heat and reduce for a further 10 minutes until thick. Drain and dice the eating apples and combine with the purée. Sweeten to taste, allow to cool slightly and mix in the cornflour. Set aside and keep warm.

2   **To make the green apple juice,** cut the apples into quarters and remove the cores, then freeze for 15 minutes. Put in a food processor with the apple liqueur, blend for 3 minutes and strain the juice into a pan. Heat to reduce to 15ml.

3   **For the bourbon vanilla cream,** whisk the egg yolks in a bowl with one-third of the sugar until pale and of a light ribbon consistency. Sift in the cornflour and mix well. Bring the milk to the boil in a pan with the remaining sugar and the vanilla seeds. As soon as it starts to bubble, pour one-third onto the egg mixture, stirring continuously. Pour the mixture back into the pan and bring to the boil over a low heat, stirring all the time. Simmer for 2 minutes and remove from the heat.

4   Soak the gelatine in a bowl of cold water for 5 minutes to soften. Warm the reduced apple juice, then squeeze the gelatine to drain it and add to the juice, stirring to dissolve. Add the juice to the vanilla cream, followed by the bourbon, to taste. Strain into a clean bowl, cover and allow to cool until tepid.

When baking the puddings, place a lightweight tray on top of them to ensure the filling does not escape.

5   **For the Italian meringue,** pour 40ml of water into a pan and add the sugar and glucose. Bring to the boil, skimming and brushing down the sides of the pan with a brush dipped in water. Cook until the temperature reaches 121°C.

6   Meanwhile, in a separate bowl, beat the egg white with an electric hand-held mixer until firm, keeping an eye on the sugar in the pan. Take the pan off the heat once the meringue has reached 121°C. When the egg white is firm, set the mixer to the lowest speed and pour in the cooked sugar in a thin steady stream. Continue to beat for about 15 minutes until the mixture is tepid. Using a whisk, rapidly beat 1 tbsp of the meringue into the vanilla cream mixture, then gently fold in another 2 tbsp of the meringue until it is completely combined. Place in a bowl and set aside.

7   **For the apricot glaze,** put 1 tbsp of water with the jam in a pan and bring to the boil. Strain and keep warm.

8   **To make the fruit bread pudding,** preheat the oven to 180°C (Gas 4). Cut out eight 5cm-wide greaseproof paper bands, each long enough to line eight 7cm-diameter ring moulds. Butter the moulds and paper strips and fit the strips inside the moulds. Lightly cream the butter with the allspice, cinnamon and honey.

9   Remove the crusts from the bread and trim into lengths to fit the inside edge of the moulds; also cut 16 discs to fit the base and top of each mould. Spread the spiced honeyed butter on both sides of the bread and first line the inside edge of each mould, slightly overlapping the ends, and then insert a disc for the base. Fill each mould with a layer of apple filling followed by a layer of cornflour-dusted blackberries. Repeat until the mould is three-quarters full and top with a bread disc. Bake in the oven for about 15 minutes until golden and crisp. Remove from the oven and allow to settle for 5 minutes.

10 **To serve,** carefully remove the puddings from the moulds and position on serving plates. Brush lightly with the apricot glaze and add a little vanilla cream. The chef suggests serving this dessert with puffed honeycomb ice, a caramel wafer and a dash of blackberry sauce (see page 6).

Serves 8

For the apple filling
2 eating apples, preferably Granny Smith
Juice of 1 lemon
Knob of unsalted butter
2 cooking apples, preferably Bramley
Caster sugar, to taste
20g cornflour
170g blackberries, halved and dusted with cornflour

For the green apple juice
2 eating apples, preferably Granny Smith
25ml apple liqueur

For the bourbon vanilla cream
2 egg yolks
20g caster sugar
½ tbsp cornflour
90ml full-fat milk
½ vanilla pod, split lengthways and seeds scraped out
½ gelatine leaf
20ml bourbon or other whisky

For the Italian meringue
60g caster sugar
1 tsp liquid glucose
1 egg white

For the apricot glaze
50g apricot jam

For the fruit bread pudding
100g butter, softened
Pinch of allspice
Pinch of ground cinnamon
1 tbsp honey
½ medium loaf of sliced white bread

PEAR RISOTTO & CARAMEL CUSTARD
with blackberry jelly doughnuts
Ron Faulkner

'While other kids wanted to be astronauts, I always wanted to be a restaurateur,' says Ron Faulkner, owner of two much-lauded Bristolian favourites, Ronnies of Thornbury and the Muset by Ronnie. Ron's distinguished career has seen him work with Anton Mosimann, whose 'exceptional work ethic' proved a great inspiration, while high-profile catering jobs, including the Prince of Wales's fiftieth birthday celebration and a banquet for the Changing of the Guard, have seen this great chef prove his mettle at the highest level.

1   **For the pear risotto,** peel and grate the pears. Melt the butter in a heavy-based pan. Add the pears, star anise and a quarter of the juice and simmer gently for about 3 minutes. Add the rice and cover with most of the remaining pear juice. Stir occasionally, adding more juice if necessary. Cook for 16–18 minutes until the rice is soft and tender. Its consistency should be fairly fluid, but not runny. Sweeten with the caster sugar, add the brandy and spread in a 30 x 20cm baking tin to cool.

2   **To make the caramel custard,** first melt 50g of the sugar with a little water in a heavy-based pan on a high heat and cook until a deep caramel. Carefully add 50ml of the cream and shake the pan gently to mix together. Bring back to a simmer, then pass through a sieve and set aside.

3   Put the milk and vanilla pod into a separate pan and bring to a simmer. Mix the remaining sugar with the cornflour, 25ml of the cream and the egg yolks into a smooth paste. Then pour the hot milk over the egg mix, constantly stirring. Pour the mix into a clean pan, bring to the boil and gently cook for 4 minutes. Remove from the heat and whisk in the caramel, cover and leave to cool. Whip the remaining 40ml of cream and fold into the caramel.

4   **For the blackberry jelly,** put the blackberries and lemon juice into a food processor with 100ml of water and blend to a purée. Transfer to a pan and bring to the boil, then push through a sieve into a heavy-based pan. Add the sugar, bring to the boil and cook for 10–15 minutes on a low heat. Pour onto a flat tray to cool (or into preserving jars if you're not in a hurry. The blackberry jelly can be made several days in advance).

5   **For the doughnuts,** mix the milk and egg together. Put the flour, yeast, salt and sugar in an electric mixer with a dough hook attached and make a well in the centre. Pour the milk and egg mix into the well and mix slowly. Increase the speed as the mix comes together and then slowly add the butter. Put the dough into an oiled bowl, cover with cling film and put in a warm place until it doubles in size.

6   Knock the dough back and knead on a floured work surface until a workable consistency forms. Divide the dough into two or three pieces and roll each by hand to a 3cm diameter sausage. Cut into 2.5cm pieces to make 12 doughnuts and place on a well-oiled baking sheet. Cover with oiled cling film and leave to prove for 30–40 minutes until doubled in size.

7   Heat the oil to 190°C in a large pan or a deep fryer and deep fry the doughnuts, in batches, for 1–2 minutes until golden brown, turning over halfway through the cooking time. Drain on kitchen paper. Put the blackberry jelly into a piping bag fitted with a narrow nozzle and squeeze some jelly into the centre of each doughnut, then roll the doughnuts in the remaining sugar.

8   **To serve,** place a small amount of the blackberry jelly into a glass and add a couple of spoonfuls of the pear risotto. Cover with caramel custard and pile the warm doughnuts on the side of each plate.

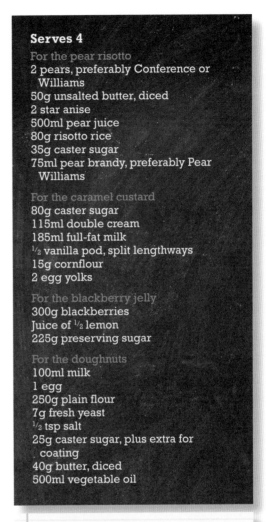

Serves 4

For the pear risotto
2 pears, preferably Conference or Williams
50g unsalted butter, diced
2 star anise
500ml pear juice
80g risotto rice
35g caster sugar
75ml pear brandy, preferably Pear Williams

For the caramel custard
80g caster sugar
115ml double cream
185ml full-fat milk
½ vanilla pod, split lengthways
15g cornflour
2 egg yolks

For the blackberry jelly
300g blackberries
Juice of ½ lemon
225g preserving sugar

For the doughnuts
100ml milk
1 egg
250g plain flour
7g fresh yeast
½ tsp salt
25g caster sugar, plus extra for coating
40g butter, diced
500ml vegetable oil

A deliciously grown-up spin on nursery classics: a delicate, sweet risotto with irresistibly moreish doughnuts.

CREAMED RICE PUDDING
with poached pear & toffee vodka sabayon
Andy Waters

Being named *The Good Food Guide's* Restaurant of the Year for the Midlands is just one of a string of accolades to have been bestowed on Andy Waters' fine-dining restaurant in Birmingham's Brindleyplace. Named after Andy's late father, Edmunds enjoys an enviable reputation for precision cooking, classical technique and all-round excellence; little wonder, given Andy's experience in five-star kitchens across Europe. Despite his classical background, Andy retains a refreshingly down-to-earth approach. 'Put what you love on a plate,' he says. 'If people love and eat it, then it is the best dish.'

Serves 4

For the diced toffee
397g can of condensed milk
100g white chocolate, broken into
  small pieces
Sea salt

For the poached pear
½ vanilla pod, split lengthways and
  seeds scraped out
125g caster sugar
½ cinnamon stick
1 pear, preferably Williams

For the bonfire toffee
125g dark soft brown sugar
Pinch of cream of tartar
30g black treacle
30g golden syrup

For the creamed rice pudding
40g pudding rice
40g caster sugar
½ vanilla pod, split lengthways
150ml full-fat milk
150ml double cream

For the toffee vodka sabayon
3 eggs yolks
50g caster sugar
Toffee vodka, to taste (optional)
Pinch of ground cinnamon
½ vanilla pod, split lengthways and
  seeds scraped out

1 **To make the diced toffee,** pour the condensed milk into a pan and heat over a medium heat for 5–8 minutes, stirring continuously, until reduced by half and slightly darkened. Remove from the heat and add the white chocolate. Stir until it has melted and then chill in the fridge for 2 hours or until it becomes fudge-like in consistency. Sprinkle with sea salt.

2 **For the poached pear,** put the vanilla pod and seeds in a pan with the sugar and cinnamon stick and 600ml of water and slowly bring to the boil. Peel and core the pear, place in the hot syrup and bring back up to the boil. Reduce the heat and simmer for about 20 minutes until the pear is soft to the touch. Allow to cool in the liquid, then drain and dice.

3 **For the bonfire toffee,** line a baking sheet with a silicone mat or baking parchment. Put the sugar and 150ml of water in a heavy-based pan and gently heat until the sugar has dissolved. Add the remaining

ingredients, bring to the boil and heat the caramel up to 160°C (soft crack). Immediately pour onto the prepared baking sheet and leave for about 10 minutes until set. Break into pieces and set aside.

4   **To make the creamed rice pudding,** put all the ingredients into a pan and slowly bring to the boil, stirring continuously. Reduce the heat and simmer for 15–18 minutes, continuing to stir, until the rice is soft. Discard the vanilla pod.

5   **For the toffee vodka sabayon,** put all the ingredients into a glass bowl and set it over a pan of simmering water. Beat the mixture for 3–4 minutes, taking care to mix evenly and scrape the edges of the bowl to prevent lumps forming. The mixture will become lighter in colour and will increase in volume. The sabayon is ready when it has a glossy, creamy consistency. Discard the vanilla pod.

6   **To serve,** put some diced toffee and diced poached pear in the bottom of four shot glasses, fill with the toffee sabayon and top with some crushed bonfire toffee. Place a spoonful of the rice pudding on each plate, dust with more crushed bonfire toffee and scatter around some of the diced toffee. Finish with diced poached pear and then add the shot glass to the side. The chef suggests serving this dish with pear ice cream and decorations of pain d'épices and a spun sugar nest (see page 6).

Divine indulgence by way of silken rice pudding with a crunch of toffee.

COCONUT RICE PUDDING
with a coconut, poppy seed & jaggery samosa
Alfred Prasad

The fact that Alfred Prasad's original career plan – to join the Indian Air Force as a fighter pilot – never took flight is a source of much happiness to diners at London's exquisite Tamarind restaurant where, as executive chef, Alfred delivers a masterclass in northwest Indian cuisine. With a culinary career that began 'as Mum's commis chef', Alfred trained in New Delhi before being head-hunted by the legendary Veeraswamy, where he developed his philosophy of cooking as the 'perfect amalgamation' of art and science.

1   **To make the coconut rice pudding,** simmer the milk with the cinnamon sticks and cloves in a pan for 10 minutes. Strain the milk into a clean pan and add the rinsed rice. Bring to the boil, then reduce the heat and simmer for 30–40 minutes, stirring occasionally to prevent the rice from sticking. Once cooked, add sugar to taste and leave to cool for 20 minutes, stirring occasionally to prevent a skin forming.

2   Open the can of coconut milk and carefully drain off the liquid to leave you with the creamy solids. Combine the whisky with 3 tbsp of the coconut milk solids and then fold this into the cooled rice pudding. Chill in the fridge for 20 minutes, again stirring occasionally to prevent a skin forming.

3   **For the coconut, poppy seed and jaggery samosas,** reserve some of the dried coconut (if using) for decoration and finely grate the rest and set aside. Cut the spring roll wrappers into strips measuring 5 x 15cm and cover with cling film topped with a damp cloth. Combine the plain flour with enough water to make a paste and set aside.

4   To make the filling, mix together the jaggery or sugar, grated dried coconut or desiccated coconut, cardamom seeds, green raisins and cashew nuts. Uncover the spring roll strips, and place one strip in front of you vertically, so you have the 5cm sides at the top and bottom. Place 1 tbsp of the filling 3cm from the top. Take the top right-hand corner and fold it across the filling to meet the left-hand 15cm side (this creates a small triangle with the excess pastry below).

Temperature is extremely important when cooking samosas. Too hot, and the pastry will cook too quickly and leave you with a cold filling. Too cold, and the pastry won't crisp up quickly enough and absorb too much oil leaving you with a soggy samosa.

Serves 6

For the coconut rice pudding
1.7 litres full-fat milk
3 cinnamon sticks
4 cloves
3 tbsp basmati rice, rinsed in cold
 water 2–3 times
2–3 tbsp caster sugar
400ml can of coconut milk (it is
 important not to shake the can)
2 tsp single malt whisky

For the coconut, poppy seed and
 jaggery samosas
1 dried coconut or 3 tbsp desiccated
 coconut
6 spring roll wrappers, each
 measuring 215 x 215mm
2 tbsp plain flour
2 tbsp grated jaggery or cane sugar
Seeds from 2 cardamom pods
1 tbsp green raisins, chopped
1 tbsp cashew nuts, crushed
500ml vegetable oil
2 tbsp poppy seeds

To decorate
8 figs
2 kiwi fruits
4 raspberries
4 strawberries, halved
Green pistachio nuts, shelled, peeled
 and halved
1 sheet of silver leaf (optional)

5   Take the excess pastry and fold it upwards over the triangle and then carefully wrap the remaining flap (on the right corner) around so you are left with the whole thing as a triangle with a small tab running along one side. Brush some of the flour paste onto this tab and seal the edge to completely close the samosa. Repeat the process for the remaining strips of pastry and set aside.

6   To cook the samosas, heat the oil to 180°C in a large pan or a deep fryer. To test the temperature, drop a spare bit of pastry into the oil. It should colour gradually as opposed to immediately. If it turns brown too quickly, remove the pan from the heat briefly to bring the temperature down, or reduce the heat of the deep fryer.

7   Coat the samosa in the flour paste and roll in poppy seeds, then deep fry one at a time for 30–35 seconds or until it turns a pale brown. Take the samosas out of the fat with a slotted spoon and drain on kitchen paper.

8   **For the decoration,** cut out one wedge from each fig, which will then be served as a whole with just the wedge removed. Peel and halve the kiwi fruits lengthways and then slice into thin half moons. Cut the raspberries and strawberries in half lengthways.

9   **To serve,** divide the coconut rice pudding between six 7–8cm-diameter ramekins and place on large plates. Decorate with pistachio halves, a raspberry and flakes of dry coconut and silver leaf (if using). Add a samosa and arrange a cut fig, kiwi slices and half a strawberry at the top of each plate. This dessert is also good topped with a teaspoon of rose sago (see page 6).

HOT CHOCOLATE PUDDING
with honeycomb ice cream
Garry Watson

Fine dining runs in the family at the charmingly intimate Gordon's in Inverkeilor on Scotland's east coast, where head chef Garry Watson cooks alongside his father, and his mother runs front of house. Garry was brought up at the stove, and his confident cooking and sensational flavour combinations work their magic on seasonal Scottish produce cooked simply, but with impressive imaginative flair.

1   **For the liquid centre,** boil the cream with 2 tbsp of water in a pan. Add the butter and stir to melt, then mix in the chocolate and whisky with a hand whisk until smooth. Pour into a small container about 38mm deep and leave in the fridge for 6 hours to set. Cut out eight small cylinders with a narrow pastry cutter and then freeze for about 1½ hours until firm.

2   **For the hot chocolate pudding,** first melt the chocolate and butter in a glass bowl over a pan of simmering water. Mix in the yolks until smooth and then add the almonds and rice. In a separate bowl, whisk the egg whites with a pinch of the caster sugar to soft peaks, then slowly add the remaining sugar, continuing to whisk, until you have a stiff glossy meringue. Fold the meringue into the chocolate mixture.

3   Preheat the oven to 180°C (Gas 4) and line eight 6cm-diameter ring moulds with baking parchment so that it stands 4cm higher than the mould. Stand a frozen cylinder (which will become the liquid centre) in the middle of each ring and pipe in enough of the pudding mix to surround and cover the cylinder, then chill in the fridge for about 20 minutes. Bake in the oven for about 25 minutes until the puddings are set on the top and around the edges, but with a slight wobble in the middle. Remove from the oven (but keep it switched on) and dust with cocoa powder.

4   **For the honeycomb,** put the honey, glucose, sugar and 75ml of water in a large heavy-based pan. Heat to just under 150°C until it forms a golden caramel. Remove the pan from the heat, mix in the bicarbonate of soda and allow to it foam. Pour onto a large baking sheet lined with a silicone mat or baking parchment, allow the mixture to spread out evenly and then leave to cool.

5   **For the ice cream,** lightly mix the egg yolks and sugar in a bowl. In a pan, boil the milk and cream with the grated tonka bean (if using). Soak the gelatine in a bowl of cold water for 5 minutes to soften. Then pour the milk and cream onto the yolks, return to the pan and gently cook until 85°C. Remove from the heat, squeeze the gelatine to drain it and add to the cream, stirring to dissolve, then allow to cool. Churn in an ice-cream machine until set. Break 50g of the honeycomb into small pieces using the end of a rolling pin, and mix it into the set ice cream. Place in the freezer to set once again.

6   **To serve,** transfer the chocolate puddings to plates and add a scoop of the honeycomb ice cream. The chef suggests serving this dessert with croquant biscuits, damson confit and white chocolate (see page 6).

Serves 8

For the liquid centre
400ml double cream
100g unsalted butter
240g dark chocolate (55% cocoa solids), broken into pieces
90ml whisky

For the hot chocolate pudding
220g dark chocolate (55% cocoa solids), broken into pieces
100g unsalted butter
4 egg yolks
80g ground almonds, sifted
20g ground rice, sifted
4 egg whites
80g caster sugar
1 tsp cocoa powder

For the honeycomb
75g runny honey
140g liquid glucose
400g caster sugar
20g bicarbonate of soda

For the ice cream
5 egg yolks
85g caster sugar
210ml full-fat milk
210ml double cream
1 tonka bean, finely grated (optional)
½ gelatine leaf

Indulge your inner child in a sophisticated homage to old-time favourites.

WHITE CHOCOLATE DUCK EGG TART
with textures of brambles
Paul Leary

The Woodhouse restaurant in the Leicestershire village of Woodhouse Eaves is owned and headed by Paul Leary, famed for his grandstanding approach to regional produce. Paul experiments with an array of flavours, textures and embellishments, demonstrated here in his white chocolate duck egg tart with textures of brambles. The choicest local and wild ingredients are used in the dish, with Paul foraging for blackberries and collecting eggs from the ducks in his back garden; though everything here can be re-created using locally bought ingredients.

1   **To make the bramble purée,** put the blackberries in a food processor and blend until smooth. Pass the mix through a sieve and measure out 100g for the leather, 250g for the sorbet and 100g for the compote.

2   **For the bramble leather,** preheat the oven to its lowest setting. Pour the 100g portion of bramble purée onto a baking sheet and leave in the oven overnight until the purée has dried out and lost its shine. Remove the dried purée from the oven and cut into pieces.

3   **To make the bramble sorbet,** first put the sugar with 120ml of water in a heavy-based pan and slowly bring it to the boil to dissolve the sugar. Then continue to boil until it forms a syrup. Add the lemon juice, glucose and the 250g portion of bramble purée and combine well. Leave to cool then churn in an ice-cream machine until set.

4   **For the white chocolate duck egg tart,** first make the pastry. Rub the flour and butter together in a bowl to the consistency of fine breadcrumbs. Mix in the salt and 40g of the caster sugar. Gradually mix in the 2 beaten eggs until a dough is formed (you may not need all of the egg), reserving some of the beaten egg for an egg wash. Wrap the dough in cling film and rest in the fridge for 30 minutes.

5   Butter a 27cm-diameter loose-bottomed tart tin and dust with flour, tapping off the excess. Roll the dough out on a lightly floured surface to 3mm thick. Line the tart tin with the pastry, pressing down into the edges and pulling the pastry over the top lip. Rest in the fridge for about 20 minutes.

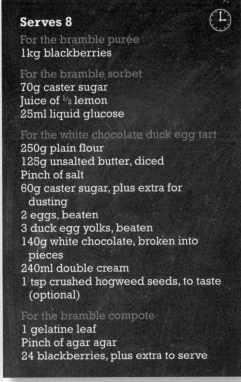

Serves 8

For the bramble purée
1kg blackberries

For the bramble sorbet
70g caster sugar
Juice of ½ lemon
25ml liquid glucose

For the white chocolate duck egg tart
250g plain flour
125g unsalted butter, diced
Pinch of salt
60g caster sugar, plus extra for
    dusting
2 eggs, beaten
3 duck egg yolks, beaten
140g white chocolate, broken into
    pieces
240ml double cream
1 tsp crushed hogweed seeds, to taste
    (optional)

For the bramble compote
1 gelatine leaf
Pinch of agar agar
24 blackberries, plus extra to serve

6   Preheat the oven to 180°C (Gas 4). Line the tart case with cling film and then baking beans and bake blind in the oven for about 25 minutes or until cooked through. Take the tart from the oven, remove the cling film and beans and then brush the inside with the remaining beaten egg. Reduce the oven temperature to 110°C (Gas ¼).

> A fantastically rich and creamy tart with a kick of tangy berries.

7   To make the filling, mix the duck egg yolks and the remaining 20g of sugar in a bowl until pale. Put the chocolate, cream and crushed hogweed seeds (if using) into a glass bowl and warm gently over a pan of simmering water. Stir the melted chocolate into the egg mixture and combine, then pass through a sieve and pour the filling into the tart case. Place in the oven and bake for about 50 minutes or until just set. Remove from the oven, trim the edges and leave to cool at room temperature for 10 minutes before chilling in the fridge. Dust the surface with caster sugar and then caramelise it with a blow torch or put the tart under a preheated grill.

8   **For the bramble compote,** soak the gelatine in a bowl of cold water for 5 minutes to soften. Put the remaining 100g portion of bramble purée into a pan, bring to the boil and then add the agar agar. Squeeze the gelatine to drain it, add to the purée and stir until dissolved. Add the blackberries and then spoon the compote into eight small ramekins. Chill in the fridge for at least 30 minutes until set.

9   **To serve,** cut the tart into eight portions and place one slice on each plate. Add a ramekin of compote next to it and then a quenelle of the sorbet topped with a piece of the bramble leather and some blackberries to decorate. The chef suggests serving this dessert with bramble foam, if you have a cream whipper (see page 6).

CARAMEL CHOCOLATE CUSTARD TART
with yogurt ice cream
Simon Christey-French

Having worked with star chefs such as Michael Caines and Phil Howard, Simon Christey-French is now head chef under Jun Tanaka at London's glamorous Pearl restaurant, where the visual impact of his dishes matches the artistry of the meticulous cooking. He says 'the sky's the limit' when it comes to taking a simple ingredient and turning it into something special.

Serves 4

For the prune purée
100g prunes
100ml orange juice

For the shortbread base
80g unsalted butter
120g plain flour
20g icing sugar
20g caster sugar
20g cornflour
Grated zest of ½ unwaxed lemon
½ vanilla pod, split lengthways and
  seeds scraped out

For the yogurt ice cream
1 vanilla pod, split lengthways and
  seeds scraped out
250ml double cream
250ml milk
4 eggs yolks
50g caster sugar
190g Greek-style yogurt
50g runny honey

For the caramel chocolate custard
  topping
1 vanilla pod, split lengthways and
  seeds scraped out
340ml double cream
110g caster sugar
8 egg yolks
100g caramel milk chocolate, broken
  into pieces

1   **To make the prune purée,** soak the prunes in the orange juice for 1 week, then blend to a purée in a food processor and pass through a sieve. Set aside. Alternatively, to speed up the process, gently boil the prunes in the orange juice for 10 minutes and then blend.

2   **To prepare the shortbread base,** line a baking sheet with baking parchment. Blitz together all the ingredients (use the vanilla seeds only) in a food processor until they reach a crumb-like texture. Mould the crumbs into a ball and roll into a thin sheet on the baking parchment. Leave to rest overnight.

3   **To make the yogurt ice cream,** put the vanilla seeds and pod in a pan with 50ml of the cream and milk and warm through to infuse. In a glass bowl, over a pan of simmering water, whisk the egg yolks and sugar until creamy, then add the infused milk mix and warm through, stirring continuously, until it forms a custard. Meanwhile, in a separate pan, bring the remaining milk and cream to 84°C and then whisk into the custard. Add the yogurt and honey and cook for a few more minutes, stirring the mix until it reaches 84°C once again. Remove the pod, allow to cool and then churn in an ice-cream machine until set.

An excessively pleasurable, creamy indulgence for the ever-so-sinful.

4   **To make the caramel chocolate custard topping,** preheat the oven to 100°C (Gas ¼) and line a 12cm-square silicone mould with two layers of cling film and a layer of foil. Put the vanilla seeds and pod into a pan with the cream and warm to infuse. In a bowl, whisk the sugar and egg yolks with an electric hand-held mixer until pale, then strain in the cream and whisk together. Stir through the chocolate until it has melted, but don't use a whisk because you don't want any air bubbles added. Pour into the prepared mould and cook in the oven for 40–45 minutes until set but with a slight wobble in the middle. Remove from the oven and place in the fridge for about 15 minutes until cooled. Gently remove the mould and cut the topping into four pieces lengthways.

5   **To cook the shortbread,** increase the oven to 180°C (Gas 4), put the baking sheet with the shortbread base in the oven and bake for about 15 minutes until golden. Remove from the oven and cut to the same size as the custard topping.

6   **To serve,** spread the shortbread bases with the prune purée and place on individual plates. Top with a custard slice and finish with a quenelle of the yogurt ice cream. The chef suggests serving this dish with poached apple balls and an apple purée, and you can decorate the tart with a honeycomb spiral (see page 6).

CUSTARD TART
with blackcurrant sorbet
Paul Beckley

Paul Beckley's fine French cuisine with a British twist graces the tables at what is surely Manchester's most opulent dining room, the French at the Midland Hotel. It's a venue with a terrific history, not least as the setting for the Beckhams' first date. Citing a stint at London's Park Lane Hotel as one of his most formative culinary experiences, Paul now takes great pleasure in mentoring young chefs in the French's famous kitchen.

Serves 8

For the blackcurrant sorbet
250g caster sugar
550g blackcurrant purée
15g sorbet stabiliser (optional)

For the custard tart base
110g unsalted butter, diced
40g caster sugar
2 medium eggs
220g plain flour

For the custard tart filling
500ml double cream
9 egg yolks
75g caster sugar
Grated nutmeg

Make sure the golden, rich custard filling has a slight wobble when it comes out of the oven. Delicious.

1 **To make the blackcurrant sorbet,** put the sugar with 500ml of water in a heavy-based pan and heat gently until the sugar has dissolved. Bring to the boil, then add the blackcurrant purée and heat through. Add the sorbet stabiliser (if using) and leave to cool. Churn in an ice-cream machine until set.

2 **To make the custard tart base,** first cream the butter and sugar together in a bowl until pale and fluffy. Beat in the eggs and stir in the flour to form a dough. Chill the dough in the fridge for 30–40 minutes until it is firm enough to roll out.

3 Preheat the oven to 180°C (Gas 4). On a lightly floured surface, roll out the chilled pastry and use it to line a 25cm-diameter loose-bottomed tart tin. Line the pastry case with greaseproof paper and fill with baking beans. Bake blind for about 20 minutes until the base is cooked, then remove the greaseproof paper and beans and bake for a further 5 minutes until the base is just firm and lightly coloured. Remove from the oven. Reduce the temperature to 120°C (Gas ½).

4 **For the filling,** pour the cream into a pan and heat for about 2 minutes until it is lukewarm (37.5°C). Remove from the heat. Beat together the egg yolks and sugar in a large bowl, then pour the warm cream over the egg mixture, stirring continuously. Strain and pour into the tart case, sprinkle with nutmeg and cook for about 25 minutes until set.

5 **To serve,** remove the tart from the tin and cut into eight portions, place on large plates and add a scoop of sorbet. To give a twist to the sorbet, the chef suggests making a liquorice sorbet after the blackcurrant sorbet (see page 6) and, when set, folding them together to form a ripple effect.

SALTED TOFFEE TART
with crème fraîche sorbet
Russell Brown

Good things come in small packages at the bijou 15-seater Sienna in Dorchester, where acclaimed chef-proprietor Russell Brown cooks his seasonally driven modern British cuisine. It's a far cry from Russell's first career running a fishing-tackle business, but technical flair and an instinctive feel for authentic flavours have garnered this self-taught chef acclaim from the highest quarters. Sienna comes in for particular praise for its desserts, and this salted toffee tart achieves exactly what Russell hopes for from his cooking: it 'makes people happy'.

1. **To make the crème fraîche sorbet,** combine the créme fraîche, milk and glycerine in one jug with 50ml of water and the remaining ingredients, except for the citric acid, in another. With an electric hand-held mixer, gradually blend the liquid ingredients into the dry mix. Pass through a sieve, adjust the acidity with a dash of citric acid or some lemon juice, if required, and churn in an ice-cream machine until set.

2. **To make the sweet pastry,** cream the butter and sugar together in a bowl and gradually beat in the egg yolk. Sift the flours together with the salt and fold into the butter mix. Bring together into a dough, wrap in cling film and chill in the fridge for 30 minutes.

3. **For the salted toffee tart filling,** combine the sugars and syrup in a small pan. Over a medium-high heat, heat the mixture to 160°C. Bring the cream to just below a simmer in a separate pan and add to the caramel. Cook over a medium heat until all the caramel has dissolved. Weigh the caramel cream in a bowl and add water to make the weight up to 285g.

4. Whisk the egg yolks with the flour and salt and add the hot cream, whisking continuously. Return the cream to a pan, bring to the boil over a medium heat and cook for around 1 minute to cook the raw flour. If the mix appears to be separating, mix in a drop of cold water. Pass through a sieve into a plastic container. Cover the surface with cling film and chill over a bowl of ice for 30–40 minutes.

5. **To assemble the tart,** preheat the oven to 160°C (Gas 3). Roll out the pastry to about 3mm thick and line four individual small brioche tins with the pastry. Chill for 10 minutes and then line the pastry cases with greaseproof paper and fill with baking beans. Bake blind for about 8 minutes, then remove the baking beans and paper and cook for a further 3–5 minutes until golden brown. Set aside to cool for 10 minutes.

6. **To serve,** fill the tart cases with the toffee filling, dust heavily with icing sugar and glaze with a blow torch. Sit a tart just off-centre on each plate and add a quenelle of sorbet next to each one. The chef suggests serving this dessert with caramel cookie crumbs and orange segments and syrup (see page 6).

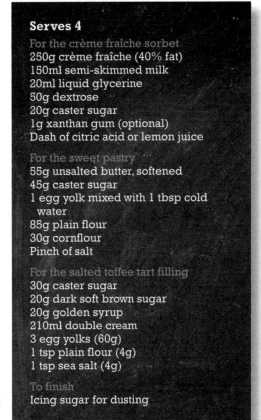

Serves 4

For the crème fraîche sorbet
250g crème fraîche (40% fat)
150ml semi-skimmed milk
20ml liquid glycerine
50g dextrose
20g caster sugar
1g xanthan gum (optional)
Dash of citric acid or lemon juice

For the sweet pastry
55g unsalted butter, softened
45g caster sugar
1 egg yolk mixed with 1 tbsp cold water
85g plain flour
30g cornflour
Pinch of salt

For the salted toffee tart filling
30g caster sugar
20g dark soft brown sugar
20g golden syrup
210ml double cream
3 egg yolks (60g)
1 tsp plain flour (4g)
1 tsp sea salt (4g)

To finish
Icing sugar for dusting

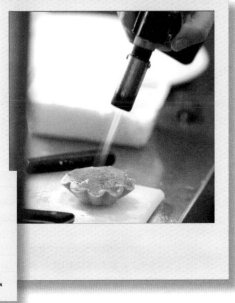

Glazing the tart with icing sugar and a blow torch gives a crisp caramel on top of the tart without overheating the filling.

BARA BRITH & BLACKBERRY TART
with Grand Marnier sorbet
Ludovic Dieumegard

Breton chef Ludovic Dieumegard has a 'French accent when in Wales, and a Welsh accent when in France'. He works this cultural mix to great effect at his restaurant Ludo's at the Coopers in the market town of Newcastle Emlyn, making imaginative use of premium Welsh ingredients in his contemporary European cuisine. He 'eats, lives and breathes food', but learnt more in his time in National Service than four years of catering college could teach him: 'You do what you're told to do; you learn to listen.'

1 **For the Grand Marnier sorbet,** put the sugar and 250ml of water into a pan and bring to the boil. Remove from the heat, add the gellan gum and mix well using a hand-held blender, then bring back up to the boil. Add the Grand Marnier and then stir in the crème fraîche. Churn in an ice-cream machine until set.

2 **To make the tart case,** sift the flour and sugar into a bowl, add the butter and work gently together with your fingertips. Then add the egg yolks and work into a pastry, taking care not to over-work the mixture. Leave in the fridge for at least 30 minutes.

3 **For the jam,** put the sugar and blackberries in a pan on a very low heat. Once the juices start to run out of the berries, increase the heat and cook for about 3 minutes until the mixture turns sticky. Take off the heat and pass through a sieve to remove the seeds. Place in the fridge immediately and leave for about 10 minutes.

4 **To make the tart filling,** put the cake crumbs into a bowl with the lemon zest. Then work in the butter, egg, egg yolk and a pinch of vanilla salt.

5 **To assemble the tarts,** preheat the oven to 180°C (Gas 4). Roll the pastry to a thickness of 3mm and use it to line six 10cm-diameter loose-bottomed tart tins. Line the pastry with a layer of cling film, add baking beans and bake blind for 10–15 minutes until golden brown. Remove the baking beans and cling film and let the pastry cool for 10–15 minutes. Generously spoon some of the jam across the base of each tart and then spread the filling over the top. Set the rest of the jam aside. Sprinkle a little more vanilla salt over the tarts and then bake in the oven for 8–10 minutes until just firm.

Serves 6

For the Grand Marnier sorbet
250g caster sugar
8g gellan gum
30ml Grand Marnier
300g crème fraîche

For the tart case
250g plain flour
75g icing sugar
125g butter, softened
3 egg yolks

For the jam
100g caster sugar
150g blackberries

For the tart filling
150g bara brith or Madeira cake
  crumbs
Grated zest of 1 unwaxed lemon
100g butter, softened
1 egg
1 egg yolk
Vanilla salt

To decorate
30 blackberries
6 liquorice sticks (optional)

You don't have to use bara brith or Madeira cake. You could, for instance, use a lemon drizzle cake as crumbs and then put lemon curd in the bottom instead of jam or Christmas cake and a sweet cranberry jelly – the possibilities are endless.

6 Dilute a little bit of the reserved jam for a sauce by adding a splash of water until it is the consistency of runny honey. If using the liquorice sticks to decorate, soak them in hot water to soften, then slice lengthways and chop each stick into four pieces.

7 **To serve,** drizzle a little of the diluted jam across six plates. Cut a wedge from each tart so you can see the purple jam and brown filling, then put on the plates. Pile eight of the soaked liquorice sticks as a pyre (if using) on each plate and top with the sorbet. Place some fresh blackberries around the side for decoration.

PUMPKIN & BLUEBERRY TARTLET with crema catalana ice cream
Ricardo Gibbs

For Ricardo Gibbs, chef-proprietor of Rick's Café in south London, cooking is a family affair: 'My Spanish mum was a great cook … even my son's a cook, so it's in the genes.' Despite its unassuming name, Rick's Café serves its loyal clientele with vibrant, global food cooked with great skill, all underpinned by Rick's philosophy of involving all five senses in the culinary experience. Renowned for his offbeat sensibility, Rick's pumpkin and blueberry tartlet with crema catalana ice cream references his Spanish heritage and gives a great twist to a seasonal favourite.

Serves 4

For the crema catalana ice cream
100g granulated sugar
¼ vanilla pod, split lengthways
600ml double cream
6 egg yolks, beaten
Grated zest of ½ unwaxed orange
30g milk powder
Small pinch of salt

For the tartlet bases
100g plain flour
50g caster sugar
50g unsalted butter
Splash of warm milk

For the filling
400g peeled pumpkin
2 tbsp runny honey
100ml double cream
1 egg
1 egg yolk
20 blueberries

1 **To make the crema catalana ice cream,** line a baking sheet with a silicone mat or baking parchment. Put the sugar in a heavy-based pan and add 60ml of water. Bring to the boil, without stirring, and continue to boil for about 5 minutes until the sugar caramelises and turns a deep golden brown. Pour onto the prepared baking sheet and leave to set. Once set, roughly break into small chunks, put in a food processor and blitz into a coarse powder.

2 Put the vanilla pod with the remaining ingredients in a pan and gently heat until warm. Remove the vanilla pod, scrape out the seeds and return these to the pan. Continue to cook until the mixture is thick enough to coat the back of a spoon. Remove from the heat and leave to cool for 20 minutes. Then add three-quarters of the burnt sugar powder, transfer to an ice-cream machine and churn until set.

3 **For the tartlet bases,** preheat the oven to 180°C (Gas 4) and lightly butter four 10cm-diameter loose-bottomed tart tins. To make the pastry, mix together the flour and

sugar in a bowl. Add the butter and rub between your fingertips until the mixture resembles fine grains. Add enough warm milk to bind the mixture into a dough, then roll into a ball and turn out onto a lightly floured surface.

4   Divide the pastry into four and roll each piece into a circle 5mm thick with a diameter of 12.5–15cm. Line the prepared tart tins with the pastry and trim the edges using a rolling pin, pressing hard over the top of each tin. Place in the fridge for 6–8 minutes to rest.

5   Line the pastry cases with greaseproof paper and fill with baking beans. Bake blind for 10–12 minutes or until the edges begin to brown. Remove the greaseproof paper and beans and return the tart tins to the oven for a further 6–8 minutes until the bases are cooked. Remove from the oven, but keep it switched on.

6   **To make the filling,** dice the pumpkin into 2cm-square chunks. Dry roast in the oven for 15–20 minutes, ensuring the flesh doesn't brown or colour. Transfer to a food processor, add the honey, cream, egg and egg yolk, and blend to a purée. Fill each case to the top with the pumpkin purée, then return to the oven for 6–8 minutes until the filling starts to set around the edges. Top up each tartlet with any remaining purée to ensure a deep filling and cook for a further 3–4 minutes. Drop fresh blueberries onto the top of each tartlet and bake for a final 3–4 minutes or until the centre of the filling has set, although there should still be a slight wobble in the middle. Remove from the oven and leave to rest for 5–7 minutes.

7   **To serve,** place the warm tartlets on plates, add a scoop of the crema catalana ice cream and dust with any remaining burnt sugar powder.

When lining pastry cases ensure you press the pastry dough right into the edges to remove any trapped air. Trim off the excess but then pull the edge back over the lip of the tartlet cases. This ensures that the pastry doesn't shrink during cooking.

TARTE TATIN OF PEACH
with lemongrass
ice cream
Daniel Green

Perched on its clifftop eyrie, the Auberge in Guernsey enjoys panoramic views, the thrills of which are matched by head chef Daniel Green's high-class modern European cooking. Daniel's classical training in the French kitchens at Harrods underpins the big flavours and clever innovation in his food, as shown in this tarte Tatin of peach with lemongrass ice cream, where a timeless dish is elevated by an exotic twist.

1   **To make the lemongrass ice cream,** first chop the lemongrass stalks into small pieces and pound using the end of a rolling pin to release the juice and bring out the flavour. Pour the cream and milk into a pan, add the lemongrass and bring to the boil. Take off the heat, cover the pan with cling film and leave to infuse for 10 minutes.

2   Meanwhile, put the egg yolks and sugar into a large bowl and whisk until pale and fluffy. Strain the cream and milk mixture and discard the lemongrass. Pour the liquid over the sugar and egg mix and place back on a low heat for 5 minutes, stirring continuously so as not to burn the cream. Remove from the heat and chill, then stir in the lemon juice. Churn in an ice-cream machine until set.

3   **To make the tartes Tatin of peach,** melt the butter and sugar in a pan until it bubbles and stir with a wooden spoon until smooth. Add the vanilla pod and the cinnamon stick and stir to combine, pressing on the vanilla pod to bring out the vanilla seeds inside. Continue simmering for about 5 minutes until caramel in colour. Stir in the brandy, lemon juice and orange zest and continue cooking for about 2 minutes more until smooth. Remove and discard the vanilla pod and cinnamon stick.

4   Preheat the oven to 190°C (Gas 5) and arrange four 10cm-diameter ramekins on a baking sheet. Pour 2 tbsp of the caramel into the bottom of each ramekin and top with half a peach in each. Pour a little more caramel over the peaches and bake for 10–15 minutes until the caramel is bubbling and the peaches are almost tender.

5   Meanwhile, use a cutter or sharp knife to cut the puff pastry into four rounds the same diameter as the ramekins. Remove the ramekins from the oven and turn it up to 200°C (Gas 6). Leave the ramekins to stand for 10–15 minutes to cool slightly. Then top each one with a round of puff pastry and bake for about 10 minutes until the pastry is golden brown. Let the tartes cool for at least 10 minutes.

6   **To serve,** place the tartes in a shallow pan of very hot water set over a medium heat to loosen the caramel. Turn upside down onto plates and add a scoop of lemongrass ice cream. The chef suggests serving this dessert with some sesame seed, salt and chilli praline together with a nest of spun sugar for decoration (see page 6).

Serves 4

For the lemongrass ice cream
5 stalks of lemongrass
250ml double cream
250ml full-fat milk
6 egg yolks
110g caster sugar
2 tsp lemon juice

For the tartes Tatin of peach
120g unsalted butter
200g caster sugar
1/2 vanilla pod, split lengthways
1 cinnamon stick
1 tbsp brandy
1 tbsp lemon juice
1/4 tsp grated orange zest
2 peaches, halved and pitted
1 sheet puff pastry

Pound the lemongrass with the end of a rolling pin or pestle and mortar to release the natural juices, which will result in a more intense flavour than simply chopping.

CHOCOLATE TART
with chocolate shavings & vanilla ice cream
Kevin Harris

Kevin Harris might keep a special place in his heart for 'good old-fashioned fish and chips', but his menus at the Seagrave Arms, a listed Georgian house in the heart of the Cotswolds, are far more ambitious. Combining the classical French skills he acquired under the tutelage of Raymond Blanc with produce sourced from nearby farms, Kevin's confident modern British cuisine has attracted accolades aplenty. A local-food champion, Kevin is committed to keeping food miles low and sustainability high.

1   **For the tart case,** put the vanilla seeds, the remaining dry ingredients and the butter into a food processor and pulse until it resembles breadcrumbs. Transfer to a bowl, add the egg, egg yolk and lemon zest and combine, then turn out onto a floured work surface and knead until smooth. Wrap in cling film and allow to rest in the fridge for 20 minutes.

2   Preheat the oven to 160°C (Gas 3). Roll out the pastry to 5mm thick, cut out 12cm-diameter circles and use these to line four 10cm-diameter loose-bottomed tart tins. Line each pastry case with greaseproof paper and fill with baking beans. Bake blind for 10 minutes, then remove from the oven, take out the beans and greaseproof paper and return to the oven for about 10 minutes until the pastry is golden brown.

3   **For the chocolate filling,** put the chocolate, butter and vanilla seeds in a glass bowl over a pan of simmering water and stir together until the mixture has melted. Put the egg, egg yolks and sugar in another bowl, place over a pan of simmering water and whisk, using an electric hand-held mixer, for about 3 minutes until the mixture becomes thick and pale yellow. Fold the

Serves 4

For the tart case
1 vanilla pod, split lengthways and
    seeds scraped out
270g plain flour, sifted
50g ground almonds
100g icing sugar, sifted
150g unsalted butter, softened
1 egg
1 egg yolk
Grated zest of 1 unwaxed lemon

For the chocolate filling
200g dark chocolate (70% cocoa
    solids), broken into pieces
150g unsalted butter, diced
2 vanilla pods, split lengthways and
    seeds scraped out
1 egg
5 egg yolks
50g caster sugar

For the vanilla ice cream
200ml double cream
300ml full-fat milk
4 egg yolks
75g caster sugar
25ml liquid glucose
1 vanilla pod, split lengthways

For the white chocolate shavings
250g white chocolate

melted chocolate into the egg and sugar mixture and pour into the tart cases. Leave to set for 30 minutes in the fridge.

4   **For the vanilla ice cream,** pour the cream and milk into a pan and bring to the boil. Cream together the egg yolks and sugar in a large bowl and stir in the glucose and vanilla pod. Slowly pour the hot cream and milk into the egg mixture, stirring continuously, then return to the pan and heat to 83°C. Pass through a sieve and cool in the fridge. Churn in an ice-cream machine until set.

A heaven-sent chocolate filling will make sweet-lovers swoon.

5   **For the white chocolate shavings,** break the chocolate into a glass bowl and melt over a pan of simmering water. Pour the chocolate onto a cool marble slab or work surface and spread out with a palette knife until it starts setting. To make the shavings, scoop up the set chocolate with a metal scraper.

6   **To serve,** remove the chocolate tarts from the tins and place each one just off-centre on a large plate. Place chocolate shavings on top of each tart and add a scoop of vanilla ice cream to finish. The chef suggests serving this dessert with an orange espuma, if you have a soda siphon (see page 6).

BITTER CHOCOLATE TART with salted caramel ice cream & popcorn panna cotta
Richard Turner

Sitting on a suburban high street in Harborne, Birmingham, Richard Turner's unpretentious restaurant is a thoroughly relaxed home for dazzling, intricate dishes of a modern European bent. Transforming the restaurant from a place where you would 'wipe your feet on the way out' into a dining experience that counts among Birmingham's elite, Richard admits that 'food and cooking consume his life'. Here, his bitter chocolate tart 'epitomises what we do at Turner's; taking something simple and making it the best dish you've ever tasted.'

1. **For the tart case,** beat the butter, sugar and vanilla seeds in an electric mixer until pale. Add the flour and mix to form a breadcrumb consistency and then add the eggs and mix into a dough. Wrap in cling film and allow to rest in the fridge for 24 hours.

2. **To make the salted caramel ice cream,** put the sugar into a heavy-based pan with 2 tbsp of water, gently heat to dissolve the sugar and then cook to a light caramel. Add the milk and leave to cool and infuse. In a large glass bowl, beat the egg yolks and stir in the infused milk together with a pinch of salt. Cook over a pan of simmering water to 82°C, remove from the heat and leave to cool. Churn in an ice-cream machine until set.

3. **To cook the tart case,** preheat the oven to 180°C (Gas 4). Roll out the pastry onto a lightly floured surface to 2–3mm thick and 25cm in diameter. Line an 18cm-diameter loose-bottomed tart tin with the dough, pressing the pastry into the sides of the tin and trimming the edges (you can freeze any pastry that is left over to use in the future). Line the pastry case with cling film and fill with baking beans and bake blind for 15–20 minutes. Remove the cling film and baking beans and then bake for a further 10 minutes or until the base is cooked through. Remove from the oven and leave to cool slightly. Reduce the oven temperature to 100°C (Gas ¼).

4. **To make the tart filling,** first put the milk and cream into a pan and bring to the boil. Put the chocolate into a bowl, then pour over the milk and cream mix and stir until the chocolate has melted. Add the eggs and mix well to combine. Pour the filling into the tart case and cook for about 20 minutes or until the filling is set but still has a slight wobble in the middle. Remove from the oven and leave to cool to room temperature.

5. **For the popcorn panna cotta,** pour the cream and milk into a pan and bring to the boil. Add the popcorn, cover with a lid and leave to infuse for 15–20 minutes. Soak the gelatine in a bowl of cold water for about 5 minutes to soften. Pass the cream and milk through a sieve into a jug and put 3–4 tbsp into a pan and warm through. Squeeze the gelatine to drain it, add to the warmed milk mixture and stir until dissolved. Return this mixture back into the remaining milk. Combine well and then pass once more through a sieve. Pour into six 6.5cm-diameter dariole moulds and then place in the fridge for 3–4 hours until set.

6. **To serve,** unmould the panna cottas by quickly dipping each mould into warm water. Invert each onto a plate and tap the mould to release. Cut the chocolate tart into six slices and place on the plates with a ball of the ice cream. Decorate with popcorn, a sprinkling of sea salt and gold leaf (if using). The chef suggests serving this dessert with toffee hazelnuts and a swirl of caramel sauce (see page 6).

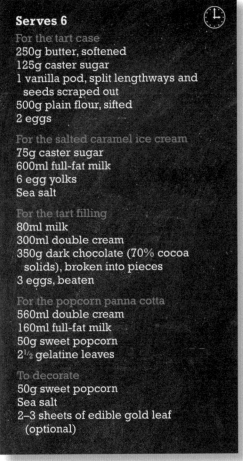

Serves 6

For the tart case
250g butter, softened
125g caster sugar
1 vanilla pod, split lengthways and
  seeds scraped out
500g plain flour, sifted
2 eggs

For the salted caramel ice cream
75g caster sugar
600ml full-fat milk
6 egg yolks
Sea salt

For the tart filling
80ml milk
300ml double cream
350g dark chocolate (70% cocoa
  solids), broken into pieces
3 eggs, beaten

For the popcorn panna cotta
560ml double cream
160ml full-fat milk
50g sweet popcorn
2½ gelatine leaves

To decorate
50g sweet popcorn
Sea salt
2–3 sheets of edible gold leaf
  (optional)

A sophisticated treat to satisfy sweet-toothed connoisseurs.

ALMOND TARTLET
with elderflower jelly & clotted cream fool
Mickael Weiss

'I know the value of food, and I don't mean price,' says Mickael Weiss, head chef at the landmark City restaurant Coq d'Argent, and passionate supporter of the charity Action Against Hunger. Leaving his native France for London two weeks before his 18th birthday, Mickael has flourished in England, working in some of the country's most famous kitchens, including Le Gavroche and Le Manoir aux Quat'Saisons. 'The French way of cooking has never gone out of fashion,' he says. 'It is the basis of food.'

1   **To make the elderflower jelly,** soak the gelatine in a bowl of cold water for about 5 minutes to soften. Warm 100ml of water in a pan. Squeeze the gelatine to drain it, add to the warm water and stir until dissolved. Add the cordial and leave to set in a flat container in the fridge.

2   **For the blackberry coulis,** put the berries in a food processor and blend to a purée, checking acidity and adding sugar to taste. Pass through a sieve.

3   **For the clotted cream fool,** whip the creams and yogurt to soft peaks and semi-fold in 100ml of the blackberry coulis. Place the rest of the coulis in the fridge for serving. Transfer the clotted cream fool to a piping bag and leave in the fridge until you are ready to serve.

> When making the jelly, make sure the elderflower cordial is chilled in the fridge just before using so it cools the jelly mixture when added.

4   **To make the almond tartlets,** cream the sugar and butter together in a bowl and add the almond essence, to taste. Add a small pinch of salt followed by the egg and yolks. Fold in the ground almonds and Amaretto, transfer the mixture to a piping bag and chill in the fridge for 20 minutes.

5   Preheat the oven to 165°C (Gas 3) and grease six 10cm-diameter loose-bottomed tart tins. Pipe one layer of the almond filling into the prepared tart tins and add a spoonful of blackberry coulis in the centre. Top with more almond mix and finish with a few flaked almonds. Bake for 14–16 minutes until golden and remove from the oven. Leave to cool and then gently remove from their tins.

6   **To serve,** place some chopped jelly at the bottom of each glass, top with blackberry coulis and then fill the glasses with the clotted cream fool. Place on large plates and add an almond tartlet to each one. The chef suggests serving this dessert with chocolate nib croustillants topped with elder sorbet and decorated with caramelised almonds as well as adding some pink candyfloss over the clotted cream fool; when elderflowers are in season, you might want to make your own cordial (see page 6).

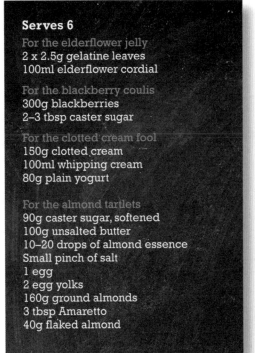

Serves 6

For the elderflower jelly
2 x 2.5g gelatine leaves
100ml elderflower cordial

For the blackberry coulis
300g blackberries
2–3 tbsp caster sugar

For the clotted cream fool
150g clotted cream
100ml whipping cream
80g plain yogurt

For the almond tartlets
90g caster sugar, softened
100g unsalted butter
10–20 drops of almond essence
Small pinch of salt
1 egg
2 egg yolks
160g ground almonds
3 tbsp Amaretto
40g flaked almond

PUMPKIN TART
with chestnut sorbet & candied walnuts
Ashley Wright

Sheltering on the edge of Dartmoor in the charming village of Chagford, the bijou 22 Mill Street has just 22 covers – each enjoying head chef Ashley Wright's dedication to the finest-quality, freshest local ingredients. 'Simple, yet effective' is Ashley's food philosophy, matching the stripped-down elegance of 22 Mill Street's restaurant-with-rooms. In devising his pumpkin tart, Ashley wanted to highlight the culinary potential of this much underrated vegetable.

1   **For the tart filling,** preheat the oven to 180°C (Gas 4). Peel and deseed the pumpkin and cut the flesh into large cubes. Bake in a covered ovenproof dish for about 45 minutes until the pumpkin is soft. Remove from the oven, but keep the oven switched on throughout the method.

2   **For the fig carpaccio,** thinly slice the figs and lay them on six large plates in a circle with the slices slightly overlapping each other. Place in the fridge until needed.

3   **To make the tart case**, rub together the flour and butter in a large bowl until it forms rough breadcrumbs. Add the egg and 25ml of water and mix until it forms a dough. Roll out the pastry on a lightly floured work surface, line an 18cm-diameter loose-bottomed tart tin and place it in the fridge to rest.

4   **For the chestnut sorbet,** put the sugar with 300ml of water in a heavy-based pan and heat gently until the sugar has dissolved. Increase the heat and boil for 5 minutes, then leave to cool. Put the chestnut purée into a bowl and add 250ml of the syrup, keeping the remaining syrup in the pan. Churn in an ice-cream machine until set.

5   **For the candied walnuts,** put the walnuts in the pan with the remaining syrup and boil for 5 minutes. Heat the oil to 140°C in a large pan or a deep fryer and deep fry the walnuts for about 5 minutes until browned. Remove from the oil with a slotted spoon and drain on kitchen paper.

6   **To cook the tart filling,** in a large bowl mix 225g of the baked pumpkin with the spices, eggs, milk and sugar using an electric hand-held mixer. Pour the pumpkin mixture carefully into the lined tart tin and bake for 45 minutes until set. Remove the tart from the oven and set aside to cool.

7   **For the tuiles,** mix together the butter, flour, sugar and egg white in a bowl with an electric hand-held mixer. Stir in the cinnamon and place in the fridge for 30 minutes to firm up. Line a baking sheet with a silicone mat or baking parchment, spread the mixture over it and bake for about 8 minutes until golden.

8   **To serve,** remove the plates with the fig slices from the fridge. Cut the tart into slices and place a slice on the figs with a scoop of sorbet next to it, dressed with a tuile. Arrange candied walnuts around the plate to finish.

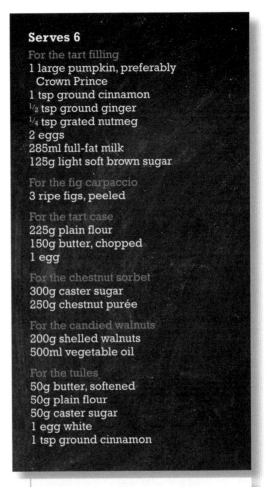

Serves 6

For the tart filling
1 large pumpkin, preferably Crown Prince
1 tsp ground cinnamon
½ tsp ground ginger
¼ tsp grated nutmeg
2 eggs
285ml full-fat milk
125g light soft brown sugar

For the fig carpaccio
3 ripe figs, peeled

For the tart case
225g plain flour
150g butter, chopped
1 egg

For the chestnut sorbet
300g caster sugar
250g chestnut purée

For the candied walnuts
200g shelled walnuts
500ml vegetable oil

For the tuiles
50g butter, softened
50g plain flour
50g caster sugar
1 egg white
1 tsp ground cinnamon

With cinnamon and ginger, a heaven-sent pumpkin tart that will melt in your mouth after teasing your tastebuds.

LEMON MERINGUE PIE with a mango parfait
Sue Ellis

Appreciative from a young age of the virtues of home-grown produce from her father's allotment, head chef Sue Ellis confesses to being 'amazed' at seeing tinned food in her friends' kitchens. She has retained that ethos of using 'only fresh ingredients, locally grown' at Belle House, where she brings her Med-influenced French cuisine to an enthusiastic Worcestershire audience. A driven, ideas-led chef, Sue honed her craft at Gordon Ramsay's Royal Hospital Road and the French Laundry in San Francisco.

Serves 4

For the lemon meringue filling
150g caster sugar
Grated zest and juice of 2 lemons
3 medium eggs
110ml double cream

For the mango parfait
1 egg
1 egg yolk
1 vanilla pod, split lengthways and
  seeds scraped out
40g caster sugar
210ml double cream, lightly whipped
50g mango purée

For the mango jelly
1 gelatine leaf
45g caster sugar
45g mango purée

For the meringue
2 egg whites
70g caster sugar
70g icing sugar, plus extra for dusting

For the shortbread bases
65g strong flour
25g icing sugar
½ vanilla pod, split lengthways and
  seeds scraped out
50g unsalted butter, softened
½ egg

1   **For the lemon meringue filling,** preheat the oven to 160°C (Gas 3). Mix all the ingredients together and pass through a sieve, then pour into a 30cm-diameter cake tin and cook for 16–18 minutes until thickened. Whisk the mixture then churn in an ice-cream machine until set.

2   Scoop the mixture out of the ice-cream machine into a plastic container and freeze for 20 minutes to firm it up. Transfer the mixture into a piping bag and pipe into four 6cm-diameter ring moulds on a baking sheet. When the moulds are three-quarters full, smooth off the top with a warm spoon and put in the freezer for 20 minutes.

3   **To make the mango parfait,** preheat the oven to 180°C (Gas 4). Whisk the egg and egg yolk in a bowl with the vanilla seeds. Put the sugar in a deep baking tin and warm in the oven for 5 minutes (if your oven is fan assisted turn off the oven before you put in the sugar). Then mix the sugar with the eggs using an electric hand-held mixer for about 5 minutes until it reaches a light, foamy custard-like consistency and has doubled in size. Fold in the cream and the mango purée, then pour the mixture into four 5cm-diameter ramekins and freeze for 2 hours.

4   **For the mango jelly,** lightly oil an ice-cube tray and soak the gelatine in a bowl of cold water for about 5 minutes to soften. Put the sugar in a pan together with 140ml of water and bring to the boil. Squeeze the gelatine to drain

it, add to the syrup together with the mango purée and stir until dissolved. Pass the mixture through a sieve and into the ice-cube tray to about 1cm deep. Put the jelly in the fridge for about 1 hour until set.

5 **To make the meringue,** preheat the oven to 120°C (Gas ½), then line a baking sheet with a silicone mat or baking parchment and lightly dust with icing sugar. Using the same sized ring mould as for the lemon meringue filling, make four outlines in the icing sugar as a guide for the meringue. Whisk the egg whites and caster sugar together in a bowl until they are stiff using an electric hand-held mixer, then fold in the icing sugar.

6 Transfer the meringue to a piping bag fitted with a small nozzle and pipe the meringue into four circles (using the excess mixture to make extra meringues to use another time). Dust the peaks with icing sugar and cook for 12–15 minutes, then freeze for a minimum of 20 minutes (they can be left in the freezer overnight if needed). Increase the oven temperature to 160°C (Gas 3).

You'll always find room for this truly scrumptious lemon pie topped with fairy-light meringue.

7 **For the shortbread bases,** put the flour, sugar, vanilla seeds and butter into a food processor and blend until combined. Add the egg and mix until it becomes a paste, then leave the mixture to rest for 30 minutes. Roll out until it is about 2mm thick and, using the same-sized ring mould as for the lemon meringue and a ramekin as for the parfait, cut out four circles in each size. Transfer to a baking sheet and cook for about 8 minutes until lightly golden. Leave to cool for about 10 minutes.

8 **To serve,** warm the lemon meringue fillings slightly with a blow torch (or between warmed hands) and dip the mango parfaits in warm water to unmould them. Place one of each size of shortbread circle on a large plate. Put a lemon meringue filling on top of the larger circle and a mango parfait on top of the smaller. Top the lemon meringues with a meringue peak, then turn the jelly out of the ice-cube tray and add some mango jelly cubes. The chef suggests serving this dish with a cucumber and lime sorbet and apricot purée, and creating a spun sugar decoration (see page 6).

WARM SEA SALT & LAVENDER BROWNIE
with chocolate ganache
Jonathan Taylor

One of Berkshire's most historic inns, the Pot Kiln dates back to the early 18th century, and head chef Jonathan Taylor stays true to the hostelry ethos, serving gloriously honest, local fare, observant of the seasons and the inn's environs. Previously of the Dorchester and Highclere Castle, Jonathan is quite clear about the whys and the wherefores of his craft: 'Chefs get obsessed with processes and techniques, but it's there to be eaten at the end; it is the enjoyment of it that matters most.'

Serves 4

For the lavender-infused olive oil
20g fresh or 10g dried lavender
   flowers
200ml extra-virgin olive oil

For the lavender brownies
250g dark chocolate (70% cocoa
   solids), broken into pieces
220g unsalted butter, diced
3 egg yolks
2 eggs
250g caster sugar
120g plain flour
40g cocoa powder
1 level tsp baking powder
Few drops of vanilla extract
60g roasted hazelnuts, chopped
1 tsp sea salt
Grated zest of 1 unwaxed orange

For the chocolate ganache
250ml double cream
250g dark chocolate (50–60% cocoa
   solids), broken into pieces
Knob of unsalted butter
Pinch of salt
Few drops of vanilla extract
   (optional)

To serve
Pinch of sea salt
Lavender flowers

1   **To make the lavender-infused olive oil,** first scrunch the lavender flowers to release their essence, cram into a bottle and fill with the oil. Leave for a day. This will keep for a long time, but remove the lavender after 2–3 days.

2   **For the lavender brownies,** preheat the oven to 180°C (Gas 4) and thoroughly butter a 23 x 23cm baking tin deep enough to hold the mix as it rises. Put the chocolate and butter in a glass bowl over a pan of simmering water. Stir the chocolate and butter until they have melted.

3   Put the egg yolks, whole eggs and sugar into a food mixer and whisk briskly for 5–6 minutes until they are light and fluffy. Slow the mixer and pour the melted chocolate and butter onto the egg mixture. When fully incorporated, remove the bowl from the mixer. Sift the flour, cocoa powder and baking powder into a separate bowl and slowly fold into the chocolate mixture. Add 1 tsp of the lavender-infused olive oil and then the vanilla extract, hazelnuts, salt and orange zest. Put the mix into the prepared baking tin and cook for 25–30 minutes until it has risen. Be careful not to overcook; the brownie needs to be quite moist and gooey in the centre.

4   **For the chocolate ganache,** pour the cream into a pan and heat it slowly until just below boiling point. Add the chocolate and whisk it until it has melted. Remove from the heat, then whisk in the butter and finally add the salt and vanilla extract (if using). Pour into a dish and allow to set.

5   **To serve,** cut the brownie into individual portions and warm gently in a low oven for a few minutes. Place on plates and use a warm dessertspoon to scoop a ball of the ganache on to the top of the brownie. Decorate the plate with a little sea salt, a few lavender flowers and a splash of lavender-infused oil. The chef suggests serving this dish with a cup of coffee jelly with malted cream piped on top (see page 6).

In place of the lavender-infused olive oil you could simply use extra-virgin olive oil.

BEETROOT BROWNIE
with a beetroot & berry compote & cardamom panna cotta
Grant Young

Faced with a choice of fixing the car with his dad or baking with his mum, Grant Young chose the latter; and he's never looked back. After stints at the esteemed Goring Hotel and Champneys Health Resort, Grant established a true local gem in Hemel Hempstead's Restaurant 65, where his deceptively straightforward, finely balanced dishes have won him national acclaim. And with five separate martial arts under his belt, we're not about to argue.

1   **To cook the beetroot,** put them in a pan and cover with water. Bring to the boil, reduce the heat and simmer for 20–25 minutes until cooked through. Drain, leave to cool and then peel.

2   **To make the cardamom panna cotta,** put the cream, cardamom pods, milk and icing sugar into a pan and warm to a simmer. Remove from the heat and leave to infuse for 10 minutes. Soak the gelatine in a bowl of cold water for about 5 minutes to soften. Squeeze the gelatine to drain it, add to the cardamom cream mixture and stir until dissolved. Strain through a sieve, then blitz with a hand-held blender and pass through a sieve into a jug. Add the yogurt and crème fraîche and combine until smooth. Pour into six 50ml dariole moulds and leave in the fridge for about 2 hours to set.

3   **For the beetroot and berry compote,** wash the berries under cold water and allow to drain. Finely dice 50g of the cooked beetroot and mix with the berries.

4   **For the mixed-berry coulis,** chop 50g of the beetroot and mix it with the berry juice in a pan over a gentle heat. Add icing sugar to taste – you want the coulis to be slightly tart, but not too tart, so add sugar accordingly. When the coulis is thick enough to coat the back of a spoon, remove the pan from the heat and, once it is cool, carefully stir a spoonful of the coulis into the beetroot and berry compote.

5   **For the beetroot brownies,** preheat the oven to 180°C (Gas 4) and line a 20 x 23cm baking tin with greaseproof paper. Put the chocolate into a glass bowl and stand over a pan of simmering water to melt. Add the egg yolks and oil and mix together. Grate 100g of the beetroot into the mix and combine well. Then add the orange zest and juice and mix together.

Serves 6

For the beetroot
2 large beetroot

For the cardamom panna cotta
50ml double cream
20 cardamom pods
100ml skimmed milk
100g icing sugar
3 gelatine leaves
100g Greek-style yogurt
100g crème fraîche

For the beetroot and berry compote
200g mixed berries, such as
   strawberries, blackberries,
   blueberries, redcurrants

For the mixed-berry coulis
20ml mixed berry juice
25g icing sugar

For the beetroot brownies
150g dark chocolate (70% cocoa
   solids), broken into pieces
50ml walnut oil
Grated zest and juice of 2 unwaxed
   oranges
75g plain flour
25g cocoa powder
100g caster sugar
3 eggs, separated
100g broken walnuts

To decorate
Sprig of mint
Icing sugar, for dusting

6   Sift together the flour and cocoa powder into a bowl and stir in the sugar, then fold into the chocolate mixture. Whisk the egg whites to soft peaks with an electric hand-held mixer and then fold them into the chocolate mixture followed by the walnuts. Combine well and pour into the prepared baking tin. Spread the mix evenly and bake for 7–8 minutes until risen and crisp on the outside but still soft in the centre – a knife inserted in the middle should come out wet but the top should be crisp. Remove from the oven and set aside to cool, then turn the cake out of the tin and cut into individual portions.

7   **To serve,** unmould the panna cottas by warming the moulds slightly with a blow torch (or between warmed hands), then turn them out onto plates. Add some of the beetroot and berry compote and a portion of brownie and drizzle the coulis around the plates. Decorate with a sprig of mint and dust with a little icing sugar.

DARK CHOCOLATE CAKE with milk chocolate honeycomb & white chocolate ice cream
Olly Jackson

Desserts have been singled out for special praise at New Yard Restaurant in Cornwall, so it's only fitting that head chef Olly Jackson presents his delectable chocolate trio here. A former coach house on the historic Trelowarren Estate, New Yard prides itself on utilising the produce from its bucolic surroundings. With over 90 per cent of his ingredients being sourced from within a 15-mile radius, Olly is a true champion of local produce.

1 **To make the white chocolate ice cream,** put the cream and milk in a pan over a low heat and bring to the boil. Meanwhile, whisk the eggs and the sugar together. When the milk and cream mix has come to the boil, pour it over the eggs and sugar, stirring continuously.

2 Pour the mixture back into the pan and return to the heat for about 1 minute until the mixture is thick enough to coat the back of a spoon. Strain it through a sieve and then add the white chocolate and stir until the chocolate has melted and is incorporated into the mixture. Put into the fridge to chill for 20–25 minutes before churning in an ice-cream machine until set.

3 **For the chocolate honeycomb bar,** line a 30 x 20cm baking tin with greaseproof paper and line a 15 x 8cm baking tin with cling film. Put the sugar, glucose, honey and 20ml of water in a pan. Bring it to the boil, reduce the heat and simmer until the temperature reaches 170°C. Remove the pan from the heat for about 10 seconds before adding the bicarbonate of soda and whisking together. Quickly pour the frothing mixture onto the greaseproof paper, leave to cool for about 20 minutes, then break into 1cm-sized pieces.

4 Warm the cream over a low heat and when it begins to boil take it off the heat and add the chocolate, allowing it to melt. Add two-thirds of the honeycomb pieces and mix together with the chocolate (store the rest of the honeycomb in an airtight container for enjoying at another time). Pour the mix into the prepared tin and place in the fridge to set.

5 **To make the dark chocolate cake,** preheat the oven to 180°C (Gas 4) and line a 23cm-diameter cake tin with greaseproof paper. Put the chocolate into a glass bowl, add the butter and melt them together over a pan of simmering water. Meanwhile, mix together the cocoa powder, sugar and egg yolks for 4–5 minutes until they are light and fluffy. In a separate bowl, whisk the egg whites to soft peaks. Stir the chocolate mixture into the egg yolk mixture, then fold in the egg whites.

6 Pour into the cake tin and bake for 30 minutes. Remove from the oven and allow the cake to stand for 10 minutes, then place a saucer on top of the cake so it sinks in the middle. Allow it to cool for about an hour and then remove the cake from the tin.

7 **To serve,** put a honeycomb bar and a small slice of the cake on each plate and add a scoop of the ice cream. The chef suggests serving this dessert with a dark chocolate and cardamom ganache and decorated with chocolate tuiles (see page 6).

Serves 8

For the white chocolate ice cream
150ml double cream
150ml full-fat milk
3 egg yolks
75g caster sugar
75g white chocolate, broken into pieces

For the chocolate honeycomb bar
80g caster sugar
2 tbsp liquid glucose
70g runny honey
10g bicarbonate of soda
100ml double cream
300g milk chocolate, broken into pieces

For the dark chocolate cake
150g dark chocolate (70% cocoa solids), broken into pieces
100g unsalted butter, diced
1½ tbsp cocoa powder
85g caster sugar
3 eggs, separated

Each part of this dish can be made individually, such as the honeycomb bar as a snack, or they can all be made in advance for the ultimate dinner party dessert.

CHOCOLATE SWEET BOX
Andrew Nutter

A healthy dose of sibling rivalry sparked Andrew Nutter's journey to professional cooking; following his sister's success in a junior Cook of the Year competition, he embarked on a mission to take the prize for his own. Taking his craft one step further as an apprentice at the Savoy, Andrew eventually opened Nutters, now housed in a Georgian manor house, where he has established a sterling reputation for adventurous and inventive modern British cuisine.

Serves 5

For the chocolate sweet box
Two 30 x 40cm chocolate transfer sheets
200g white, milk or dark chocolate pistoles or drops (to match the transfer)
1 tsp popping candy pellets

For the brownie slab
2 medium eggs
170g caster sugar
Few drops of vanilla extract
90g butter, melted
140g dark chocolate pistoles (70% cocoa solids)
40g plain flour
40g cocoa powder

For the chewy flapjack
60g unsalted butter, softened
50g golden syrup
25g light soft brown sugar
60g porridge oats
25g plain flour
40g dried mango, diced
40g dried blueberries, diced
40g dried cherries, diced

For the classic honeycomb
160g caster sugar
25g runny honey
60ml liquid glucose
8g bicarbonate of soda

1   **To make the chocolate sweet box,** cut out five 7 x 23cm strips from the transfer sheets. Pour the chocolate into a glass bowl and melt in the microwave on a medium setting for 10 seconds. Remove from the microwave, stir and put back in the microwave for 10 seconds; remove and stir. Continue this process until the chocolate is shiny and tempered to 34°C.

2   Spread about 2 tbsp of the melted chocolate over each strip. Leave to set slightly, then form each strip into a cylinder shape and place in a 7cm-diameter ring mould to help the setting process and hold it in place. Place for 10 minutes in the fridge to set.

3   To create a lid for each box, cut five 7cm-diameter discs out of the transfer sheets. Spread about ½ tbsp of the melted chocolate over each disc. Leave for 10 minutes in the fridge to set. Then peel the transfer sheets off each cylinder and disc to reveal your finished pieces. Set aside.

4   **To make the brownie slab,** preheat the oven to 150°C (Gas 2) and line and butter a 20 x 20cm baking tin. Put the eggs and sugar into a large bowl and, using an electric hand-held mixer, whisk them together for about 5 minutes until pale and fluffy. Whisk in the vanilla extract. In a separate bowl, pour the melted butter over the chocolate and leave until partially melted. Add to the egg mixture and continue mixing the ingredients together for about 1 minute.

5   In another bowl, sift together the flour and cocoa powder. Reduce the speed of the mixer, add the sifted flour and cocoa to the eggs and sugar and mix well for about 1 minute. Spoon the mixture into the prepared baking tin, spread evenly and bake for about 15 minutes until the chocolate brownie is set but still squidgy. Remove from the oven and set aside to cool. Using a 7cm-diameter cutter, cut out five brownies.

6   **For the chewy flapjack,** preheat the oven to 180°C (Gas 4) and line and butter a second 20 x 20cm baking tin. Melt the butter, golden syrup and sugar together gently in a pan for 3–4 minutes until foaming. Remove from the heat, stir in the remaining ingredients and transfer to the baking tin. Cook for about 12 minutes until golden and chewy, then leave to cool for 10 minutes and cut into chunks or bite-sized pieces.

7   **For the classic honeycomb,** put the sugar, honey, glucose and 60ml of water into a large heavy-based pan. Bring to the boil, then reduce the heat and simmer for about 5 minutes until it turns a light toffee colour. Remove from the heat and quickly whisk in the bicarbonate of soda. Leave it to grow – the mixture will treble in size, so be careful it doesn't spill everywhere. Pour out onto a silicone mat or baking parchment, leave for about 10 minutes to cool and then break into shards.

8   **To serve,** fill the box with alternating layers of the brownies, flapjack and honeycomb, scatter over the popping candy pellets and then top off with the lid. The chef suggests serving this dessert with chocolate sauce, some marshmallow fluff and nutty brittle (see page 6).

TEXTURES OF ENGLISH PEARS WITH PARSNIP & VANILLA
Michael Bremner

From the time his mum handed him a rose made out of a tomato, the young Michael Bremner was hooked on the possibilities of food; to this day he enjoys 'forward cooking', using modern techniques to extract optimum flavour from local Sussex ingredients. Head chef at Due South, on the Brighton sea front, Michael is passionately committed to sustainable sourcing, working closely with artisan producers, fishermen and farmers from within a 35-mile radius of the restaurant.

Serves 8

For the parsnip purée
200g parsnip
200ml full-fat milk
½ vanilla pod, split lengthways and seeds scraped out

For the stock syrup
160ml caster sugar
50ml liquid glucose

For the pear sorbet
2 large pears
1 tbsp pear liqueur

For the poached pear fluid gel
2 underripe pears, preferably Conference or Comice
150g caster sugar
2 star anise
½ tsp ground ginger
4 cloves
2 tbsp runny honey
250ml red wine
1 tsp agar agar

For the parsnip cake
3 eggs
1 egg yolk
60g caster sugar
60g plain flour
Salt

1   **To make the parsnip purée,** peel, core and chop the parsnip. Add to a pan with the milk, vanilla pod and seeds. Bring to the boil, then reduce the heat and simmer for about 10 minutes until the parsnip is soft. Purée the mix with a hand-held blender and then pass through a sieve and allow to cool.

2   **To make the stock syrup,** put the sugar and glucose with 290ml of water in a heavy-based pan and heat gently until the sugar has dissolved. Bring to the boil for 5 minutes.

3   **For the pear sorbet,** peel and chop the pears and put into a bowl with the pear liqueur and 250ml of the stock syrup. Purée together with a hand-held blender. Churn in an ice-cream machine until set.

4   **For the poached pear fluid gel,** peel, core and quarter the pears, then put them into a pan with the sugar, spices, honey and enough red wine to cover. Bring to the boil, then reduce the heat, cover with a lid or piece of greaseproof paper, and simmer for 5–7 minutes until just tender. Carefully remove the pears, leaving behind the star anise. Strain the mix, keeping the liquid, and use

enough of it to purée the pears until smoothie-like with a hand-held blender.

5   Weigh out 500g of the purée into a clean pan and add the agar agar. Bring to the boil and then remove from the heat. Transfer to a bowl and place in the fridge for about 10 minutes to set, then purée again with the hand-held blender to obtain a fluid gel. Keep in the fridge.

6   **For the parsnip cake,** preheat the oven to 180°C (Gas 4). Beat the eggs, egg yolk and sugar in a bowl until pale and fluffy. Sift in the flour and a pinch of salt and fold through. Then fold in 150g of the parsnip purée and pipe into four 5cm-square moulds standing on a baking sheet and bake for about 12 minutes until firm and pale gold. Leave to cool slightly in the moulds on a wire rack.

7   **To serve,** drizzle some poached pear fluid gel on each plate. Tear the parsnip cake into uneven chunks and put four on each plate and finish with balls of sorbet. The chef suggests serving this dish with pear jelly, poached pear balls, parsnip crisps and vanilla dressing (see page 6).

> This cake method can be used with other ingredients such as chocolate, courgettes or carrots. They're all great speedy cakes that can also be baked in a traditional fashion.

WARM PISTACHIO CAKE
with goat's cheese mousse
Jim Key

Jim Key is head chef at Aiden Byrne's Church Green restaurant in Lymm, Cheshire. Jim has worked in some of the country's leading restaurants, including the Devonshire Arms and Tyddyn Llan, the realisation of a dream that began as a four-year-old, when Jim informed his mum of his intention to become a chef. His ambitious, creative take on modern British dishes has won this committed chef much acclaim. 'There are no rules,' he says. 'You are a free man in the kitchen. There aren't many jobs where you can say that's true.'

1   **For the filo pastry,** first ensure the pastry is always well covered with a slightly damp tea towel. Preheat the oven to 140°C (Gas 1). Place a sheet of greaseproof paper on a baking sheet and cover with a sheet of pastry. Brush with just enough melted butter to cover the pastry, then sprinkle with a small amount of sugar and then one-third of the thyme leaves. Place another filo pastry sheet on top, then brush with butter and sprinkle over sugar and thyme, as before. Lay a third sheet on top and again brush with butter. Cover with another sheet of greaseproof paper and then a second baking sheet and place an ovenproof heavy weight on top to press down firmly.

2   Put in the oven and bake for 20–25 minutes. Remove from the oven, take off the top baking sheet and layer of greaseproof paper. While the pastry is still warm, cut it into eight strips measuring about 20 x 1.5cm. Leave to cool on a wire rack.

3   **For the warm pistachio cake,** increase the oven to 160°C (Gas 3) and line a 15 x 18cm baking tin with greaseproof paper. Whisk the butter and sugar together in an electric mixer and add the eggs, one at a time. Mix in the ground almonds and the pistachio paste and then fold in the flour. Pour the cake mixture into the prepared tin and cook for about 35 minutes until it springs back to the touch. Let the cake cool in the tin, then turn out onto a wire rack and set aside.

4   **To make the crème anglaise,** put the egg yolks and sugar in a glass bowl and, using an electric hand-held mixer, whisk until smooth and creamy. Pour the cream and milk into a pan and bring to the boil, then pour the hot cream and milk over the eggs, whisking continuously. Return to a clean pan and cook over a low heat, still stirring continuously, until the temperature reaches 73°C. Do not allow it to boil. Pass through a sieve.

5   **For the pistachio cream,** soak the gelatine in a bowl of water for about 5 minutes to soften. Gently warm 200g of the crème anglaise and whisk in the pistachio paste. Set 4 tbsp of this aside for dressing the plates. Squeeze the gelatine to drain it, add it to the remaining anglaise mixture and stir until dissolved. Pass through a sieve and allow to cool. Once set, fold in the lightly whipped cream, place it into a piping bag with a small nozzle and keep refrigerated.

6   **To make the goat's cheese mousse,** soak the gelatine in a bowl of cold water for 5 minutes to soften. Warm the milk in a pan, squeeze the gelatine to drain it, then add to the milk and stir until dissolved. Put the goat's cheese in a food processor and blend until smooth, then whisk into the warmed milk. Fold in the lightly whipped cream and keep refrigerated.

7   **To finish the filo pastry,** pipe the pistachio cream onto four of the filo pastry strips and sandwich with the remaining strips.

8   **To serve,** cut the pistachio cake into small portions and, if necessary, reheat in a warm oven for a couple of minutes before dividing between large plates. Spoon on the goat's cheese mousse and top with a filo pastry strip. The chef suggests serving this dessert with cherry sorbet, poached cherries and cherry brandy jelly (see page 6).

Serves 4

For the filo pastry
3 sheets of filo pastry
25g unsalted butter, melted
Caster sugar, for sprinkling
Handful of thyme leaves

For the warm pistachio cake
200g butter, softened
200g caster sugar
4 eggs
200g ground almonds
50g pistachio paste
50g plain flour

For the crème anglaise
4 egg yolks
35g caster sugar
60ml double cream
360ml semi-skimmed milk

For the pistachio cream
1½ gelatine leaves
150g pistachio paste
100ml double cream, lightly whipped

For the goat's cheese mousse
1 gelatine leaf
50ml milk
125g mild soft goat's cheese
50ml double cream, lightly whipped

Sandwiching the filo pastry strips between baking parchment and two baking sheets removes the air bubbles and ensures you have a flat piece of pastry when cooked.

APPLE & PARSNIP 'GATEAU' with candied walnuts & apple sorbet
Brittany Manning

An infectious welcome is to be had at Guy and Brittany Manning's Wiltshire pub, the Red Lion, where Brittany's innovative desserts have helped to make this country inn a firm foodie destination. Brittany is inspiring in her use of vegetables in desserts, as exemplified by this apple and parsnip 'gateau', which showcases her talent for bringing together seasonal flavours.

1 **To make the honey sponge,** preheat the oven to 160°C (Gas 3) and butter a 27 x 33cm baking tin and line with baking parchment. Put the eggs, sugar and honey in a bowl and whip together until very light. Sift in the flour, baking powder and a pinch of salt and then fold in the milk followed by the butter. Transfer to the prepared baking tin and cook for 15–20 minutes until firm. Remove from the oven and allow to cool before turning out onto a wire rack, then cut into long narrow strips.

2 **For the candied walnuts,** put the sugar and 250ml of water in a heavy-based pan and bring to the boil to make a stock syrup. Add the walnuts and cook for about 20 minutes until the syrup has penetrated the nuts and reduced. Heat the oil to 180°C in a large pan or a deep fryer. Drain the walnuts, then deep fry for 1–2 minutes until the syrup has hardened. Remove the walnuts from the oil with a slotted spoon and spread them out on a baking sheet lined with greaseproof paper. Season with salt.

3 **To make the apple sorbet,** warm half of the apple juice in a pan, add the glucose, sugar and vitamin C, stirring to dissolve, and then add the remaining juice. Allow to cool; reserve 50ml for the honeyed green apples, then churn the rest in an ice-cream machine until set.

4 **To make the parsnip cream,** put the parsnips, vanilla pod, milk, cream and honey in a pan and bring to the boil. Reduce the heat to very low, lay a disc of baking parchment over the parsnips and gently simmer for 15–20 minutes until soft. Drain the parsnips, but reserve the milk. Put the parsnips into a food processor and blend until smooth. Season with salt and then add the butter and some of the reserved milk and process further until very smooth.

5 **For the honeyed green apples,** put the reserved sorbet base into a bowl with the honey. Peel and cut the apples into crescents and add to the bowl. Mix thoroughly.

6 **For the fresh green apples,** cut into quarters, remove the core and then cut the flesh into thin slices. Use a small round cutter to cut out coin-sized pieces of apple. Combine the vitamin C powder with 100ml of water and put the apples into the solution to prevent them from oxidising.

7 **For the red apples,** just before serving, put the sugar, vitamin C powder and vanilla seeds into a bowl and mix together. Then toss the apple matchsticks in the mixture.

8 **To serve,** spread the parsnip cream across each plate, followed by a slice of sponge. Place the various apples on top to create a 'salad', then sprinkle the walnuts around and put a scoop of sorbet to the side. Drizzle the honey over the dish and decorate with wood sorrel (if using).

Serves 4

For the honey sponge
2 eggs
45g caster sugar
55g set honey
90g plain flour, sifted
½ tsp baking powder
Salt
40ml full-fat milk
40g unsalted butter, melted

For the candied walnuts
250g caster sugar
75g walnut halves
500ml vegetable oil

For the apple sorbet
500ml unsweetened apple juice
130ml liquid glucose
100g caster sugar
2g vitamin C powder

For the parsnip cream
200g parsnips, peeled and chopped
1 vanilla pod, split lengthways
250ml full-fat milk
250ml double cream
50g runny honey
30g unsalted butter, softened

For the honeyed green apples
20g runny honey
2 green eating apples, preferably Granny Smith

For the fresh green apples
1 green eating apple, preferably Granny Smith
Pinch of vitamin C powder

For the red apples
20g caster sugar
1g vitamin C powder
½ vanilla pod, split lengthways and seeds scraped out
2 red eating apples, preferably Braeburn, cut into matchsticks

To serve
1 tsp honey
4 sprigs of wood sorrel (optional)

Puts the 'oh' into gateau – a dessert that layers honey notes with crisp fresh apple.

BITTERSWEET CHOCOLATE CAKE with cinnamon ice cream & cookies
Chris O'Halloran

The stunning Highlands landscape provides a glorious backdrop for the Green Inn, where chef-patron Chris O'Halloran's much-lauded modern Scottish cuisine 'with a French twist' takes centre stage. Citing Raymond Blanc as one of his culinary heroes, Chris is a passionate connoisseur of fine dining. This dessert finds its inspiration in the chocolate and ice cream that he loved as a child; here he reinvents the dish for a more sophisticated palate.

1   **To make the chocolate cake,** stand six 8cm-diameter ring moulds on a baking sheet. Using a balloon whisk, whisk the egg whites with 65g of the sugar over a bowl of simmering water for 3 minutes until the mixture is slightly warm and foamy and the sugar has dissolved. Take the bowl off the heat and continue to whisk on a medium speed for 5 minutes until soft peaks form.

2   Soak the gelatine in a bowl of cold water for 5 minutes to soften. Pour the milk into a pan over a low heat, then add the remaining 80g of sugar with the cocoa powder, flour, a pinch of salt and egg yolks and whisk until it becomes thick like a pudding texture. Remove from the heat and whisk in the chocolate. Squeeze the gelatine to drain it and whisk into the chocolate mixture, then fold in the whisked eggs. Pour the mixture into the ring moulds and put in the freezer for 30–60 minutes.

3   **To make the cookies,** mix both flours with the baking powder, cinnamon and a small pinch of salt in a bowl and then beat in the butter, sugars and honey with a wooden spoon until it turns into an almost pastry-like dough that can be kneaded. Roll out the dough with a rolling pin until wafer thin and place in the freezer for about 1 hour. Preheat the oven to 180°C (Gas 4) after about 40 minutes.

4   Remove the dough from the freezer and put it in the oven for 8 minutes. Remove and then cut into twelve 8cm-diameter cookies and six 6cm-diameter cookies. Return these to the oven for a further 3 minutes. Keep the oven switched on.

5   **To make the cinnamon ice cream,** put the milk, cream and cinnamon stick into a pan and bring to a simmer, then turn off the heat and leave to infuse for 10 minutes. Remove the cinnamon stick and add half of the sugar, then put the pan back on a low heat and stir until the sugar has dissolved.

6   In a separate large bowl, whisk the egg yolks and the remaining sugar until slightly thickened and pour half of the hot milk mixture into the eggs. Then pour this back into the remaining milk in the pan. Return to a very low heat and gently simmer for 5–10 minutes until the mixture is thick enough to coat the back of a spoon. Pour it into a bowl and leave to chill in the fridge for 30 minutes before churning in an ice-cream machine until set.

7   **To finish,** remove the chocolate cakes from the moulds and place each one on top of a large cookie, put on a baking sheet and bake for about 14 minutes.

8   **To serve,** put the remaining larger cookies on plates, add a ball of ice cream and then top with a small cookie. Put a chocolate cake next to each ball of ice cream and finish with a dusting of icing sugar. The chef suggests serving this dessert with chocolate sauce (see page 6).

Serves 6

For the chocolate cake
3 eggs, separated
145g caster sugar
1 gelatine leaf
160ml full-fat milk
25g cocoa powder
20g plain flour
Salt
30g dark chocolate (64% cocoa solids), broken into pieces

For the cookies
100g plain flour
40g wholewheat flour
¼ tsp baking powder
¼ tsp ground cinnamon
85g unsalted butter
30g light soft brown sugar
30g granulated sugar
1½ tsp honey

For the cinnamon ice cream
250ml full-fat milk
250ml double cream
1 cinnamon stick
45g caster sugar
5 egg yolks

To serve
Icing sugar, for dusting

Partly bake the cookies before you cut them into circles to help them maintain a perfect shape when cooked.

FEUILLANTINES OF RHUBARB
with ginger jelly
Jake Saul Watkins

With his parents inviting up to 150 guests for supper each Christmas Eve, Jake Saul Watkins was well-versed in the association of food with pleasure at an early age. Having cooked with culinary heavyweights such as Heston Blumenthal, he is now chef-proprietor at Petersfield's elegant 17th-century inn, JSW, where guests marvel at the precision cooking and the awe-inspiring wine list. Jake's feuillantines of rhubarb is inspired by fond memories of fruit picking with his father as a young boy.

Rhubarb and ginger is a classic flavour combination that still excites – especially in this delicately textured and intricately designed dish.

1   **To make the rhubarb compote,** dissolve the sugar in 125ml of water in a heavy-based pan over a low heat. Put the rhubarb in the syrup and poach for about 2 minutes until soft. Drain the fruit and leave to cool in a bowl. Put one-quarter of the rhubarb in a food processor with some of the syrup and blend to make a purée. Mix the purée through the remaining diced rhubarb. Set aside.

2   **For the dried rhubarb,** use a potato peeler to peel at least 16 strips of rhubarb each about 10cm long and poach in the remaining syrup for about 30 seconds. Do not overcook. Lay the rhubarb on a silicone mat or baking parchment and dry in a warm place until crisp. It will take about 8 hours in a hotplate drawer or up to 48 hours in an airing cupboard.

3   **For the ginger jelly,** mix the ginger beer with the agar agar in a bowl and leave for about 20 minutes to set. Whisk the jelly to form small pieces and then set aside in the fridge.

4   **For the feuillantines,** preheat the oven to 200°C (Gas 6). Cut the filo pastry into eight sets of 10cm, 8cm, 6cm and 4cm squares. Lay the squares on a board and brush one side with melted butter and dust with icing sugar. Turn the squares over and repeat, then pair the squares so that each square is double layered. Cook between two flat baking sheets for about 3 minutes until golden (keep an eye on their progress, as the mixture burns very easily). Remove from the oven and transfer immediately to a wire rack.

5   **To serve,** whip the cream with the vanilla seeds and the caster sugar until stiff. Pipe a small amount of cream in the centre of each plate. Place the largest feuillantine on top of this with another blob of cream in the centre. Spoon some of the compote around the cream and add pieces of jelly. Repeat this process with the next two feuillantines in descending order to form a pyramid. Place the smallest sheet on the top. Lean one piece of dried rhubarb up each corner of the rhubarb stack, as in the photograph, secured with a little cream.

Serves 4

For the rhubarb compote
125g caster sugar
150g rhubarb, diced

For the dried rhubarb
1 straight thin rhubarb stick

For the ginger jelly
400ml ginger beer
10g agar agar

For the feuillantines
100g filo pastry
50g unsalted butter, melted
Icing sugar, for dusting

To serve
100ml double cream
1 vanilla pod, split lengthways and
  seeds scraped out
75g caster sugar

TASTE OF BONFIRE NIGHT
John Robinson

John Robinson's Whites Restaurant in
Beverley, Yorkshire, is striking for the
intimacy of the 28-cover, lovingly run dining
room; a space as sympathetically designed
for complete enjoyment as the food itself.
John opened the restaurant when he was just
23 years old, and his attention to detail and
commitment to bringing fine-dining to the
area have marked this ambitious young chef
as a name to watch. John sets out to serve
food that 'exceeds expectations in every
way' – and delivers by the plateful.

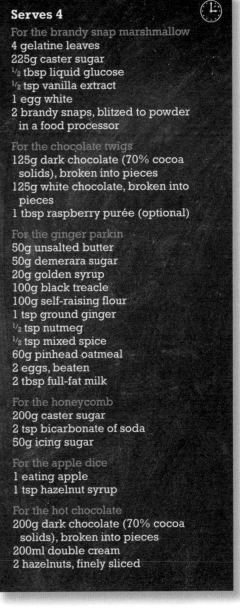

For the brandy snap marshmallow
4 gelatine leaves
225g caster sugar
½ tbsp liquid glucose
½ tsp vanilla extract
1 egg white
2 brandy snaps, blitzed to powder
   in a food processor

For the chocolate twigs
125g dark chocolate (70% cocoa
   solids), broken into pieces
125g white chocolate, broken into
   pieces
1 tbsp raspberry purée (optional)

For the ginger parkin
50g unsalted butter
50g demerara sugar
20g golden syrup
100g black treacle
100g self-raising flour
1 tsp ground ginger
½ tsp nutmeg
½ tsp mixed spice
60g pinhead oatmeal
2 eggs, beaten
2 tbsp full-fat milk

For the honeycomb
200g caster sugar
2 tsp bicarbonate of soda
50g icing sugar

For the apple dice
1 eating apple
1 tsp hazelnut syrup

For the hot chocolate
200g dark chocolate (70% cocoa
   solids), broken into pieces
200ml double cream
2 hazelnuts, finely sliced

1   **To make the brandy snap marshmallow,** first soak the gelatine in a bowl of cold water for about 5 minutes to soften. Put the sugar, liquid glucose and vanilla extract into a pan together with 100ml of water and bring to the boil. Remove from heat, squeeze the gelatine to drain it and add to the pan. Whisk until it is fully incorporated. Put the egg white into a clean bowl and whisk with an electric hand-held mixer until stiff, then pour the sugar mix into the egg white and whisk until stiff again. Whisk in the brandy snap powder, then pour into a shallow container and leave, covered and at room temperature, to set overnight. Slice into 5cm squares.

2   **For the chocolate twigs,** melt the dark chocolate slowly in a glass bowl over a pan of simmering water, then pour onto greaseproof paper and leave to cool. Repeat with the white chocolate, adding the raspberry purée at the end (if using) before pouring. Once set, cut into 'twig' shapes. Set aside.

3   **For the ginger parkin,** preheat the oven to 180°C (Gas 4) and line a 15 x 10cm baking tin with greaseproof paper. Put the butter, sugar, syrup and treacle into a pan and bring to the boil. Mix together the flour, ground spices and oatmeal in a large bowl and pour the butter mixture on top. Stir to combine, then mix in the eggs and milk. Pour the mixture into the prepared tin and bake for 20–25 minutes until risen and golden.

4   **To make the honeycomb,** line a baking sheet with a silicone mat or baking parchment. Combine the sugar with 1 tbsp of water in a pan and heat until the mixture reaches 138°C. Then add the bicarbonate of soda. Tip the mixture onto the prepared baking sheet and leave it to cool for about 5 minutes. Roughly break up the honeycomb, then put two-thirds of the smaller pieces into a food processor with the icing sugar and blend to a powder. Set the bigger pieces aside. Take the marshmallow squares and coat them in the honeycomb and icing sugar mix.

5   **For the apple dice,** peel, core and dice the apple. Toss the dice in the hazelnut syrup in a bowl and leave to marinate.

6   **Make the hot chocolate** just before serving. Put the chocolate into a large bowl. Pour the cream into a pan, bring it to the boil and then slowly pour over the chocolate. Whip until it reaches a creamy consistency.

7   **To serve,** stack the chocolate twigs in a bonfire shape on large plates, then pour the hot chocolate into mugs and top with the hazelnuts. Arrange some marshmallow on the 'bonfire', and place a ginger parkin square and finish with some apple dice and broken pieces of honeycomb. If you like, place a glass cloche over the bonfire and insert smoke with a smoke gun. The chef suggests serving this dish with apple jelly and a toffee apple sauce, and you may also want to make your own brandy snaps for the marshmallow (see page 6).

GOAT'S CHEESECAKE
with walnut crumble
Mark Constable

Island food is the mainstay of head chef Mark Constable's menus at the Isle of Wight's Seaview hotel, where the restaurant's own private fisherman, Captain Stan, provides the catch of the day. Playing with texture and flavour is central to Mark's culinary style, and this dish of goat's cheesecake with walnut crumble is a witty play on 'cheese and biscuits', subverting expectation by transforming savoury ingredients into a sweet dessert.

A sweetly playful take on 'cheese and biscuits'.

Serves 4

For the cheesecakes
250ml double cream
250g soft goat's cheese
125g icing sugar
2 gelatine leaves

For the walnut crumble
60g unsalted butter, diced
60g plain flour
60g wholemeal flour
60g demerara sugar
120g walnut halves

For the candied grapes and celery
1 celery stick, cut into very fine strips
Icing sugar, for dusting
16–20 red grapes, peeled

For the syrup
250ml red dessert wine
80g caster sugar

For the red grape jelly
2 gelatine leaves
250ml red dessert wine

1 **To make the cheesecakes,** put the cream into a bowl and whip to soft peaks. Then crumble in the goat's cheese, add the sugar and cream together until smooth. The texture should be quite stiff. Soak the gelatine leaves in a bowl of cold water for about 5 minutes to soften. Warm 3 tbsp of water in a small pan. Squeeze the gelatine to drain it, add to the water and stir until dissolved. Incorporate the gelatine into the cheese mixture, then spread it evenly between four 8cm-diameter ring moulds. Place in the fridge for at least 30 minutes to set.

2 **For the walnut crumble,** preheat the oven to 180°C (Gas 4). Rub together the butter, both types of flour and the sugar in a bowl to a crumble consistency. Spread the crumble on a baking sheet and cook in the oven for about 10 minutes until golden. Remove it from the oven and allow it to cool for 10–12 minutes. Keep the oven switched on. Transfer the crumble to a food processor, add the nuts and blitz to coarsely chop. Then return it to the oven on the baking sheet for a further 5 minutes. Remove and allow to cool for 10–12 minutes and blitz once more. Reduce the oven to its lowest setting.

3   **For the candied grapes and celery,** blanch the celery in boiling water for 1–2 minutes and
    refresh in cold water. Drain well, dust with icing sugar and place in the cool oven for about
    10 minutes. Re-dust with the sugar and return to the oven for $1\frac{1}{2}$ hours to dry out. Halve the
    red grapes, removing any pips, and dust with sugar.

4   **To make the syrup,** put the red wine and sugar into a pan over a medium heat. Bring to
    the boil then reduce the heat and simmer for 8–9 minutes until it has reduced to a syrup
    consistency. Set aside to cool.

5   **For the red grape jelly,** line a medium-sized flat container with cling film. Soak the gelatine
    in a bowl of cold water for about 5 minutes to soften. Bring the red wine to the boil in a pan.
    Squeeze the gelatine to drain it, add to the wine and stir until dissolved. Pour into the prepared
    container and place in the fridge for 10–12 minutes to set. Cut into 5mm squares.

6   **To serve,** gently remove the cheesecakes from their moulds and roll the edge of each one in
    the crumble mixture. Place a cheesecake in the middle of each plate and scatter the rest of the
    crumble mixture alongside. Dot squares of jelly around the plates, top each with a grape and
    then pieces of candied celery. Dot the syrup around the plates to finish.

WHISKEY CREAM LIQUEUR CHEESECAKE
with dark chocolate caramel mousse
Maciej Bilewski

Inspired by his grandmother, Maciej Bilewski has been experimenting in the kitchen from a young age. After five years at catering college, Maciej has settled at the Anchor Inn in Sutton Gault, where he enjoys 'trying new things, new styles; trying to find new ways to do things.' While looking to Europe for culinary inspiration, Bilewski remains a champion of fresh, local produce. He cites Gordon Ramsay as his main inspiration, admiring his passion and tenacity. 'He makes food look sexy,' the young chef remarks.

1   **For the cheesecake base,** melt the butter in a pan. Put the biscuits into a plastic bag and crush with a rolling pin. Transfer to the pan with the butter, add the mint leaves and mix together. Pour the mixture into four 8cm-diameter ring moulds and put in the fridge for 5–10 minutes.

2   **For the cheesecake topping,** put all the ingredients (using only the seeds from the vanilla pod) in a large bowl and whisk together with an electric hand-held mixer until light and fluffy. Use a spatula to spread the mixture on top of the cheesecake bases.

3   **To make the dark chocolate mousse,** melt the chocolate in a glass bowl over a pan of simmering water, stirring occasionally. In a separate bowl, whisk the egg whites with the sugar until they form stiff peaks. Remove the chocolate from the heat and mix in the egg yolks, cream, cocoa powder and egg white and sugar mixture.

Serves 4

For the cheesecake base
80g unsalted butter
200g digestive biscuits
A few mint leaves, chopped

For the cheesecake topping
200g soft cheese
150g crème fraîche
Juice of 1 lemon
2 vanilla pods, split lengthways and
    seeds scraped out
110g caster sugar
4 tbsp Irish whiskey
4 tbsp whiskey cream liqueur
80ml double cream

For the dark chocolate mousse
120g dark chocolate (70% cocoa
    solids), broken into pieces
4 medium eggs, separated
4 tsp caster sugar
100ml double cream, lightly whipped
1 tsp cocoa powder

For the caramel
150g caster sugar
Juice of 1 lemon
40g unsalted butter, melted
20ml double cream

To decorate
Icing sugar, for dusting

Divide the mousse between four glasses and chill in the fridge for 15–20 minutes.

4   **For the caramel,** put the sugar, lemon juice and 2 tbsp of water in a pan and cook over a medium heat for about 10 minutes until golden brown and, having reached a temperature of 178°C, remove the pan from the heat and mix with the butter and cream. Allow to cool to room temperature. Store any caramel that is left over in an airtight container to prevent it from becoming sticky. It will keep for up to two weeks.

You need to work swiftly when making caramel because it sets quickly. If it starts to harden before you've finished using it, gently reheat in the pan until it is warm.

5   **To serve,** unmould the cheesecakes by warming the moulds slightly with a blow torch (or between warmed hands) and place them on plates. Add the chocolate mousse glasses, top with 1 tbsp of the caramel and dust the plates with icing sugar. The chef suggests serving this dessert with salted caramel and praline ice cream decorated with praline (see page 6).

Specific equipment

For ease, we have listed below the recipes that require specific equipment – although this is by no means comprehensive and we would recommend that you read a recipe thoroughly to make sure you have all the materials to hand.

In addition to the list of specific equipment given below, most of the desserts include an ice cream or sorbet, for which an ice-cream machine is required. Likewise, many of the recipes include specific temperatures for optimum results. A digital thermometer, which is readily available online and from good cookery shops, is the most efficient and accurate device to use.

MAINS

Page 12: Four 225ml metal pudding basins
Page 14: Deep fryer (optional)
Page 16: Six individual pie dishes
Page 22: Pasta machine; deep fryer (optional)
Page 26: Pasta machine; ravioli wheel
Page 30: Four individual pudding moulds; large and small cutters
Page 32: Deep fryer (optional)
Page 42: Deep fryer (optional)
Page 48: Deep fryer (optional)
Page 62: Mandoline
Page 64: Four 6cm-diameter ring moulds
Page 66: Mandoline
Page 68: Melon baller; four individual ovenproof dishes
Page 70: Four individual ovenproof dishes
Page 74: Deep fryer (optional)
Page 80: Deep fryer (optional)
Page 86: Pasta machine; 5cm-diameter cutter
Page 90: Pasta machine; 8cm-diameter cutter
Page 94: Four 8cm-diameter ring moulds
Page 100: Deep fryer (optional)
Page 108: 12cm-diameter cutter; four 10cm-diameter ramekins
Page 114: Stove-top smoking box with hay; Deep fryer (optional)
Page 118: Four ovenproof tea cups; mandoline
Page 120: Small round cutter; stove-top smoking box with 6 tbsp white oak smoking chips; 14 x 8cm container

DESSERTS

Page 124: 28 x 22cm baking tin; four 5cm-square by 2.5cm-deep metal frames
Page 126: Acetate
Page 130: Set of lollipop moulds
Page 132: Four 8cm-diameter ramekins; 15 x 8cm baking tin; 15cm-diameter loose-bottomed cake tin
Page 134: Four 7–8cm-diameter ramekins
Page 136: Six small coffee cups
Page 138: Eight 5cm-diameter dariole moulds; small round cutter
Page 140: Four 7cm-diameter and 5cm-deep ring moulds
Page 142: 15 x 20cm baking tin
Page 146: Eight 10cm-diameter ring moulds
Page 148: 8cm-diameter cutter; four 8cm-diameter ring moulds
Page 150: 20 x 40cm baking tin; mandoline; three 7.5cm-square metal frames
Page 152: Eight 6cm-diameter ring moulds
Page 154: Four to eight square or round 5cm moulds
Page 156: Six 130ml soufflé moulds
Page 158: Four 9cm-diameter and 7cm-deep soufflé moulds
Page 160: Mandoline
Page 162: Six pieces of 9cm-square acetate; 5cm- and 4cm-diameter cutters
Page 164: 17 x 7 x 8cm baking tin
Page 166: Four 10cm-diameter ring moulds
Page 170: Mandoline
Page 172: Melon baller
Page 176: Twelve 5cm-diameter dariole moulds
Page 178: Eight 7cm-diameter ring moulds
Page 180: 30 x 20cm baking tin; deep fryer (optional)
Page 184: Deep fryer (optional); six 7–8cm-diameter ramekins
Page 186: Small, approximately 38mm

deep container; narrow cutter; eight 6cm-diameter ring moulds
Page 188: 27cm-diameter loose-bottomed tart tin
Page 190: 12cm-square silicone mould
Page 192: 25cm-diameter loose-bottomed tart tin
Page 194: Blow torch; four small brioche tins
Page 196: Six 10cm-diameter loose-bottomed tart tins
Page 198: Four 10cm-diameter loose-bottomed tart tins
Page 200: Four 10cm-diameter ramekins
Page 202: 12cm-diameter cutter; four 7.5cm-diameter loose-bottomed tart tins
Page 204: Six 6.5cm-diameter dariole moulds; 18cm-diameter loose-bottomed tart tin
Page 206: Six 10cm-diameter loose-bottomed tart tins
Page 208: Deep fryer (optional); 18cm-diameter loose-bottomed tart tin
Page 210: 30cm-diameter cake tin; four 6cm-diameter ring moulds; four 5cm-diameter ramekins
Page 212: 23cm square baking tin
Page 214: Six 50ml moulds; 20 x 23cm baking tin
Page 216: 30 x 20cm and 15 x 8cm baking tins; 23cm-diameter cake tin
Page 218: Five 7cm-diameter ring moulds; two 20cm-square baking tins; 7cm-diameter cutter
Page 220: Four 5cm-square moulds
Page 222: 15 x 18cm baking tin
Page 224: 27 x 33cm baking tin; deep fryer (optional); small round cutter
Page 226: Six 8cm-diameter ring moulds; 8cm- and 6cm-diameter cutters
Page 230: Smoke gun (optional); 15 x 10cm baking tin
Page 232: Four 8cm-diameter ring moulds
Page 234: Four 8cm-diameter ring moulds

Index

Main entries for chefs and restaurants are in **bold**